The Ultimate Digital Marketing Book

Nick Smith and Jane Heaton

Nick Smith runs a successful online marketing consultancy advising companies how to increase sales and profits using the power of the Internet and by leveraging forgotten assets hidden in their business. Companies hire Nick and his team to devise effective traffic strategies using a combination of paid marketing sources, search engine optimization and social media marketing. In addition, Nick is considered to be one of the leading direct response marketing consultants in the UK after logging more than 33,000 hours implementing successful online marketing strategies during the past 12 years. In his spare time, Nick writes for his blog (NickTheGeek.com) and also maintains CamStudio (CamStudio.org), the world's most popular free desktop recording software downloaded 100,000 times every week.

Jane Heaton is a marketing consultant, content specialist and writer who helps people master the principles and practice of marketing and communications, from strategy to execution. A member of the CIM and a Chartered Marketer, Jane developed her business and marketing expertise in a small ad agency, in regional newspaper publishing and for brands such as Shell and Cable & Wireless – through hands-on experience and setting up and leading marketing teams. She started Jane Heaton Associates in 2000 to give businesses of all sizes access to expert marketing advice and skills – easily and cost effectively. As marketing becomes more complex, Jane believes marketers must be able to confidently apply the essential core principles of marketing and think in a joined-up way in order to manage the growing choice of tools and tactics and deploy them successfully. Today she uses her wide-ranging experience and a blend of consultancy, mentoring, training and coaching to enable individuals and teams to create wellwritten, well-produced content as part of a clear, focused marketing strategy. Find out more at:

www.janeheatonassociates.com

LinkedIn https://uk.linkedin.com/in/janeheaton

Twitter @janeheaton

The Ultimate Digital Marketing Book

Teach Yourself®

Succeed at SEO and Search, Master Mobile Marketing, Get to Grips with Content Marketing

Nick Smith and
Jane Heaton

First published in Great Britain by Teach Yourself in 2023

An imprint of John Murray Press

A division of Hodder & Stoughton Ltd,

An Hachette UK company

1

Based on original material from *Successful Digital Marketing, Successful SEO and Search Marketing, Successful Content Marketing, Successful Mobile Marketing*

A CIP catalogue record for this title is available from the British Library

Paperback ISBN 978 1 473 68841 4

eBook ISBN 978 1 473 68842 1

Typeset by KnowledgeWorks Global Ltd.

Printed and bound in Great Britain by Clays Ltd, Elcograf S.p.A.

John Murray Press policy is to use papers that are natural, renewable and recyclable products and made from wood grown in sustainable forests. The logging and manufacturing processes are expected to conform to the environmental regulations of the country of origin.

John Murray Press

Carmelite House

50 Victoria Embankment

London EC4Y 0DZ

www.teachyourself.com

Contents

PART 1
Your Digital Marketing Masterclass

Introduction

This Part is what I consider essential basic training for every small business owner or department manager before they hope to trek deeper into the marketing woods. I'm giving you the broad strokes to train you in the basics of what you need to know to survive and thrive with marketing in this digital age.

More than just that, of course, this Part gives you the low-down on all the topics you will need:

- social marketing
- search engine optimization
- 'paid' advertising on Google/Facebook, and so on
- creating the perfect website that makes sales
- and more ... (lots of tips and tricks on everything from Yahoo Answers to press releases).

CHAPTER 1

Building the ultimate sales website

Welcome to the starting line of your 'digital marketing' race.

This is more of a marathon than a sprint but as the saying goes 'The journey of a thousand miles begins with one step'.

So take what you learn in this Part and *apply it* as this can change you and your business for the better.

And so to begin, before we get into the 'sexy' stuff, like social media marketing and search engine optimization, we need to talk about some far more important things.

First, we need to talk about your website, because all the traffic in the world will not make you money if you have a crappy website that can't convert all those visitors into buyers.

This is where you really start to make money.

At the same time you don't want to spend too much time trying to fine-tune every detail on the site but not enough time on generating traffic.

The key here is to practise a little 'Kaizen'– the art of continuous improvement.

Just get started with a decent (though not perfect) website and make small improvements when you need to as your traffic grows and builds over the long haul.

Look and feel

So first off you need to find your perfect 'look and feel'– what should this be?

Check out your competition to see what kind of 'look' their websites have. Take notes of what you like and what you don't.

Take a look at company websites in different sectors. Is there anything you like on those sites that your competition *aren't* utilizing?

Now ask yourself a question ... Who are you? What makes you unique in this world? What's your personality? Sarcastic? Funny? Thoughtful?

The perfect look and feel for you and your business is a combination of all these things.

It should be a reflection of what makes you unique in this world. If you're an accountant with a great sense of humour, inject a little of that into your website. Accountants don't have to all be boring (kidding).

For a perfect example of this, take Sir Richard Branson. His various Virgin websites are still very corporate looking but have enough of his personality in them to make them stand out.

Why can't you do the same?

Organization

Next your website needs to be easy to move around. Your visitors want to quickly find what they're looking for. Once they come to your site and you're able to answer their questions and show them what they need, they may want the answers to other questions as well.

So make it as easy as possible for them. Interlink within your posts to other posts at the beginning, at various places in the middle and also at the end.

Essentially be plugging your other content as much as possible without going overboard.

Lay out your navigation bar logically and make sure that your most popular pages are highlighted.

This will get people clicking around your site, which looks good to Google, which looks great to your bottom line.

If you need help with this, again check your competition and other websites not in your sector for ideas.

Landing pages and sales pages

First some definitions.

A landing page is where your visitor enters your site and a sales page is where you offer to sell them something and they make the choice to buy or not.

The two aren't necessarily the same thing, although they can be.

It depends on what you're promoting, and whether your potential visitors are likely to be offended with a gentle sales message as soon as they get to your website and so on.

The 'sales funnel'

The idea with the sales funnel is to guide your visitors through your site to eventually land on a related sales page where you can try to persuade them to buy your product or service. How do you get them to do this? The question you need to ask is 'What do my visitors really want?'

If they've just done a search on Google for 'dog grooming service Hoboken', they probably don't need educating as to the benefits of professional dog grooming, they're ready to hire, so take them to a page with a little sales copy explaining why they should hire 'you' and a 'buy' button or your phone number so they can get in touch.

If they searched for 'dog grooming techniques', then the landing page could be a nice article explaining some basic techniques that owners could use and then maybe offer a free video showing you doing the techniques in exchange for their email address (building a prospect list) enabling you to follow up with them via email, increasing your chances of getting a client or making a sale.

(I talk about email marketing in Chapter 6.)

TIP Money making ninja tip

If you can also capture the visitor's state/province/county at the same time as capturing their email address, you could earn additional revenue by taking those leads you would normally ignore and selling them on to non-competing 'dog grooming' businesses in different locations.

Speak to your techie about this – it's really easy to do and could be very profitable.

Anyway, you get the picture.

The only exception to this would be if you are an online company, perhaps a software company, and all you do is sell your software and have other people educate for you and send them to your sales website.

But, in that case you are probably not reading this book anyway!

So as you can see there are essentially two main sales funnels, direct and indirect, via email. I recommend having both for your business.

A third model – the webinar

There is a third model that is a mix between email and sales and that is the webinar model.

A webinar is just like a presentation that you do online (you talking into a webcam and/or a slide-based presentation) and that can be watched and listened to by hundreds of people at once.

This works particularly well if you offer a high-ticket product or service. You promote a special event giving away some excellent information for free that solves a big problem for your visitors and then, at the end of the webinar, you make attendees aware of your product or service (with a corresponding high price tag) for those that are interested, with no pressure.

You can add the names of those that sign up to attend the webinar to a mailing list so the other email marketing rules still apply and, while the sales volume may be lower, the actual money made can be higher, depending on the business.

In the dog groomers example, this could be a week's vacation for their pooch including grooming, pampering, special training and so on.

If you sell a physical item, maybe bundle it up with other items or partner with someone who can offer a related service and split the profits.

Any business can offer a 'premium' version of their product or service. It just requires a little thought.

Once you know what you're selling, what next?

Tracking

Now is the time to start tracking the visitors to your website.

- Where do they spend the most time?
- How many pages do they view?
- Where do they land the most frequently and from there where do they click?
- Are your visitors mostly mobile?
  And of course the most important question:
- What percentage of visitors buy?

All these and more are questions that you must answer to have the ultimate sales website.

Only in this way can you see what is really working and what isn't. You may be getting a lot of traffic to one page but the visitors end up leaving quickly or not going to another page. Why? Who knows but you need to find out. Go and check out that page, and see whether you can spice it up.

Actually, you can do all this by having analytics software installed on your website.

This is very easy to do – literally copying and pasting a code into every page you want to track or into your website's design template (if you have software like WordPress or Magneto eCommerce).

I recommend using either Google Analytics (GA) or Clicky.

GA is free and can directly interface between your Google AdWords and Google Webmaster Tools accounts to get the maximum amount of data possible.

Clicky is perfect if you're worried about information overload because the interface is a lot simpler.

Spend time getting to know the interface and go through the settings one by one. There are lots of settings and I could write a full book on them alone.

Google provides a couple of excellent free resources where you can learn everything you need to know to get up to speed with GA:

www.youtube.com/googleanalytics?hl=en

www.google.com/analytics/learn

You can sign up for Clicky here: http://clicky.com

There are lots of tutorials on YouTube for both Clicky and GA – just do a search for 'Clicky analytics' or 'Google Analytics.'

If you use WordPress to power your website, you can integrate both their GA and Clicky in just a couple of mouse clicks by installing related plug-ins.

Use analytics to track the changes that had a positive increase on your pages, then replicate them on others and see what happens.

Split testing

Once you have traffic and are tracking where your visitors come from, where they go on your website and what kind of conversion rates you get, it's time to start split testing your sales and order pages.

One simple way is to use Content Experiments by Google Analytics. It's pretty easy to set up and once you have done so, each of your visitors will be shown one or other of the pages in the Experiment automatically. When set up correctly, you'll be able to track right the way through to a sale or whatever the action is that you want to track.

(Again there are videos on YouTube showing you how to do this, or hire a geek on a freelancer site like UpWork.com or eLance.com to do it for you.)

When you do this, don't send them to two entirely different pages. Only make a small change to the second page, that is, change the 'buy now' button to an 'add to cart' button or change the button colour. Small changes like this can make a huge difference.

Change the font to something easier to read. Change the headline at the top of the page. And on and on.

Keep in mind that you should *only change one thing at a time*. If you change multiple things at the same time, there is really no way to know why the page is doing better or worse than the other page.

There's a great Content Experiments tutorial video here courtesy of Robbie Richards:

https://goo.gl/yl9EEo

In conclusion

The key is to start getting your website out there. A perfect site doesn't exist. But imperfect sites make money every single day if they get traffic.

So make a site that matches your personality and get going.

I was once involved in a project back in my beginner days with a doctor who wanted the 'perfect' website. He paid upwards of $20,000 for everything he wanted custom made. Problem is when he opened up the site he found out nobody really wanted what he offered. He eventually ran out of money and had to go back to work as a doctor.

Don't be that person.

Summary

If you go through the things recommended in this chapter, you should have a website capable of making sales within a short period of time.

But don't just rest on your laurels. Keep tweaking, testing, tweaking and testing until it becomes second nature.

If there is one constant in marketing, it is that you and your market will always be changing!

Things that worked a year ago don't work now. Those that work now might not work as well a year from now.

So keep an eye on your website (or hire someone once it is making money to do that for you) and it will be a source of income for years to come.

Fact-check (answers at the back)

1. When building your site, you need to have:
   a) The ultimate sales website right out of the gate ❑
   b) A good site to start and the ultimate site later ❑
   c) A bad site to start and the ultimate site later ❑

2. Landing pages are:
   a) Pages that are fallen on sometimes, causing them to break ❑
   b) The first page your visitor sees ❑
   c) The place where you sell your visitor stuff ❑

3. Sales pages are:
   a) Pages that people should come to first ❑
   b) Pages that people should come to second· ❑
   c) Pages that people should come to when ready ❑
   d) Pages that are basically the same as landing pages ❑

4. How many sales funnels are out there?
   a) 1 ❑
   b) 2 ❑
   c) 3 ❑
   d) 4 ❑

5. These sales funnels include:
   a) Immediate 'buy now' pages ❑
   b) An email follow-up series ❑
   c) Webinars ❑
   d) All of the above ❑

6. The website tracker of choice is:
   a) Google Analytics ❑
   b) Anything that you can get a hold of that costs money ❑
   c) Whatever works best for you: do your research ❑

7. The best way to get to know GA is:
   a) Use it ❑
   b) Use it a lot ❑
   c) Go through everything many times ❑
   d) Watch the video tutorials ❑
   e) All of the above ❑

8. When you find a page many are going to but are then leaving, what can you do?
   a) Spice it up a bit ❑
   b) Force your visitors to visit a new page with ninja mind tricks ❑
   c) Change your site completely ❑

9. When split testing:
   a) Test only one thing at a time ❑
   b) Test two entirely different pages each time ❑
   c) Change at least two things on the new page you are testing ❑

10. There is a point at which you can just stop testing and learning new things:
    a) True ❑
    b) False ❑

CHAPTER 2

SEO: The backbone of any digital marketing strategy

In this chapter we're going to be covering the first basic step of digital marketing and that is search engine optimization (SEO).

This is the solid base that, if you get it right, will help all your other areas of marketing.

Why?

Because just as digital marketing is a holistic (complete) approach to marketing in a primarily digital age, *SEO is also becoming more and more a holistic website experience for the user.*

If you want to sell online, you need to have a good website with good SEO backing it up.

SEO defined

SEO can be defined as the things you do for the pages on your website so that they are found by Google and to ensure that they show in the top ten results when people search for something related to your business.

For instance, this may include being found when your customers type into Google the keywords 'chiropractor Dallas TX', 'dog grooming supplies' or 'cute kitten photos' (if that's what you're trying to make into a business).

This in turn brings you a lot of traffic and, depending on how valuable those keywords actually are, this can then in turn bring you new customers and clients.

So yes, this is pretty awesome but, as I will show later, it is not the only way that your customers find their way to your door/website. Nor is it necessarily always the *best* way for your customers to come to you. In fact, depending on your market, it might not even be the best place to start.

But SEO is an essential skill to learn and it's not that difficult (regardless of what high-priced SEO consultants may lead you to believe) so let's get into it, shall we?

So exactly how does SEO work?

People and SEO consultants have a million theories as to how exactly to go about doing this, but what really works?

I have written a whole book on this subject, which of course I recommend you read for more info, but here is the basic idea in a nutshell.

First look at it from Google's perspective: they want their results to be the best of any search engine, because the best results mean more users of their service, which means more eyeballs on their site and more eyeballs means that more users will click the paid ads on the right-hand side.

Google is continuously fine-tuning the number and types of factors they use to determine whether a page gets into the top ten results for a certain search phrase, like looking at how long people stay on your site, how fast your webpages load, the number of people who like and share your content on Facebook, Twitter or Google+ and so on.

But when you boil it all down, essentially what Google and the other search engines are looking for is a *great user experience.*

Note

As soon as you start looking into Search Engine Optimization, within a very short period of time you'll start seeing references to 'Penguin' and 'Panda' penalties.

These are ongoing updates to Google's index they implemented to stop people from 'gaming' their search results using webspam techniques, like creating thousands of low-quality and/or irrelevant links from 'dodgy sources' to point to all their webpages and 'keyword stuffing' their webpages using tiny/hidden text to try and trick Google into ranking their webpage for competitive search terms.

If you follow the guidelines below, you really won't have to worry about penalties as my guidelines don't try to *trick* Google, they just aim to get its *attention.*

To sum it all up there are three aspects of your site that you need to keep in mind when developing it. If one is missing, you will not have the success you want out of your website in the long run.

First, you need to think about your on-site goals.

This means that your site should load quickly, look good and be logically laid out so people can find your content in the easiest and quickest manner possible.

Next, your site needs every page to be in some way related to your site's overall theme (e.g. dog product-related if you are selling dog products) and every page needs to be optimized for just one keyword phrase (more on this later).

Third, you need to take care of your off-page criteria.

If you have heard about SEO at all, you might have heard that getting high in Google is pretty much just about getting links.

And you'd be correct. However, the real power is by getting what are known as 'authority' links pointing to your pages and your website.

'Authorities' are websites and pages that Google deems highly trustworthy on your subject matter.

So for example, if you are a website selling accessories for iPods, iPads and iPhones, the ultimate (albeit unlikely) dream would be for Apple to link to you in some way.

But even if you're unable to get an 'Apple' level of authority linking to you, if enough people link to a page then that page will be seen by Google as an 'authority' on the subject and (all things being equal) they will move it up the rankings for certain keywords and search terms.

Although this extra 'weight' is not as high as it used to be, it is still there. However, if you want your site to *last* it is not all you should focus on.

Super ninja trick

Create your own 'authority' site. How can you do this? Create pages on something that Google sees as an 'authority' already!

The best site for this right now is YouTube and another one is Google+. There are a few others out there but these two are the most effective.

Create a business page on Google+ then post good YouTube videos using the same account. Send links to those videos and you will be amazed at the authority boost you will get now that these two authority pages are linking to you.

SEO guide

Now you know a bit more about SEO, what are you to do about it?

We see that search engines are looking for a great user experience. So what does this mean for you and your business?

Let me present to you 'Nick the Geek's guide to solid SEO', the sure-fire steps to SEO that gives your website the best shot possible. (I can't guarantee anything though, since I don't own Google. I can dream though ...)

First step is that your website's HTML code – the markup language used to build webpages – should be fully validated with W3C standards (speak to your techie about this).

Your website should load as fast as possible and should look good. It doesn't have to be the Sistine Chapel to start off but it shouldn't scare people away either and needs to have a good amount of content (at least ten optimized pages and five to ten optimized blog posts).

Load times can be improved by getting good-quality web hosting (it is definitely not all the same – drop me a line and I'll tell you who I use).

Keep your webpages' file sizes as small as possible to help load quickly and your images should also be optimized for the web (I tend to use JPEGs wherever possible at 60 per cent compression – again, speak to your techie).

W3C compliance and load speed can both be covered by using a content management system like WordPress (free from WordPress.org) and getting a good premium theme from them that matches your business and goals (this will take care of the coding).

Premium themes average approximately $50 and will look like your website had thousands of dollars spent on it.

If you have a website already, go to http://webpagetest.org/ and test your site out for free (you want the load speed to be less than seven seconds to be good, fewer than five seconds to be the best).

Websites generally tend to have static, unchanging content on them, so to continually give Google and the other search engines a reason to keep visiting your website to index it in their huge databases, I recommend having a blog somewhere on your domain.

The search engines all tend to prefer new and timely content, so the more often new content is added to your site, the more the search engines will like it. And the more the search engines like it, the more often they'll add new pages from your site (your blog posts) into their databases and you then increase the chances of your website being shown to someone looking for what you offer.

More content = more chances to be found. Easy, isn't it?

Content

If your website were a building, then content is the foundation that makes that website robust.

Not just ordinary content but great content.

Why?

Because this is what your website visitors really want; they don't really care about your super-slick graphics, or your sci-fi looking interface. They want the answer to their question. They want information they can use.

If you give it to them, you will be rewarded by Google for it.

So not only do you want good content, you want good content that will match your ideal visitors' needs and desires. If you do it well, you will meet your visitors' needs and desires at a stage before they want to buy from you.

You also want, as much as possible, for *every* page of your site to be optimized for at least one keyword. Even if it is a keyword that is only searched 100 times a month. Every page should have some key phrase that you are trying to win for.

Definition

'Optimized' means the main keyword you'd like the webpage to rank for in Google. So for example, let's say you want to target the keyword/search term 'Vietnamese dog brush'. First of all, put the keyword as the filename (or the permalink if you're using a CMS) so it looks something like:

http://yourdomain.com/vietnamese-dog-brushes or
http://yourdomain.com/vietnamese-dog-brushes.html

You need the title of the page to use an H1 HTML tag (ask your techie) and contain your keyword within it but *not* be the exact keyword.

Something like 'high quality Vietnamese dog brushes'.

You should make sure that this 'close keyword' is mentioned first on the page, and once every 200 words or so in the content.

You should have at least one picture on the page that has a filename of the 'close keyword' and it is always good to have a video embedded on the page about the dog brush as well (more on this when we talk about YouTube later).

Note

Don't try to win for more than one phrase per page. Google gets easily confused and wants it to be clear what the page is about.

At the same time it doesn't want to be tricked so don't write 'Vietnamese dog brush' a million times on the page and think you will win. Just make it natural and mention it every couple of hundred words or so. (No more than 2 per cent of your text should be your keyword.)

This requires a plan

First, do a bit of thinking about what your visitors want. This is key at this point; don't think about what *you would want* but what a *visitor wants*. These will often be two different things. You are the expert in this area (hopefully) and as such you have a lot more knowledge than your visitors.

For instance, say you are a chiropractor; you may search for 'chiropractor', while your prospective visitor may look for 'back pain specialist' or 'what to do to help a sore back'.

You will use acronyms and other jargon. For example, I would use SEO or PR (page rank), or *'ranking* a website' in my searching but you might use 'being found by Google' or 'online marketing' in yours.

Learn what this means for your potential customers and you will go somewhere others haven't gone.

Super ninja tip

Google had a significant update in August 2013, known at the time as 'Hummingbird' but this is now the name given to Google's actual ranking algorithm due to the size of the changes made. In late 2015, Google also released information on an Artificial Intelligence function within Hummingbird called 'RankBrain'. These updates (and no doubt other secret functions) are designed to analyse not just keywords in the query but the context of the query. To give you a sense of how important this update was, other updates like Panda and Penguin generally affect 4–5 per cent of search queries: Hummingbird has been said to have affected 90 per cent of search queries.

With more and more people using Google on their mobiles, voice search queries are becoming more popular and as such, search queries are becoming longer and more conversational (e.g. 'Where can I find an emergency plumber in Hoboken, New Jersey?') and less keyword-orientated (e.g. 'emergency plumber Hoboken NJ').

Hummingbird is designed to pay more attention to every word in a query and to determine the meaning of the sentence as a whole and the intent of the searcher – not just the 'what' but the 'why'. It's not outside the realms of possibility to suggest Google ranking Hummingbird-friendly webpages higher than other non-Hummingbird friendly content.

To take advantage of this major update fully, I suggest doing lots of research using Google's Keyword Planner, discussion forums etc., for common questions your target market has relating to your subject, and create content answering them.

Next, think about what your customers search for before they come to you. Looking for a chiropractor, maybe they will search for 'back pain home remedies'. Now, meeting this need may send some customers away (because the problem may be fixed), but those who find no relief or only some relief will now know who to visit for full professional help.

Say you make Facebook apps, maybe you can make a page on 'how to make a Facebook app'. People may be searching for them and a few will make their own app. But many of these just want to know the details and will then give you the money to do it for them because they can tell that you know what you are talking about.

Google Keyword Planner

Take these ideas for content and load them into the Google Keyword Planner tool. This will give you a bunch of additional ideas as it will spit out the related keywords to the phrases that you already have in mind.

What you are looking to get right now is both lower and higher demand. Look at the general search volume for the term. You should have a good mix of 100–500 per month and 1,000–5,000 per month related searches with which to begin your site (only do with less than this if you can afford to make fewer sales; if you make $1,000 per sale then you can live very well off of a 5 per cent conversion rate on 500 people).

What you *don't* want to do with your content

Don't go out and put random content on your site just because a lot of people are searching for it. If you go out and rank for, let's say, 'underwater hang-gliding' and you are a chiropractor, when people land on your site they're going to be understandably confused and will probably leave faster than you can say 'Jack Robinson'.

This is the equivalent of putting a huge '**Free sex**!' at the start of a newspaper ad and then saying 'Now I've got your attention ...' Don't do it.

What you *do* want to do with your content

Make your content high quality and every last word worth reading (or every last second worth watching if it's a video).
Some ideas for content:

- Videos – these are hugely advantageous when used creatively. Don't just post bland boring stuff; don't be afraid to show your fun side! Videos are great and can really drive people to your site (more on this later).
- Informative text content, ideally over 1,000 words long (Google likes more content on a page).
- High-quality images (like infographics) – use these as much as possible to explain what you do or an important aspect of your niche.
- Audio recordings – of you talking in a radio talk show format or interviews with other leading experts, and so on.
- Case studies of clients or customers that show their success with your product/service.

Next steps

Now you have a plan for your content, a well-designed and running site with a blog. The next step is to start getting people to the site (all the prettiness in the world won't make people visit).

One of the best ways to start doing this is going out and getting links that people click. But how to get these? They are actually embedded in the above content ideas.

For instance, if you create videos you can upload them to YouTube and as soon as you post them you should always put the link to your site as the first line in the video description and also encourage people to visit in the video.

If your videos are good, you will start getting clicks on this link and Google will quickly reward you for that.

This is a traffic source that I see many, many people surviving off **alone**. They don't even really need Google traffic. Though you should go after both of course!

When you do audio podcasts, you can then go out and submit your site to podcast directories, which in turn will link to your site and drive people back to your site.

When you interview an expert in your field, you'd better believe they will probably link back to you.

Building this way takes a bit of time and doesn't happen overnight but will establish solid links and traffic that will last a lifetime if done right.

Another way to get links and traffic is to just be active in your niche reaching out to related businesses cross-promoting each other. This is particularly powerful for local businesses that require foot traffic to their door, such as doctors.

In the case above, it wouldn't even have to be related so much as just another business in the area. Google sees those links almost as recommendations from friends.

Keep it up tip

Be constantly experimenting with and expanding the variety of your links. Don't just keep going back to YouTube or any other single source of links over and over again.

It is important to diversify and get as many different sites as possible linking to you.

After a certain point you can scale back but never stop completely.

Ignore the siren call to use software to blast millions of links at your site and then stop.

Conclusion

I hope I didn't blow any brain cells with the above and if so I apologize (a little).

The bottom line is you need to take care of two things. First what is on your page (your on-page criteria). You need to make sure that the words that you want people to find your page with are in the right places on your site.

Secondly, you need to make sure that you are being linked to from good quality places out on the web (your off-page criteria) which will bolster your reputation in Google's eyes, rewarding you with improved rankings and, all things being equal, sending you more visitors.

Summary

The following is a summary of what I suggested above in the SEO area:

1 Get a fast-loading well-designed site.
2 Create great content that your customers and potential customers will love, that meets a need they have (whether they know it now or not).
3 Become active in your niche (and area if you are a local business) and reach out to the established people around you to start getting links and traffic. Comment on other blogs in your niche (giving valuable insight) and leave your link.

That is it ...That is pretty much SEO. In Chapter 3 we will talk about the next traffic source – social media.

Fact-check (answers at the back)

1. SEO stands for:
   a) Super epic organization ❏
   b) Search engine optimization ❏
   c) Send error out ❏
   d) Search engine opposition ❏

2. Digital marketing is:
   a) A holistic approach to marketing in a primarily digital age ❏
   b) A great way to trick people into buying from you ❏
   c) The ultimate way to make lots of money overnight ❏
   d) Pure magic and impossible to learn ❏

3. SEO is:
   a) A game where you learn to get one over on Google and get free traffic to your site ❏
   b) The only way to get traffic to your site ❏
   c) Becoming more and more a holistic website experience for the user and is only one of many ways to get traffic ❏
   d) The be-all and end-all of digital marketing ❏

4. Keywords are:
   a) Words shaped like a key ❏
   b) Special magic words ❏
   c) Words that you repeat three times and get traffic to your site ❏
   d) The words that people type into Google/Yahoo to find your site ❏

5. There are two areas you need to keep in mind when you want to start getting traffic. These are:
   a) Nice-looking websites and cool graphics ❏
   b) The latest cutting-edge technology and a private server ❏
   c) On-page and off-page criteria ❏
   d) You should have done the Google rain dance and worn your lucky Google pin while turning around three times before sitting at your computer ❏

6. One key to reaching customers is:
   a) Finding them after they have purchased from a competitor ❏
   b) Reaching them before they even know they need your product/service ❏
   c) Brainwashing them from birth to want your product ❏
   d) Being really nice ❏

7. An optimized page is:
   a) A page that looks nice ❏
   b) A page that has been customized ❏
   c) A page that has your keyword choice strategically put all over it (not too much though) ❏
   d) A page made to trick the search engines into thinking that your page is perfect for that keyword ❏

34

8. You should optimize each page for how many keywords?
a) 1 ❏
b) 2 ❏
c) 3 ❏
d) 4 ❏

9. Great ideas for content are:
a) Interviews with related experts ❏
b) Videos ❏
c) Long articles (1,000 plus words) ❏
d) All of the above ❏

10. My recommendations for CMS and hosting are:
a) WordPress and a Cloud server on Hostgator ❏
b) Custom made and GoDaddy ❏
c) Custom made and a private server privately run ❏
d) None of the above ❏

CHAPTER 3

Social media marketing madness

I want to make this whole Part as user-friendly as possible, which is why I don't get very technical and am trying on focus on the concepts that really work.

It's great to see you continuing to learn the tips and tricks to getting buyer traffic in this day and age and I actually have some particularly cool stuff in this chapter.

We are going to cover social media marketing or SMM for those who do this professionally. (What can I say? We love our acronyms.)

If SEO is a lot about your relationships within your marketplace (i.e. the related but-not-competing links that point at your site), then SMM is more about your relationship with your actual customers.

In fact, one of its primary and most effective uses for business is as an instant online customer support centre (more on this later).

What is social media?

Social media is defined as content that is generated and interacted with by the participants and the generators of said content.

To give you an example, say you take a picture (create content), you post it on Facebook (publish it on a social platform), a million people comment on it, like and share it with their friends.

You generated the content but the other participants interacted with it and in so doing spread it all over the world. In so doing, they became *content amplifiers*. This is one of the huge potential powers of social traffic.

They willingly spread your message and voice for you, amplifying what you could never have done at all on your own.

Now getting shared a million times is a rare thing (it's what you might have heard referred to as going 'viral').

But it can and does happen many times every single day.

However, that *shouldn't* be your goal for using social media because if it is you're going to be disappointed once you find out your funny cat video only got a hundred views (which is the YouTube average).

Why you need to be on social media

1 Your customers are there (*billions* of people around the world have a social presence of some kind on a social network).
2 See point 1. That is about it.

Seriously, don't give me anything about Facebook takes your identity or anything like that. If you are a business, you need to be where your clients and customers are, and you need to be interacting with them where they feel comfortable interacting.

So, now that that is out of the way ...

What different platforms are there?

There are literally hundreds of tiny social networks out there. Some exist just for small-business people or particular countries.

The main ones that you need to concern yourself with to start are:

- **Facebook** I know big surprise right? Well it has over 1 billion users so it is a pretty big deal.
- **YouTube** This is the second most searched site in the world, making it the second biggest search engine in the world and is also Google-owned.
- **LinkedIn** Particularly good for business-to-business operations but also good for any business as a place to be found by other business people who may just want your service or you might want to use theirs.
- **Google+** Not only good for social traffic, also has some SEO benefits that will be talked about later in this chapter.
- **Twitter** More specialized but still very useful.
- **Pinterest** An image-based social platform with a very high female demographic of 85 per cent, that is fast gaining popularity and value with retailers – as you can well imagine.
- **Instagram** An image- and video-based social network popular with the tech-savvy demographic because it's a smartphone app.

If you only could choose three to start, I would choose Facebook, YouTube and Google+ for the normal business; for the business-to-business company, replace Facebook with LinkedIn.

Now let us determine what SMM is good for and what it isn't good for so you can start to have an idea about how you can use it for your own business.

What social media is good for

1 Social media is a great place to interact with your customers on a personal level.

They can be made to feel comfortable posting questions on your timeline or as comments to updates you've posted.

On Twitter, the tagline is 'It is all about the conversation' and that is the truth, not only on Twitter but on Facebook, YouTube and all the other social platforms out there.

If you ship products as part of your business, you can be sure to get a few 'where is my package?' Facebook page posts now and then. As well as other product-related questions ...

2 Social media is also a great place to get social proof.

Everyone always goes where the crowd is just to see what they are looking at.

It's the same for your social efforts: build up your fan base and more people will follow, just to see what is going on, and they may also end up being customers.

3 Social media is good for lead generation (prospecting).

This is not to say that social media is good at direct selling (see number 1 in the next section) but it is a great place to find people who are willing to find out more about you before buying.

4 Social media is great for product demonstrations and service descriptions.

This is where YouTube shines and, by extension, provides something you can share on Facebook and Twitter, that is, the ability to demonstrate how something works and explain it in detail. Whether this is the latest do-hickey that you came up with or how a divorce settlement really works, this is a good place and way to illustrate it and make it clear for people to understand.

What social media is *not* good for

The number 1, and I repeat, the number 1 thing you need to know about social media is that it is not a good place for:

1 Selling directly and incessantly

As you can imagine, I'm on one social media platform or another pretty much constantly and the one thing I continually see is businesses that do nothing but broadcast their latest promotion ... **all the time**!

I mean, this is alright if you're a deals site like Groupon or something like that. But if you're not, you're just going to turn your prospects off and then you've lost them for good (if you're lucky); if you're not lucky you'll get your account banned for spamming.

Just the other day I saw someone in a £185/month private Facebook mastermind group spam twice within an hour with their first two ever posts. Crazy.

No one likes to be sold to while hanging out with their friends.

That is what you are doing if you do nothing but broadcast sales messages and nothing will banish you to social oblivion faster as well.

So don't do it.

Now, thinking about the above scenario, say you became friends with a member of the staff of a company and one day they suggested to you, 'Come check out this sale my company is having'.

That is a completely different matter.

So the occasional sales message combined with good interaction skills is all right.

Just for heaven's sake don't do it all the time! Try to limit it to once a month, if at all.

2 Social media is not a place for blah content

You have to excite your users the second they lay eyes on your post.

You want them to be hitting the share button before they even know what they are doing because what you share is that cool.

They don't want the latest blah article you found via Google search. They definitely don't care about your tenth anniversary of being in business ... Really they don't care ... Seriously ...

Super ninja trick
Take what your customers don't care about and make them care about it.

What do your customers care about? They care about what is in it for them or how their lives are affected or can be improved.

So to turn around the ten year anniversary of your business say 'We are celebrating giving dogs the best cuts in the New York area for the last ten years' - make them care!

Lead with why they should care and they will do just that.

How to get started

Go to all of the sites above (whether you plan on using them immediately or not) and register your unique name.

Otherwise, you may find that the name you want is gone before you get there.

Next, choose your starting three (for this example, I will use Facebook, YouTube and Pinterest as Facebook/Google+/ LinkedIn are similar).

Facebook

For Facebook, LinkedIn and Google+ (G+), you first have to get a personal account before you can register your business name and get yourself a page for your business.

I recommend that if you already have a personal account then great, go ahead and create a business page.

Next you need to populate all three of these pages with as much useful information and content as possible.

No one likes walking into a ghost town page with just a headline and an 'under construction' sign.

If you are a business with any history whatsoever, it should be relatively easy for you to create content here.

Put it all down in chronological order. (They all let you do this.)

For instance, put in when certain products became available, any awards you have received, any conventions you have been to, major partnerships you have started and so on.

Anything that just shows you are a real company. Photos. Videos. Audio. Scans of newspaper clippings. Anything.

Done well, this will have your potential customer scrolling through your history thinking 'this is one accomplished company'.

Note

Don't make stuff up. Nothing can be worse than lying on social media. You **will** be found out. A good word travels at light speed, a bad word at warp speed!

If you're a new company, that doesn't mean you don't put up information, but put up information about your planned ventures, and your accomplishments so far. Even if it is only joining your local chamber of commerce and hiring some cool people at the local job fair.

Be real and share your company's life (if ever so short) there.

Now get some fans. I recommend getting all your employees and their family, your family (even the mother-in-law if you dare) and past/current clients and customers to like your page on Facebook.

Then, run a short 'like' campaign using Facebook Pay Per Click Adverts targeting people within your local area who might be familiar with your company. Aim to get more than 25 likes as this will give you the ability to choose a 'vanity' URL for your page.

Something like: facebook.com/dog-supplies-inc.

It will also show that you are a happening place and moving and grooving company, at least in people's minds at this point.

Now you need to start producing content.

> ## Note
> LinkedIn and G+ are different in the way you get to know people, join and create 'groups' related to your business and start posting good content.
>
> It won't take much to have an effect in those places.

Producing great content on Facebook

Creating good content on Facebook is not as difficult as it may seem but it can be a case of trial and error depending on your customers.

So how to really make good content?

Think emotional.

What gets your customers/clients emotional? Not just nice, but in an emotional moment. Do you have a pet service? Maybe some pictures of kittens ...

For instance, a day-care centre could post pictures of cute kids, have inspirational stories of parenthood, money-saving deals you've found on clothes, toiletries and so on.

Maybe, though you don't have such a specific group of people, you still have a group of people. Like teenagers or young adults. What gets them excited and emotional? (Teenage boys of course don't get 'emotional'–'stoked' or 'blown away' maybe ...)

Those are the things you need to think of to make great content on social networks that get shared over and over again.

Your latest doo-hickey to get Fluffy's hair straight will get trumped *every* single time by that picture of a dog and cat snuggling together with 'friends forever' written underneath it.

The more that people read and share your emotion-inciting posts, the more people will remember you and see your other posts later when you mention a sale that you have just for your Facebook friends.

That being said, the three best formats for getting an emotional response for the most part are:

- pictures/other images
- videos
- everything else.

See, a picture is really worth a thousand words.

Producing great content on other social networks

For G+, you should do the same emotion-impacting things that you put on your Facebook page. But LinkedIn is a different animal. The content that needs to be talked about there needs to show people your company and you contributing in big ways to the community as a whole.

You need to start groups and contribute good content to related groups.

For example, if you are a lawyer consider starting a group in your area of expertise to answer people's questions, then *really* answer people's questions.

Many businesses start these things but then promptly forget that they did and get 'too busy'. If you want to see growth on LinkedIn, you need to be willing to contribute to the conversation.

If you aren't able to find time, consider outsourcing (covered later).

YouTube content creation

Here you need to be creating things that your customers are looking for and this really depends on your market.

'How to' videos may really work for you here or instructional videos on how to use your products. Other things that help are to create videos about subjects that people would look for before coming to you. Perhaps 'back pain remedies' if you are a chiropractor or 'how to fill out small claims forms in your state' if you are a lawyer. Almost any business can profit from this kind of advertising, because almost everything can be portrayed by a good video.

There are some rules.

Set and follow a set flow with every video. Here is my suggested flow:

1 Introduction with music and logo with brief intro to yourself
2 Then tell them what you are going to explain/do
3 Explain/do it
4 Sum it all up with a conclusion
5 Put a call to action (visit your site, download your report, etc.)
6 Don't be boring
7 Don't be boring
8 Don't be boring

That is about it, be yourself (unless you are boring); in that case find someone else who can show enthusiasm.
I am currently working with a client who is not a naturally exciting individual, so I asked him to actually put his employee in the videos.

Don't take it personally, it is how it is. You need to show excitement or people will think you are in it only for the money (which may be the case but don't *show* them that).

It will be trial and error, at least to start with, to find the content that people want but here is a secret to success.

After producing your first ten videos, which will establish you as an expert, you can ask your viewers what they want you to talk about.

Do those things, then ask again, 'Now what do you want me to talk about?'

Some of the best YouTubers never have to 'figure out what to do' because all they do is ask their viewers what they want and give it to them.

You must remember this is a two-way street, you are not just broadcasting these videos (or those pictures on Facebook) to faceless millions. You are broadcasting them to specific people that have an interest in you and your company.

If you ask them what they want, they will probably tell you (unless you are producing such boring content that they might not even be seeing your requests). Maybe you only get a few responses to your first request. Do them and you will win the business of those who requested them.

Then, when people see that you are listening, more people will speak up next time.

Success is never instant on social media. You need real people talking about you to get other real people to come.

Why you need to be on Google+

You may have noticed that Google+ (G+) is in all of my recommendations and you might wonder why. If you track these things at all, you might know that there is not necessarily as big an audience there as there is at Facebook.

Well there is one reason and that is SEO.

Here is one of the places that SEO and social media intersect. The only reason that there is SEO is because of Google. Google is 63 per cent of the US market and 90 per cent plus of all the other markets.

Here is an example.

A little while ago I had a website where I posted a link on my G+ to a site that I own in Brazil. Recently doing a search for that term on Google, I realized that my comment for that link is *above* the actual site itself!

This is just part of the power of G+ though. You need to realize that G+ has the potential to be a real authority builder and a way for Google to 'verify' your identity, so to speak.

They give you a bit of code now that means if you post on any site you own, you can link back to your G+ profile and get 'credit' for that post even if it isn't on your site.

This has huge potential as now Google has to do a lot less guess work and will start seeing you as a real authority the more you do this, with your site and other authority sites in your niche.

Being on G+ is also essential for your local profile in that Google Local is now rolled up in your G+ business profile.

So all you need is one personal G+ account, one business G+ page and, optionally, one personal G+ page. When Google sees that you are linking to your website and other sites, it will credit you for posts there and it therefore becomes one big SEO feedback loop.

The extra visitors from social media will just be icing on the cake.

More advanced image tips

As I showed above, images are the number one thing being posted to Facebook at this time.

Now the best way to put images on a social network is to put images on two other specific networks at the same time.

These were not recommended above because it is usually best not to bite off more than you can chew to start with and posting images on Facebook alone is just fine if you want to test the waters.

To do images right and get the maximum exposure for your image efforts, post them both on Instagram and Pinterest at the same time.

Pinterest is mostly aimed at the desktop crowd (though there are many mobile users) and Instagram is almost completely aimed at the mobile crowd. In fact, without a mobile device you can't really use Instagram properly. You can view images using sites like:

http://websta.me (Webstame)
https://pro.iconosquare.com (Iconosquare)

However, you can upload any photos you have to Instagram by simply emailing them to your phone email address or saving them on an SD card and putting them on your phone and/or tablet.

So after you have tested out your images on Facebook, head over to Instagram and Pinterest and get to gramming and pinning. They are truly a match made in heaven.

Summary

Be real and interactive on your social media accounts and post things that people get emotionally involved with, and you will be light years ahead of your competition.

Focus on not being boring and check your updates constantly. If you don't hire someone to be doing it on a continual basis, there are many places online like UpWork.com where you can find people who will do it for a reasonable monthly fee.

Be involved in as many platforms as possible from Facebook to YouTube and everything in between. This gives your customers multiple ways to interact with you and also gives you authority in Google's eyes.

Be sure to include getting on Google+; whether you actually get traffic itself, this more then anything else can get your business noticed by Google and can get you listed in two spots on the first page of Google if you do it right.

Big things now include images and videos but mostly images are king now. The latest updates Facebook just made increase the up front and centre position that Facebook was already giving images.

So images are not going away anytime soon.

Fact-check (answers at the back)

1. SMM stands for:
   a) Super Monday madness ❏
   b) Sonic music monotone ❏
   c) Social media marketing ❏
   d) Social money mayhem ❏

2. One of the main uses for social media is:
   a) To make massive amounts of money from people who trip over themselves to buy in your sales ❏
   b) To be a customer support centre ❏
   c) To build an email list ❏
   d) Both b and c are correct ❏

3. Social media is:
   a) All websites in the world ❏
   b) Sites where users and creators interact seamlessly ❏
   c) Only Facebook ❏
   d) Only special sites named social media ❏

4. The main social sites are:
   a) Facebook ❏
   b) YouTube ❏
   c) LinkedIn ❏
   d) Pinterest ❏
   e) Google+ ❏
   f) Twitter ❏
   g) All of the above ❏

5. Social media is ideal for direct sales:
   a) True ❏
   b) False ❏

6. Social media is a great place for social proof:
   a) True ❏
   b) False ❏

7. The best type of social content is:
   a) Lots of related articles every day ❏
   b) Pictures ❏
   c) Videos ❏
   d) Emotionally moving pictures ❏

8. Google+ is ideal for:
   a) Social and SEO ❏
   b) SEO only ❏
   c) Social, SEO, and 'author rank' ❏
   d) None of the above ❏

9. After expanding in your top three networks:
   a) Stop there and keep going ❏
   b) Move on to Pinterest and Instagram ❏
   c) Go really deep to niche-specific ❏
   d) Work on the hundreds of other social networks out there ❏

10. The most important thing is to be 'Real'!
    a) True ❏
    b) False ❏

CHAPTER 4

Pay per click (PPC) simplified and explained

In this chapter we are going to discuss another tool that should be in every digital marketer's toolkit and that is pay per click (PPC) marketing.

SEO and social media are great ways to get traffic for 'free' – although not totally 100 per cent free because you're spending time that not all business people have to spare to be able to create content, get links, likes and shares and so on from your marketplace.

Sometimes it is nice just to click a couple of buttons and get visitors and this is exactly what PPC can do for you, but only if you do it right.

Don't go crazy now and say I told you PPC is a magic button to make money online. Far be it from me to say such a thing. What PPC can do is make money on demand if you do it right. This, like anything, requires work plus knowledge and analytical ability to read numbers, and then you need to apply those numbers.

First, let's talk about the state of the PPC market and then get into how to do it right.

PPC ads in a nutshell

It should come as no surprise that Google is number one in this arena. Google's AdWords (PPC) system is the primary revenue stream for Google ($59 billion in 2014 – almost 90 per cent of their total revenue) – well, at least until their driverless cars and other projects are available to the public.

Facebook is Google's next major competitor in the PPC space but their revenue is just a tenth of Google's and uses a different system (which I personally think is better) that we will get into later in this section.

And also you have the smaller players like Yahoo Search Marketing, and Bing PPC that all have their place.

Google search ads

When someone types in keywords, the first two to three listings are ads as well as all the links on the right side of the page.

This is Google's Search Network.

You can see a sample screenshot of those ads below in the highlighted boxes:

Also Google has its tentacles (shh don't tell them I said that, I mean its ads) on millions of websites across the web.

This is known as Google's Display Network. Website owners can apply to Google to have these ads on their websites via their AdSense Program and this is a legitimate way to help monetize a website.

You can learn more about Google's Ad Networks here: http://adwords.google.com

So how does PPC marketing work?

There are two main types of PPC – keyword related and demographically related.

Keyword related is how Google does it in their Search Network.

You bid on which keywords (search terms) your ad will show up on the right-hand side of and you pay $x.xx or just $.xx every time your advert is clicked.

You can find out the average cost per click (CPC) for each keyword using either the Google Keyword Planner or Google's Traffic Estimator tool (accessible only from within a paid AdWords account).

The price you pay is a combination of the amount of competition for the keyword and how popular your ad is. The more times your ad is clicked in your PPC campaign, the more Google rewards you by ever so slowly nudging you up the paid ad rankings.

So if your ad was initially placed fourth and ended up getting more clicks than the third, second and first place ads, it's possible that your ad will jump the queue into first place and you'll still be paying the same amount as you were when you were in fourth place.

Once again, Google rewards relevancy with ranking, and because ads in first place generally get more clicks than lower-positioned ads (assuming it does get the clicks), you'll end up sending more traffic to your website at a lower cost than your competitors!

Google's Display Network

This is a bit different from the Search Network for two reasons:

First, with the Search Network you're limited to only using text ads. But because the Display Network is made up of external websites, you can use a text ad, a banner image ad or a video ad.

Second, you don't bid on keywords shown up from a search; instead you bid to show your ad on pages Google deems relevant to a keyword.

And with the Display Network, you can either pay CPC or CPM. CPM is Cost Per Mille, the cost per 1,000 impressions. So when Google shows your ad 1,000 times, you pay $x.xx regardless of whether your ads are clicked or not.

Facebook ads

Facebook does both PPC and CPM but they are demographic-based. Their PPC network used to only work inside of Facebook, but at the time of writing they are in the process of setting up their own 'Display Network' to compete with Google where Facebook ads show up directly on external websites.

You can already run 'retargeting' campaigns with Facebook, where each new visitor to a website gets a small file called a 'cookie' placed in their browser enabling the website to show their ads on other websites in the same network, Facebook Exchange (FBX).

And because Facebook's PPC network is 'demographic-based', this means that instead of targeting what people are *searching* for, you can target people according to *who they are*, for instance, the things they like, their occupation, their age, their sex and so on.

Although you can do this type of demographic targeting in Google, it's nowhere near as detailed as it is in Facebook, because Google simply doesn't have the data. This might possibly be another reason why Google+ was created. Maybe, just maybe ...

The problem is that some people don't even know that Facebook has ads. I mentioned to my Mum recently I was running ads on Facebook and she said, 'Really, do they have those? Where are they?' Ad blindness strikes ...

The others

I have tried Yahoo/Bing ads that follow pretty much the same rules as Google, as well as other small players, and I'm not very impressed by them or their conversion rates although Yahoo/Bing was OK (your mileage may vary).

Facebook and Google are where you should focus your effort if you choose this path. You want to reach as many people as quickly as possible with this method, so go with the big boys first. So why would you choose this path? Let's look at the pros and cons.

Pros

You know that people are at least vaguely interested in what you have.

They went and clicked your ad so they must be at least curious to see what is on the other side (if you wrote your ad right, that is; more on this later).

You can really focus down to the nitty-gritty for your visitors.

If you want people from North Dakota who like bubble gum and rock and roll, you can definitely find them with Facebook, not quite in such detail as with Google, though you could find people who are searching for particular terms around rock and roll or bubble gum, just not both in the same campaign.

You can say with (almost) certainty that you will get traffic.

When they're on the ball, both Google and Facebook can approve an ad very quickly – I've personally had ads approved and live in less than ten minutes before but it's normally within an hour or two.

Cons

Costs per click (CPC) are rising generally and can be unnaturally high unless you do proper research, choose your correct keywords or demographics and also point ads to a specific page on your site, not your homepage.

Both Facebook and Google are now public companies, answering to shareholders and having to go out of their way to make sure that they are profitable.

And that means extracting as much money as possible from advertisers.

CPCs can range from anywhere between 5 cents to 50 dollars *a click* and sometimes more. It all depends on the market and keywords being bid on. So you really have to do your research into every word you are bidding for to make sure that you are getting the amount you can afford.

Even this can get really expensive really fast.

Luckily, both Google and Facebook allow you to set daily budgets that you cannot go over, so you shouldn't have to sell a kidney or your first born to pay your PPC bill.

But that daily limit needs to take into account the number of clicks you want, clicks sending people to your website.

Slight aside

PPC works really well, especially if you're doing any type of testing as you can find out pretty quickly what is working.

You need to keep in your mind though that you should aim to generate at least 200 visitors a day to your test URLs so you can be reasonably sure which item you're testing is the winner.

Here's a great online calculator that will help to tell you whether your testing results are statistically significant:

http://goo.gl/4UMIr

Also make sure that you set your daily budget high enough so you can get at least 200 daily visitors.

PPC requires a lot of research and tracking

Some keywords may be expensive but might end up converting less well for you than other cheaper keywords or vice-versa.

So you need to do research combined with a lot of tracking. Tracking is where you see where the traffic is coming from and how well it converts (how many people do what you want them to). Compare the keywords to other keywords and narrow down exactly what you need.

Both Facebook and Google have free tools that will allow you to track sales, leads or other outcomes and so on.

That is the list of pros and cons. Now you may wonder why anyone would go through the hassle. When would it be a good idea to do PPC?

When to do PPC

First when **not** to do it (so we get it out of the way): don't ever do PPC just to get visitors to your homepage. You need a real reason and purpose for your visitors to put together any kind of PPC campaign that has any sort of effectiveness because you need to know exactly how much is going out and how much is coming in. Here is my list of services and products to sell via PPC (along with some exceptions).

Subscription services

One situation is if you have a product that is a monthly paid subscription, a service to which customers will be loyal or is a high converting high-ticket item that you don't spend a lot of money to get.

For instance, say you are an online service writing press releases for companies. You have a monthly service that releases a certain amount per month or you know that, when you write for companies, they tend to stick with you because you do such a good job. Either way, depending on how much you charge, you now have an idea how much you can afford to spend to get one customer (this is called the client lifetime value).

So if you charge £49.95 a month for your subscription and you know that on average a customer will stay with you for 12 months, then the lifetime value of that customer is 12 × £49.95 = £599.40.

Why is this important? When you know how much each customer is worth to you, you can figure out how much you're prepared to spend to acquire each new customer.

If you're just starting out with a new business and website, you won't have this initial data, so just concentrate on coming up with a compelling offer at a great price, make a great looking site, and direct traffic to a landing page that presents your offer well (more on this in the next section about landing pages), and see whether anyone is interested enough to buy.

Keep track of your results and as you discover over time how long customers stay with you, you'll be able to gradually increase your spending to acquire new customers.

Big ticket items

The next area this could help with is if you have a big ticket item, which could be consulting of some sort or even a high-ticket physical item, like a swimming pool. Either way, let's imagine the item is priced at $5,000.

If it costs you $1 per click to get people to your sales page and if one out of every 500 buys what you're offering (which is an awful conversion rate, but still) it might have cost you $500 to get that new customer, but you still made $4,500 gross profit and you now have that person in your customer database to sell more to down the line and maybe get referrals so more ka-ching!

Social experimentation

Another place it could work in the short term is getting people's opinions.

For instance, say you are writing a book and you want to know if people are interested in your subject of hang-gliding in the Andes mountains. You put together a little $50 campaign that has hang-gliding and Andes mountain-related keywords with its title, 'Hang-glide the Andes mountains?' You can then judge by how readily people click on the ad whether they are interested or not.

Expert marketing tip alert
You could also put on the landing page a place for people to ask their most burning question about hang-gliding in the Andes and now you know exactly what people will want to see in your book (that isn't even ready yet) and you'll have a list of people to email when your book is ready for a quick burst of sales.

The same theory applies to product retailers and service providers. If people often ask the same questions before they purchase what you're offering, put up a Frequently Asked Questions page answering them.

Book titles

This tip can also work if you are writing a book and are wondering what the most effective title is. Take the best ones you have come up with, put them together on a landing page and send people via Facebook or Google PPC to vote on the title they like best.

You could also have them enter their email address to get the results and also add them to an 'early bird' notification list where you give them a substantial discount (or even a free copy) as a thank you.

Getting subscribers

One other place you can use PPC is for a small niche product to get subscribers to your email newsletter.

This is where you can really use the fact that you are a small site to your advantage. I heard about someone who once did a small Facebook PPC campaign to their niche bulldog website. It had one focus, getting newsletter subscribers; they spent $20 but ended up with 100 subscribers, several comments on how nice their site was and even a couple of sales.

Likes to Facebook fanpages

As said earlier in the social media section, it is sometimes good to get those first few fans with a quick campaign targeting people that will be interested in your page in the first place.

I've done this very successfully with many, many fanpages. On one video-game related fanpage, I've added nearly 200,000 fans in just a couple of months for less than $200. (For more social media strategies see below.)

PPC advertising strategies

So now you have a focus, how do you set up your campaigns?

First you *need* to watch the relevant tutorial videos provided by Google and Bing to show you the *mechanics* of creating campaigns and ad groups:

http://google.com/adwords/onlineclassroom
http://advertise.bingads.microsoft.com/en-us/new-to-search-marketing

(Click the Getting Started tab on Bing for even more video tutorials.)

Now you've watched them, let's talk about structuring PPC ad campaigns on the Google and Bing search networks.

The most common way is to use the 'long tail keyword' approach by creating multiple ad groups, each revolving around a main root keyword and having similar keywords in the same group.

If we go back to the dog grooming example we used previously, and I type the keyword 'dog grooming' into Google's Keyword Tool, I get a series of keywords all grouped together by theme like:

KIT:
dog grooming kit
dog grooming kits
grooming kits for dogs
dog grooming kits for sale
dog grooming starter kit

TUBS:
dog grooming tubs
dog grooming tub
dog grooming bath tubs
dog wash tub
dog grooming tubs for sale
used dog grooming tubs
dog bath tub
dog grooming baths

CLIPPERS:
dog grooming clippers
best dog grooming clippers
dog grooming clippers reviews
wahl dog grooming clippers
clippers for dog grooming
dog grooming clippers australia
best dog clippers
dog grooming clippers for sale
clippers dog grooming
dog grooming clippers uk
Plus a lot more ...

Once you've selected the keywords and ad groups you want to use, you can transfer them into an existing campaign in your Google AdWords account (if you're already logged in) with a couple of mouse clicks by selecting the Add To Account button.

Bing doesn't use quite as refined a process as Google so what I generally do is to use the exact same keywords and ad grouping in Bing.

If you use the free Google AdWords Editor and Bing Ads Editor software programs, you can easily export your Google campaigns and import them into Bing quickly and easily.

Just search in Google for 'Bing Ads Editor' and 'Google AdWords Editor' to get the download links for your country.

Some quick dos and don'ts.

Do:

- Set a daily amount you can afford even if it doesn't convert at all.
- Have an open mind and test out different headlines and body copy of your ads and see which work out and which don't (this could be the exact opposite of what you think will happen).
- Try and focus on the *exact* keywords that you want to get clicks on. The more specific these are, the cheaper and more effective the click becomes.
- Wherever possible, point an ad to a landing page on your website that is related to your ad.
- Always try to get at least an email address for your efforts.
- Follow the search engine or social network's guidelines to the letter.

Don't:

- Make the click go to a one-page website. This will never be approved by Google, Bing or Facebook. Instead have it focused on a landing page somewhere in your site where the focus is what you want the visitor to do.
- Try to get clicks so that you can send the visitor to a page where you try and get them to click another ad. This is known as 'arbitrage' and sooner or later you will end up having your account banned.
- Make low-quality landing pages that are not directly relevant to the ad text. For more information on best practices for landing pages, refer to this guide by Google: http://bit.ly/ReH2nd.
- Write headlines or body copy that is written just to get clicks. Clicks are not the point; the point is to get people that are already interested in what they will get on the other side.

PPC strategies for Facebook

As I mentioned before, Facebook is a different beast because there are no keywords as such to bid to show your ad for.

Instead, you need to target people interested in related subjects, located in a certain geographic area, by the college or university they went to, their sex or any other combinations of demographic information.

Based upon my own experiences with Facebook PPC, here's how I recommend you structure your campaigns.

Where possible, link your ads to a Facebook page. People don't really like it when you take them outside of Facebook. In my tests, the costs per click of my campaigns halved when I sent people to a Facebook page instead of an external URL.

If you intend to run a PPC campaign to generate likes for your company's Facebook page, also consider creating a Facebook page for a celebrity or subject that has a broad appeal and is somehow related to your product or service *and then* running a PPC campaign to generate likes for *that* page too.

For example, if you were a weight loss consultant who specializes in helping women lose weight and get fit, you might create a fanpage around a female celebrity who has successfully lost weight and now looks great, for instance Jennifer Hudson if you're in the US or maybe Davina McCall if you're in the UK.

Piggy-backing on a celebrity or broad subject like 'weight loss' should make it easier to generate likes for *that* page, targeting people using your criteria (local area, sex, age, etc.) and then you can send occasional 'promoted posts' to your fans with special offers on your company Facebook page.

Something to ponder

If you have a lot of fans/likes for your broad subject Facebook page, you might be able to sell 'promoted posts' to other companies not in direct competition with you, generating another revenue stream. Just a thought ...

Boomerang ninja PPC trick

This is a technique that few marketers will share with you because it is so powerful and that is retargeting or what I like to call 'boomerang ninja marketing'.

What this means is that if someone visits your site they are automatically given a little code and when they visit other sites on the web they will start seeing your display ads. This can be on everywhere from other Google sites, on Facebook, as well as Yahoo.

As approximately 98 per cent of those people that visit your website through social media/SEO and PPC will not actually buy, this means that those potential customers will now have a chance to come back when they are ready to buy without having to actually remember your website's name.

This tool is ninja-like in that, whether consciously or unconsciously, your visitors suddenly start seeing your ads at their favourite web news site and the sites they visit every day like Facebook.

This causes them to slowly but surely begin to trust you more and more and see you as an authority if only because they saw your ad on the *New York Times* website ...

The services I use for this are:

http://adroll.com
http://perfectaudience.com

Both of these offer simple and elegant solutions and reach a lot of websites around the world.

Video PPV on YouTube and Facebook (the next big thing?)

As I have stated elsewhere in this Part, YouTube is the second biggest search engine in the world and it is totally worth your time to create videos to get traffic. Now though, with their new pay-per-view program (PPV), they have become even more potent.

Say you create a video but you are wondering if it converts real fast.

Spend $20 and get a bunch of views to it and see!

Out of those views, how many clicked through to your page? How many of those became customers? At this point you might want to optimize it more and edit it a bit. With YouTube's average view time, you can see where people start to drop off and it might give you an idea of what to change. Or it might make sense to leave the ad up and continue to pay for views.

Otherwise, if it still converts and retains your audience but not enough to make sense continuing the ads, just keep it up on YouTube and get natural views.

Either way it is a win-win for you by saving time and helping you improve at the same time.

Once you get a few good videos converting well on YouTube, consider setting up a campaign on Facebook as well, driving dirt-cheap clicks to these.

This way you can get multiple uses out of your successes.

Ninja tip

When a potential customer watches a video, they become an 'educated prospect'; that is, they know about you, what you do and what problem your product solves.

They will still not convert 100 per cent but some studies have shown educated prospects to be worth 10 times what an uneducated click is worth.

Now combine this with the boomerang marketing technique detailed in the previous section (targeted just to those educated prospects who land on that page) and you may just have an unstoppable PPC force!

Summary

PPC can be done on the cheap or it can be expensive if you don't have a specific goal. Either way if you keep the focus right you can make it profitable.

The key is to make everything measurable. If it's not measurable you are spending money without any idea of whether you're making a profit or losing your shirt.

Focus on your keywords and get ads that get clicks and make sales. Once you determine those and get your percentages, you can pour money into them as you know how much you can afford to spend to get one person to buy.

Then you can branch out and start experimenting with different keywords where the return is not so guaranteed.

And on and on it goes.

Experiment – do 'split tests' (i.e. run two different landing pages targeting the same keyword and see which does better).

Test run 'boomerang' (retargeting) ads and definitely give video PPV marketing a spin (huge potential).

In everything start small (100–1000 clicks/ views) and make sure it is profitable before you commit your life savings to the Google gods.

Fact-check (answers at the back)

1. PPC stands for:
   a) Perfectly politically correct ❑
   b) Payment potentially
      considered ❑
   c) Pay per click ❑
   d) Panning people consolidated ❑

2. The main PPC giants are:
   a) Facebook ❑
   b) Google ❑
   c) YouTube ❑
   d) Bing ❑
   e) Everybody else ❑
   f) Both a, b, and c ❑

3. Be sure to place a daily
   limit based on:
   a) How much you expect to make ❑
   b) The size of the market ❑
   c) How much you can afford
      to completely lose ❑

4. Subscription services:
   a) Are a good service to use
      PPC to get clients ❑
   b) Are a bad idea to drive PPC
      traffic to ❑
   c) May or may not work ❑

5. Your homepage:
   a) Is a good page to use PPC
      to get clients ❑
   b) Is a bad idea to drive PPC
      traffic to ❑
   c) May or may not work ❑

6. When you do PPC, it is good
   to have the focus of those
   clicks to be:
   a) Four different options ❑
   b) Three different options ❑
   c) Two different options ❑
   d) One measurable thing that
      you want them to do ❑

7. Before you start some PPC
   campaigns, you should know:
   a) Your lifetime client value ❑
   b) How much you are willing
      to spend ❑
   c) What you want the click
      to do ❑
   d) What you are going to do
      with the information
      you glean ❑
   e) All of the above ❑

8. Always try in your PPC
   campaign to:
   a) Make sales for your efforts ❑
   b) Learn everything about your
      clients for your efforts ❑
   c) Get at least an email
      address for your efforts ❑

9. Landing pages are:
   a) Where the potential client
      'lands' after clicking on
      your ad ❑
   b) One-page sites that your
      clients want to visit ❑
   c) Only for users of private
      planes ❑

10. Retargeting ads means:
   a) Someone visiting your
      website will now see
      targeted ads on other pages ❑
   b) You will know where they
      live to set up your sniper
      nest ❑
   c) You can now find out
      everything about this person ❑
   d) b and c are correct ❑

CHAPTER 5

Mobile optimization and getting mobile users

You cannot miss this, the Internet world is changing and it is changing quickly. Times are changing so fast, that today is the day you need to make the changes I am going to be talking about.

This is not something to do next month, this is not something to put off until you have time. This is something that you must do if you want to have a digital marketing business at all.

What is this essential bit of tech?

Mobile technology

I'll give you some stats to back up my statement in a minute; first though, what are the immediate steps you need to take today?

Making your website ready for the mobile generation

First, if your products or services are mobile related OR are something that mobile users could be interested in (i.e. not things like Windows and Mac software downloads) then your website must be ready for mobile users.

In April 2015, Google released a seismic update to their index called 'The Google Mobile-Friendly Update' (or 'Mobilegeddon' if you write for the tech and marketing sectors). As you can guess from the name, the point was to reward websites with better rankings if their websites gave their mobile visitors a great user experience. By default websites whose mobile user experience wasn't great would be pushed down the rankings.

And if you think about it, this type of update makes sense with Google seeing nearly 30 per cent of all searches done on a mobile device.

And yet, according to one survey by Adobe and E-consultancy, just 45 per cent of marketers polled have a mobile-optimized website.

My personal feeling is that this figure is actually much lower but I don't have any data to back this up, it's just a hunch from the many websites I have visited; many of those that think their website is ready probably don't know what 'mobile optimized' means.

Regardless, if you're optimized for mobile your **whole business** will gain a *huge* advantage over your competition just for being first in line for mobile users.

Now you need to know some numbers to get this into perspective and understand why I sound so serious.

Currently there are 2.4 billion Internet users worldwide.

When it comes to growth, the most is now happening outside the West. China, in the last four years, added more Internet users then there are people in the USA.

But the Internet penetration of the USA still stands at an all-time high of 83 per cent, while China is only at 45.8 per cent at this point.

What does this mean?

This means that the Internet is still growing, and still has plenty of space to grow further, covering only about 25 per cent of the total population on the planet.

This also means that having international visitors will become more and more commonplace.

Great but what does this mean to you as a small business in Bithlo, Florida?

What you need to focus on are the numbers in the USA. While still growing slowly, nearly 83 per cent of the US population has an Internet connection.

This means that if you don't have a website, you are missing out big time.

Now let me qualify that statement above: if you don't have a high-performing, quality website that is optimized for getting traffic, you are missing out.

If all you have is a website with contact information and a little bit about who you are and a place to sign up for a newsletter that you never really put out, then you are missing out nearly as much as those that don't have a website at all.

But this is only the beginning. Let's get into the rest of the data. While the Internet market is still growing steadily, the mobile market is simply exploding.

The venture capital firm KPCB published a report called 'Internet Trends' and in it analyst Mary Meeker says that mobile devices now account for 45 per cent of all Internet browsing.

The report also says, 'Mobile is huge, it's going to get tremendously larger, and will soon become... The Primary Way Most People Experience The Internet!'

It even goes so far as to say 'the Mobile Internet is becoming THE Internet'.

The mobile market in the USA is currently at 189 million people and, according to comScore, in March 2015 mobile-only usage overtook desktop-only usage for the first time ever:

> 'Just a year ago, there was still nearly twice the percentage of desktop-only Internet users (19.1 per cent) as mobile-only users (10.8 per cent). While the share of mobile-only users has climbed over the past year to 11.3 per cent, the desktop-only population has drastically declined to just 10.6 per cent. Of course these numbers also tell us that the vast majority of the digital population (78 per cent) is multi-platform and goes online using both desktop and mobile platforms.'

You can read the full report here: https://goo.gl/rXWSW0

The world's largest PC manufacturer Lenovo now sells more smartphones than PCs and during 2014, total worldwide smartphone sales to end users totalled 1.2 billion units – an increase of 28.4 per cent from 2013.

So it's only a matter of time before the majority of visitors coming to your website, Facebook page, or whatever presence you have, will be via one mobile device or another.

What exactly this means for your business

This means that you need to start thinking about how best to cater to these visitors. We recently had a real estate client who said that 40 per cent of his traffic was mobile!

And it's now common for sites to experience nearly 20–35 per cent of their traffic coming from mobile platforms.

Some points to consider:

Data from Google shows that 79 per cent of US smartphone users (iPhone, Android, Blackberry, etc.) use their browser **daily**.

Also from Google, nearly a third of all UK page views are from mobiles and tablets.

And people are not just searching and reading with their mobiles and tablets ... they're buying with them.

According to ComScore research, Amazon (the Internet's largest retailer) has had year-on-year growth of sales made via mobiles of 87 per cent and Apple is seeing a 75 per cent growth of sales made via smartphones and tablets.

If you sell a product or provide a service, you need to make sure that your website can be easily viewed on a smartphone and tablet.

How do you find out whether you're already getting mobile visitors? Check your analytics software (or speak to your geek and get them to find out).

TIP

If you don't have analytics set up, either use Google Analytics or another personal favourite, Clicky (Clicky.com). When you evaluate your data, you should be able to easily see visitors from mobile traffic and it can even be broken down by individual devices.

*If you **are** getting mobile traffic (and you probably are), see how long they are staying on site compared to the rest of your visitors. If they aren't staying as long or not visiting as many pages as your other visitors then you probably have a problem.*

Alright so, maybe you are getting a lot of mobile traffic.

Do you know what to do with it?

Of course, if your mobile visitors aren't staying as long, you might need a better website with 'responsive design'.

This is when your website design files contain special code that detects what size screen and operating system the visitor is using. If it's one that could match a mobile device, it automatically gives that device the 'mobile' optimized version of the site.

Besides that, you might be tempted to treat them just like any other visitor to your site.

Why this is a bad idea

While a few of these visitors are probably browsing from home on their iPad, many of these (particularly those on their phones) may be checking out your site from across the street! Or while they are out and about and looking to purchase. These users then have massive potential for you and your local business.

For my real estate client, this meant that many people were seeing his 'for sale' signs and they were searching that address while looking at his sign.

Creating ads for mobile users

Create offers just for these visitors and pages that only they can see perhaps.

Think about what these visitors want from you and your business. Maybe you are a dog grooming business and you have a lot of mobile visitors. These visitors might have their mangy pooch sitting next to them in the car looking for a good service.

At the top of your mobile page should be something like 'Come to our location today, check in with Foursquare (or Facebook) on your mobile and get 20 per cent off!'

How likely would those visitors be to go and do that? How many dog owners do you think will come just because of that little ad? They might sign up for a Foursquare account just to get the discount ...

Well you won't know if you don't offer the option. Have a brainstorming session with your staff, and think about what someone who is sitting across the street would need to take action and give you a chance.

Another necessity of the mobile market

As well as your website needing to be mobile ready and having specific mobile ads, you also need to be checking your reputation on places like yelp.com and other local sites like Google Places.

These are most (if not all) mobile users' places of choice when it comes to finding a lot of businesses within a specific area from which to choose. With the right amount of SEO and some good reviews, you will be at the top of the search in no time.

Some of the key points on these sites are the following.

1 Make sure that you define the area you serve well.
  Don't target everyone within 1,000 miles (at least in the beginning). Aim for everything within 20–30 miles of your place of business.

You do this by working on your site first, putting a page on your site targeting each area or sub-area within that bubble. Also in the footer of your site, add all the zip codes (or post codes) with city names of the areas that you cover.

2 Next, register with Google Local, Yelp, Yahoo Local and Bing Local and set your area of service to the same 20–30 mile radius.

3 Next, start getting good reviews.

How to do this? Well asking for them helps. The tip is here: right after giving great service, as customers are on their way out the door, train your personnel to say that if they appreciated your service you would appreciate a quick review on X (where you need reviews at that point) service.

If you did a good job, many may whip out their smartphone right there and give the review.

You can also ask for these reviews via your email and address list as needed.

Start expanding

As you get a solid grasp of your core area, start expanding 10 miles or so at a time. Each time you do this, you will find it easier and easier to find new business. All the work you have done before will be building behind you.

These local strategies above, combined with a big social push on Facebook/LinkedIn with YouTube and a blog, are absolute gold for your business as those services are very mobile-orientated as well (so everything you are learning in this Part builds on this).

Run mobile ads/contests

If mobile ends up being big for you and your business, consider running ads targeting mobile users only on Facebook, Google Adwords and more. These customers, compared to how much time they spend on their mobiles, are only **10 per cent served**.

This means that mobile ads have little to no competition. Compared to the other areas of advertisement, this is almost the only area of real opportunity.

For instance, in newspaper advertising, compared to how much time people on average spend in the medium, it is saturated with over ten times more ads then the time warrants.

Note

A note for you if you are running newspaper ads. Now is probably the time to drop them unless you know that they are bringing in more business than they are costing.

Taking this to the next level

Okay, so you now have some ideas to start engaging the mobile user but there is a whole other level of integration that takes place when you enter a mobile user's life.

First some more stats to chew on:

- Mobile units (smartphones/tablets) overtook desktop/ notebook computers in total amounts of shipments in 2010.
- With the resurgence of mobile operating systems, Android and Apple are now shipping more operating systems per year than Windows.
- This doesn't mean they are going to overtake Windows in installed bases soon but what it does mean is that Windows has a long way to go to break into the mobile market (as they have tried and so far failed to do) and even buying up Nokia's smartphone division may be too little too late.

With this mobile marketplace, people are now taking everything mobile. Now I want to talk a bit about where we see this shift in culture today.

Knowledge is now mobile

A recent study showed that while people were unlikely to know certain well-known facts, 90 per cent of the people who didn't know those facts knew where to find the answer online quickly if they had to.

This is also happening in the mobile world. People increasingly don't know where your business or others really are. But they do know where to go to find that information.

Now, instead of having to know everything they can whip out their mobile phone and do a search for up-to-date information.

Do you remember the last time you looked at an *Encyclopedia Britannica*?

Nope, me neither. They don't print them anymore. They went the way of the dodo with the advent of Wikipedia and Google.

Photographs have gone mobile

Instagram, Facebook, Flickr and more all cater to a market that uploads photos on the go, and every smartphone produced now has a camera in it that can take high-quality photos just like digital cameras.

In fact, stand-alone digital cameras are becoming more of a professional product then a consumer product as shipments of all stand-alone cameras peaked four years ago and have yet to recover.

Super ninja tip

Create a contest with photos where people put in a tag and do something with your product. For instance, taking the example of a pet grooming service, it could be 'Take the best photo you can of your freshly shaved pooch and get the most likes on Facebook and Instagram and your next shave is free!'

Books are going mobile

E-book worldwide sales have exploded during the last five years from $1.3 billion in 2009 to an estimated $16 billion in 2016.

As nice as it is to snuggle up with a book, people find it just too much to cart around many hardcover books. It is much easier to buy a book online and download it on any device they happen to have handy.

Navigation is becoming mobile

Just as stand-alone digital cameras are dying so are stand-alone GPS systems. Waze (which is a program that crowdsources mobile devices such as Android and iPhone), recently added more users than there were individual GPS devices shipped.

This is not counting mobile technology or people using Google or Apple Maps as a whole but just one app that helps with directions.

Notebooks/cabinet files are going mobile

Not only are the obvious things going mobile but even note-taking via Evernote, Dropbox, and other services are making documents and notes you have made accessible by just a few taps of your finger.

Wonder if that invoice has been paid? Check your Dropbox ...

Magazines/newspapers are mobile

Print is dying ever so slowly but pretty much everything is going online and by extension everything is also going mobile. Why wait monthly to find out the colours for this season if you can log on right now and find them out as you are putting on your make-up at the mirror?

Why wait until tomorrow morning to find out what is happening in the news today when you can find out instantly on Twitter from the very people making the news? Or via the online versions of the newspapers?

All brought to us by mobile technology.

What this really means

The reason I have gone to such great lengths is to show that everything that can go mobile is going mobile. So what does this mean for your business?

This means that you should go mobile as much as possible. Position yourself early or you will find yourself playing catch up.

As you hopefully see by now, this means much more than just having a mobile-enabled website.

Level 1 Mobile integration with your business

This means, using the example of the dog grooming service, that you might consider doing an on-demand service actually going to your clients' homes. To make it even easier, provide a subscription service for those that want it and set times when you will come to their house to shave their beloved pooch.

These are the things that the mobile generation desire. They want something that does what they want when they want it. They want something that does everything in one thing, that is, the iPhone.

For those businesses without a physical service, you can start meeting your customers and demonstrating your services and products while they are on the go. Using such methods as GotoWebinar or Google Hangouts, you can meet your customers online and give them a presentation, with you and them being located anywhere in the world.

So, how you can start doing something now can be summed up in one sentence: Find out how you can go to your customer where they are now – without them having to come to you.

Level 2 Mobile integration

This means getting involved in your clients/customers lives on a very real level without having to 'do' anything.

This involves a few different working parts that automate your business to an almost absurd degree.

For the physical service

For instance, with the dog grooming service, create an app, that:

1 Reminds the customer that it is time for a haircut for their dog.
2 Allows them to choose which cut they want on their dog this time. It should also give an option to write in what they want if the pre-selected options you have don't quite fit.
3 Gives a way to order right from their phone (if they aren't subscribed already).

See how this integrates you into their lives? They never have to see it done; they could be off in Africa for all you know but you have the order, the payment and what to do without doing anything but having an app made.

For the service provider

Let's say you are an accountant. You could create a similar app that could:

1 Remind clients to send in their monthly figures.
2 Notify them of upcoming changes to laws.
3 Give them the ability to upgrade/downgrade their service level directly via the app.
4 Publish exclusive special reports or white papers to only those people with the app. Use titles like '3 Ways To Legally Keep An Extra £5,000 in Your Pocket At Year End'.

I mean who wouldn't want to download an app just to read that?
   Once again, you integrate yourself into their lives so that it becomes seamless.
   This is just the tip of the iceberg. Sit down and brainstorm this hard until you figure out how you can position your business for the mobile explosion before it is too late!

Summary

Mobile is here and it is exploding at an incredible rate that may make the Internet explosion look like a firecracker in front of a nuclear bomb (OK a little over the top but give me a break, I thought it was cool).

You need to get on the band wagon right now otherwise you will be one of those that get left behind scratching their head wondering at other businesses' success.

Get moving, start looking around at all the things that are going mobile and align yourself and your business to cater to mobile users. They want things right now and on their terms. They want to push some buttons and forget about it. They don't mind paying a little more if they have to think a little bit less and get the job done.

Take these underlying themes and run with them. If you position yourself just right at this point you can ride this wave for many, many years ahead.

Fact-check (answers at the back)

1. Mobile technology is:
   a) Essential ❑
   b) Optional ❑
   c) Boring ❑
   d) Rude ❑

2. You should put off changing to meet the mobile wave for:
   a) Months ❑
   b) Years ❑
   c) Days ❑
   d) Minutes ❑

3. In the next 1–2 years:
   a) Things will be about where they are now ❑
   b) Mobile users will outnumber desktop users ❑
   c) There will not be desktops anymore ❑

4. Amazon purchases via a mobile device have increased:
   a) 25 per cent ❑
   b) 52 per cent ❑
   c) 60 per cent ❑
   d) 87 per cent ❑

5. You should treat mobile visitors like any other visitor to your site.
   a) True ❑
   b) False ❑

6. Mobile ads are only how many per cent served:
   a) 5 per cent ❑
   b) 10 per cent ❑
   c) 30 per cent ❑
   d) 50 per cent ❑

7. Foursquare and Facebook are both:
   a) Social media ❑
   b) Good for getting people to check in at your location ❑
   c) Places that your business should be findable on ❑
   d) All of the above ❑

8. 90 per cent of people didn't know basic information but those same people:
   a) Had no idea where to find it either ❑
   b) Knew where to find it online ❑
   c) Guessed good and got close ❑

9. What has gone mobile in one way or other?
   a) Navigation ❑
   b) Notebooks ❑
   c) Books ❑
   d) Notes ❑
   e) Knowledge ❑
   f) All of the above ❑

10. What should you consider to get mobile clients?
    a) Meetings with Gotowebinar ❑
    b) Creating an app ❑
    c) Being more 'on demand' ❑
    d) Being more flexible and going to your customers ❑
    e) All of the above ❑

CHAPTER 6

Email marketing – why you should do it no matter what

OK so that title may seem pretty bold but it really isn't.

Email is often overlooked as an effective marketing medium because it just isn't as 'sexy' as tweeting or Facebooking, Instagramming, or whatever other social network updates you do, but the truth is email marketing is far and away the best way to reach consumers on a personal level.

If you call your customers, they hate you for bothering their day and if you write them a letter, while cool (and a great potential way to break through the 'noise'), it costs actual real money to send to large numbers of people.

If you're targeting potential clients to offer high-end services, I recommend using personal letters or even FedEx to really get their attention, but for the average value client or visitor, I recommend email every time.

Email

Some facts on email that could blow you away:

- Email marketing's return on investment (ROI) for 2011 was $40.56 for every $1 invested. The figure for 2012 was slightly worse at $39.40, when email accounted for $67.8 billion in sales.
- A 2012 survey of consumer channel habits and preferences found that 77 per cent preferred to receive permission-based promotions via email: 6 per cent preferred such messages via social media. A similar survey of UK consumers found 69 per cent with a preference for email as the channel for brand communications.
- The 2012 Marketing Channel and Engagement Benchmark Survey found that 63 per cent of respondents cited email as the channel offering the best ROI.
- A survey of online marketing managers at the end of 2011 found 89.2 per cent said that email is the same or more important to their overall marketing strategy when compared to two years ago.
- In April 2011, 79 per cent of search marketers said that email had grown in importance as a source of leads.
- 72 per cent of respondents to an E-consultancy survey in early 2011 described email's ROI as excellent or good. Only organic SEO scored better.

Email needs to be done right though.
 If it's done incorrectly, it's worse than not doing it at all.
 It really breaks down into two separate categories:

1 Make sure that your email is received.
2 Next, make sure that your email is read *and* responded to.

Making sure that your emails are received

If you go to all the trouble to write emails, you had better make sure that they actually hit your prospects' and clients' inboxes.
 While this isn't so much of an issue when emailing directly from you to them, when you want to send messages to multiple

respondents at the same time (for example, if you're sending out an email newsletter), then things get a little sticky.

Most Internet service providers (ISPs) will limit the number of emails that you can send out per hour and per day, so you can't just repeatedly blind carbon copy the 5,000 people in your prospect email database and hit send in Microsoft Outlook.

Even if you manage to get the emails sent, if you keep doing it you run a very good risk of having your company's domain name (the one you use in the From: setting in your email software) added to email spam blacklists that ISPs use to block emails from reaching their customers.

You also run the risk of your ISP thinking that you're spamming and simply disconnecting your Internet access.

To eliminate this possibility, you have two real choices.

Sign up with a dedicated email marketing service provider like Aweber.com, GetResponse.com, iContact.com, Mailchimp.com. They have arrangements with the major ISPs that enable you to increase the chances of your email getting to your prospects and clients.

You benefit from the trust that the ISPs have with these email marketing service providers that they monitor and will stop as much spam as possible from being sent in the first place.

With most email marketing service providers, every email you compose will be evaluated for trigger words and phrases that could unintentionally flag your email as spam, enabling you to rewrite them accordingly.

You will also be evaluated by the number of 'spam' reports your emails generate from users, which will see your deliverability numbers diminish and then, ultimately, your account will be shut down.

Roll your own email marketing solution

There are a number of software programs out there that can be installed onto your website or separate server that will enable you to run your email marketing system.

Two excellent programs I can recommend are ARPReach and Interspire Email Marketer. Both of these are very high-quality offerings with lots of features and functions with excellent support and installation help.

In years gone by, you would have needed a very high-end server set up to be able to run an email marketing system using this type of software but now with the advent of third-party email sending services like SMTP.com, Amazon SES and SendGrid.com, you can get the best of both worlds.

Both ARPReach and Interspire Email Marketer are able to directly interface with these external email sending services so you have 100 per cent control over the data; services like Amazon SES handle the server-intensive tasks of actually sending the emails and you benefit from their similar arrangements with the main ISPs.

Which route you take, email marketing service provider or roll your own, is up to you. If you don't have technical people on staff or you're not technically minded, go with option 1, otherwise take a serious look at option 2.

How to minimize your undeliverable emails

One way is to make people confirm their subscription request (sometimes known as 'double' opt-in).

This is when a visitor submits their details and then is told to click a link in an email just sent to them to confirm that they want to receive your emails.

Confirmed opt-in email subscribers have much higher engagement rates and email open rates, not to mention deliverability.

However, there is a drawback. In my experience only around half of the people who are told to confirm their request will actually do so, so you *will* lose some subscribers, either because it's 'too much effort' to go back to check their email and click a link, or they just never receive that confirmation email.

You can't really do anything about it if they never receive the confirmation email but another way to stop them from *not bothering* to confirm is to make sure that they have something significant to *gain* by subscribing.

My advice is don't bother with trying to get people to subscribe to receive an email newsletter.

Newsletters are seen as 'boring' and unless yours has amazing information in it every issue, people just won't subscribe. Better to just send them great, actionable information on a regular basis.

Send reports, white papers with cutting edge info and links to YouTube videos you've uploaded with ground-breaking news that directly affects them.

Think about how best to stand out from others in your industry and make sure that whichever method your 'ethical bribe' content is released by, it's not just vague, general information but very *specific* to the kind of client or customer you're looking for.

Marketing tip

One tactic that some business owners are beginning to use is to write a quality report on their area of expertise and publish it in Kindle format on Amazon.

There are lots of videos showing you how to do it on YouTube and it can be done totally free (if you're doing it yourself) or you can hire someone from a freelancer website like UpWork.com or eLance.com who will format and set up the book on Amazon.

Why go to the trouble to do this?

Because then you can give the book/report away for free with a 'As sold on Amazon for $x.xx' statement on the page.

Do you see the power of this? First, it uses Amazon's credibility to build yours (you're a published author now) and at the same time gives the information an actual $$ value, regardless of the value the reader will get from the information within.

Whether you actually sell books on Amazon is irrelevant. Your visitors now have a good reason to jump through one extra hoop to get your book.

Getting your emails read

So now you know your preferred clients got your free 'ethical bribe' with $x.xx – now what?

Ask them to buy something!

Noooooooooo! Don't do it! (reaches out hand in slow motion) Resist this temptation like the plague – this just isn't cool.

You don't propose to someone on the first date. You need to build up a relationship with the other person before you go down on bended knee, so to speak.

Give even more quality, useful and helpful information for free to your potential clients. With the email marketing service providers and the two software programs I mentioned before, you can pre-load entire sequences of emails to be sent automatically over a period of time, each and every time someone signs up.

Don't worry about giving away too much information. There's no such thing. If you're a service provider, you may be concerned that all your subscribers will simply take all the information you give them and do it all themselves.

They won't. Not everyone has the time or the inclination to figure stuff out on their own, especially if you're marketing to business owners. Of course some will, but most won't and those are the people who will seriously think about contacting you for help.

Fill in the holes and give further advice regarding the issue or good idea that you solved in the first give-away product.

 If you're still not 100 per cent sure about giving away lots of free information, don't go into deep specifics – just tell them 'what' has to be done to get the benefits but not exactly 'how' to do it.

Make them look forward to seeing your brand name in the inbox. This 'trains' them to always open your emails. Now when you send them that offer for a discount on your product or consultation, they will hear you out.

Don't stop sending good information. Make it a habit to continually be sending out good information to your email list.

One publication I follow sends out a 'reading list' of things across the web that he has found during the past week that are good reading for his particular audience.

It is a mixture of stuff from his own hired bloggers and other websites and is usually pretty informative.

 ## Marketing tip
If you happen to find a sale or an offer that works really well for your list, don't keep broadcasting it. Make it an occasional email in the pre-loaded automatic follow-up sequence that new sign-ups see. When you keep broadcasting your offers, it has the faint whiff of 'desperate' and also begs the question, 'When is your stuff not on sale?'

Other ideas for fun and profit

Depending on the type of business you have and who your customers and clients are, you might be able to build up engagement and rapport with your subscribers by:

- Running competitions like 'xx of the Month' or 'Funniest xx' and share the results on your Facebook page.
- Posting links to interesting videos you find on YouTube created by others (who aren't in direct competition with you) and explain exactly why people should watch them.
- Finding other people offering similar services that don't directly compete with you who might want to reach your subscribers, and cross-promoting one another to each other's lists by offering useful information.

If I had to start over

If Google blasted my websites into oblivion, Facebook banned my fanpages, and my dog abandoned me the only thing I would really need are my trusty email lists.

Those lists are all I really need to generate revenue because they are people who are interested in the things I am interested in.

I know what they probably want and from that list I could make money to keep me going until I got a new website and a new fanpage.

Your prospect and client email lists are an essential business asset that you should be building, because they really are the foundation of digital marketing and where all the money is at.

Summary

The difficult part is finding the perfect mix of information and sales pitch. Try and lean as far you can to information first and test out various levels of 'sales' to make sure that you don't overdo it with your particular market. Each one has their own tolerance level for sales but can never get enough good information from an expert for free.

Don't worry if you slightly overdo it; just go back into educational mode and people will quickly remember why they joined your list in the first place.

Remember: good information, good information, good information, sell.

Wash, rinse, and repeat.

The thing about lists is if you treat them right they can be responsive for years and years.

If you treat them badly or neglect they will quickly unsubscribe and spam folder your emails (simply because they might forget signing up to get your emails).

Fact-check (answers at the back)

1. Email is often overlooked because:
   a) It isn't 'sexy' ❑
   b) It's boring ❑
   c) People think it bothers people ❑
   d) All of the above ❑

2. ____ per cent of people prefer email though (according to some studies):
   a) 73 ❑
   b) 35 ❑
   c) 56 ❑
   d) 96 ❑

3. You need to be sure with email that:
   a) Your email is received ❑
   b) Your email is read ❑
   c) Your email is responded to ❑
   d) All of the above ❑

4. It is recommended that you get the following if you don't have a tech team:
   a) Aweber or equivalent ❑
   b) ARPReach ❑
   c) Interspire ❑
   d) All of the above ❑

5. The best opt-in is:
   a) Double opt-in ❑
   b) Single opt-in ❑
   c) Personal preference ❑
   d) Secret opt-in ❑

6. Giving something away of value to get people to opt-in is:
   a) A bad idea ❑
   b) A waste of time ❑
   c) Smart ❑
   d) Sort of cool but not that cool ❑

7. After people opt-in:
   a) Send them an offer ❑
   b) Send them 500 offers one after the other until they buy ❑
   c) Never send them any offers, just wait until they ask to buy from you ❑
   d) Send a bunch of more free amazing content, then an offer, followed by more free content and another offer ❑

8. Free information (including telling your clients exactly how to do what you do):
   a) Is a good idea ❑
   b) Makes them less likely to pay you ❑
   c) Makes you appear to be the expert ❑
   d) a and c are correct ❑

9. If they don't buy the first time you email them:
   a) Take them off your list ❑
   b) Keep sending good info ❑
   c) Curse them ❑
   d) Send them a virus ❑

10. If I had to start over, I would need:
    a) SEO ❑
    b) Social media pages ❑
    c) My email lists ❑
    d) A website ❑

CHAPTER 7

Other marketing tricks and tips in the modern world

Up until now, we have talked about the basic foundations of digital marketing today. First, build a killer sales website, then get traffic to your website with SEO, social media marketing and then pay per click paid traffic.

After that, we talked about the two other ways to reach your customers – leveraging the huge growth in mobile usage and, possibly one of the most overlooked ways, email marketing.

In this chapter, I want to talk about several other methods you can use to get traffic that, when combined, can really generate a ton of traffic.

Online press releases

Many people will tell you that these are old-fashioned and to leave them alone if you want to reach people.

This is not the case.

People still want news, they want to know the latest gizmos, gadgets, and trends.

As such, press releases might not be for every business, though you are probably different as you are reading this book.

If you follow my advice from the last chapter, you might create an app. If you have created an app, why not create a press release: 'Want to pamper your pooch by phone? NY dog grooming service says "There's an app for that!"'

This is news that is worth reading and worth spreading around. Other people will read this even if they aren't dog owners, just to see the latest trend. You could even end up in the *New York Times* if you play your cards right (see instructions below).

Press release best practices

1. Always be newsworthy

When you start talking about online press releases, there are many SEO benefits as well. Do your best to ignore these and just produce real news.

Feature other related businesses to highlight a trend or do something a bit crazy to get publicity or maybe broadcast how you are giving back to your community with free dog bath Saturdays or something.

Be unique but, most of all, actually *be* interesting news. This will come in handy later.

2. Keep it short and also have video and pictures

This is the best way to make your press release stand out and get attention.

- Make it about 300 words but then include great images (worth a thousand words) and a short video less than three minutes long (worth a million words).
- Newsreaders and, more importantly, reporters have incredibly short attention spans and you will lose them really fast unless you write copy that is short and to the point, and include attractive photos. If they are really interested, they can then watch your video.
- Even if they don't use the video and pictures should they cover your story, it can be worth it just to get their attention.
- If you need help writing and promoting your press release, you can Google search terms like 'press release services' or go to a freelancer site like UpWork.com or eLance.com and hire someone to write and promote it for you.
- If you fancy taking a crack at it yourself, there are tons of books on Amazon on press releases and getting free publicity and you can search on Google for terms like 'free press releases templates' and 'how to develop a press release hook'.

3. Release at 10 a.m. on Tuesday

Why then? Because it is most likely to be noticed at that time due to the lack of other news going on. This time is usually when 'the lag' hits in the week, despite the fact that news is a 24-hour business.

4. After the release do a little leg work

Sometimes, even if you make your press release interesting and do the above, it still won't get noticed because of all the 'noise'.

Have a list of the top publications that your customers/ clients will most likely read; for example, for our company in New York, their clients probably read the *New York Times* and a few other local papers.

Literally call these places, right after the release (remember it is during a lull, so you should get through).

Go directly after the most relevant reporter (for instance, if you're an independent financial advisor, the reporter will be the one who writes about personal money matters).

Call attention to your press release and tell them what it's about. If they want to look at it right away, then be sure to have the release already featured on your home page. So all you have to do is give them your cute URL for them to see it immediately.

Be sure and get their email during this exchange as well (for the future).

Whether they end up publishing or not, you now at least have an email address to send to the next time you have a release.

In conclusion to press releases

Doing the above can bring massive traffic and credit in the eyes of the world and Google.

Only do it when your website is in good shape with lots of content and you have all the other foundation pieces in place that we have mentioned in previous days.

Otherwise your well-earned traffic will be wasted.

Yahoo Answers and Quora

These are both places people go for answers to questions and a great place to establish yourself as an expert.

Quora in particular is increasingly becoming the mobile and social media answer of choice, and the best place for you to really customize your image, because they allow a lot to be placed in your profile page, though Yahoo Answers is still often at the top of Google for many searches.

Both are still valuable and worth looking into for your business.

How to use them

Give insightful and detailed answers only to questions in your specific niche. Use your equally insightful and relevant blog post as a source on Yahoo Answers (be sure and write out the link with http:// included) or as a 'for more info click here' link on Quora.

That is about it.

Pros and cons

If you look at the most popular posts on Quora, you will see that they use mostly images, and long detailed answers to get to the top. But getting yourself to the top is well worth it.

When a post gets popular on Quora, there is an email that goes out to everyone who has expressed interest in that subject and you will be amazed at the traffic you can attract to your site.

Yahoo is not so drastic or immediately evident but requires less of an investment in time (the questions are usually very much to a specific solution, not so broad and deep as Quora questions).

Sample Quora question:

What is love?

Sample Yahoo Answers question:

How do I get rid of this zit on my big toe?

(This is a bit of a generalization because there are bigger questions on Yahoo Answers too!)

In my tests and former projects, however, I have seen ten visitors or so a month per question answered.

This may not seem like much but if you answer 100 questions (not hard to do) this means around 1,000 visitors a month.

Plus there are even ways to outsource Yahoo Answers as there are established and professional 'answerers' out there willing to plug you into their answers. (This is not something you would want to do on Quora however.)

In conclusion

These two sources of traffic aren't good for every business. Be sure and check them out if you decide to use them. Give incredible content and answers and you will have fantastic results, both with real quality traffic *and* your SEO efforts as the links do count despite the fact they are 'no follow' (at least according to my tests).

Guest blogging

This is all the rage right now – both rightly and wrongly so. The idea is essentially finding an authority blog in your niche and then writing a high-quality post for that site to get a link and bring traffic back to your site.

This is good when starting out but they aren't everything to traffic and SEO that others make them out to be.

So you do get credit for the post both in Google's eyes with G+ and the readers there. But it still also gets credited to the blog you posted on and the click through rates on blog posts tend to stink. (They are not that much better than Yahoo Answers.)

They require a lot of time and effort both to get the post and to create the perfect content. And wouldn't it be better if you spent that time on your site and business? Just a thought ...

The best way to make this work I would think is to outsource it. Have 5-10 fantastic pieces of content created with pictures and everything. Then have someone look around for a blog willing to post them.

That should be all you need for credibility in this arena with Google and should let you know whether they are worth it (use Google Analytics to track which authority blogs are sending you traffic and which aren't – concentrate on the ones that are).

HARO (help a reporter out) http://helpareporter.com

This is a great site that allows you to sign up both to be a source for a reporter's story and also a place to find people to write stories about on your site.

How does this work?

Well first you go and sign up. Once you reach a certain level of traffic (lower than a million on the Alexa.com scale at the time of writing), then you can be a reporter.

There are no restrictions for being a source.

What happens is that there will constantly come into your mailbox 20–30 reporters asking for certain types of people to be 'sources' for their stories. This is one of the many places that all the experts end up with by lines on online stories.

Becoming a source is good if you are dedicated to it. Essentially you will have to constantly check the emails as they come in and apply to each one that you are suited for. It is usually good to offer your services on one unique subject as well, as otherwise you will not stand out to the reporter (they get hundreds of responses).

They usually then ask you a set of questions and you get a mention in their article with a byline.

Cool.

But the most power comes from actually being the reporter. I once had it set up with one of my projects that I would put out a call for a certain group of people and suddenly I had my pick from all sorts of well-qualified people to appear on my blog.

The way I set it up was to give them a full interview either over the phone or just via email.

This got me absolutely tons of exposure, not just for my website (where I started ranking for these people's names), but also exposure on their websites, as many of them promoted my website as a place where they were featured.

I ended up interviewing one of the biggest names in this field with this technique on the first try, and ended up getting a free pass (retail value $1,000) to a conference in my area.

So, once you get the traffic, start running interviews on HARO – you'll be amazed where it can get you.

Rolling with the Twitter giants

Twitter is a great place to get people following your brand but it is an even better place to find big names in your industry with whom to interact and get them to literally promote you to their followers.

So how this works is, first of all, research your niche. For our usual example of the dog groomers in New York, they might look for dog trainers in New York, or reporters that write about pets and/or the home, or even celebrities who have dogs in New York.

Find them and start following them (don't start spamming them or anything – nothing will get you removed faster).

Get to know them and the things they tweet. During this time, share your own musings and good content as well connecting with your followers (i.e. keep it real).

Then when you see something pretty cool or related to you, retweet it, or write a comment to it. Do this consistently and do it well and you will see them eventually check you out and, if you have good content, they will follow you.

Now as the relationship deepens you can @ sign them on things that you know they will find cool (remember, you have been watching them, you little stalker you).

Eventually you will be landing deals, getting retweets and getting featured in newspapers that you would never believe possible and wouldn't be possible any other day except today.

You may end up like the guy who asked Kate Upton to the prom and actually got a call, only cooler because you will make money from it, not just high fives from all your friends.

Viral marketing

Ah, the holy grail of digital marketing, how we all long for our material to go 'viral'. For those unsure of what this means, it means that your stuff gets shared, then shared, then shared some more and next thing you know you are on *Good Morning America* yucking it up with Oprah.

While there is really no way to know if something is going to go viral or not, there are some things to do to give it your best shot. (Below I will use the example of videos, but the things talked about can be any medium, from a blog post to an image you produce that gets shared a million times on Facebook.)

Looking at the list of most viral YouTube videos of 2012, you can note that most of them were well-produced videos.

In other words, they were professionally produced pieces that appealed to the video maker's followers immediately.

This is a good place to start. Don't try to make something that goes viral by being stupid and putting up junk funny videos unrelated to your niche.

Make sure that your videos will appeal to your kind of people first. This way, if it does go viral your kind of people will like it and want to visit your website.

Also, even if it doesn't go viral the views/traction you do get will only build your brand more for the next try.

Next, you will note that many of the videos that went viral were funny. Particularly the number 1 most viewed video of all time.

Humour really gets people to take notice and everyone likes to share something that makes them laugh.

As long as it isn't racist, sexist, or anything with else with '-ist' at the end of it, let your sense of humour be on full display. Don't be that boring guy who takes everything so seriously.

If humour is not your style, then hire someone who can be more light-hearted if you want any chance at viral success.

TIP *Go to your local comedy club and watch a few of the acts. See who you like and see whether you can have a quick chat with them afterwards. You'll be surprised how cheaply you can hire someone to help you come up with a funny approach.*

Next, make quality content to the right length. This can't be overemphasized. Make them as long as they need to be; there is no magic cut-off point for length. One of the top ten videos from 2012 was over 30 minutes long! So this could mean making your viral blog post 2,000 words long.

If you follow the above steps, it will not guarantee that you will go 'viral' but it will guarantee that you resonate with your fans/followers and so on – which is never a bad thing. Eventually, no matter how you slice it, you will get traffic from it.

So at the point that you finally go viral, it might just be the icing on the cake and not so much a necessity for fame and fortune.

Summary

These were my super tips for building your brand and name. Use them for good and not for evil!

1 There will always be more and possibly better websites that may replace those I have mentioned. If you find them, jump in with both feet when you get a chance.

2 'There is no such thing as bad press' rings true even here. The more you get your name and brand out there the better.

3 For those new sites you may find and for the sites I mentioned, remember it is always good to give a lot of good content and link to your website when it calls for it and always in context. You never know where some of these rabbit holes will lead, but I can say with certainty if you don't go out and promote yourself on these places and others, no one else will do it for you.

4 At least to start you are your own best promotion machine. Depending on how well you do it, it will pay off for years at a time, because most of what you do on the sites I mentioned will stick forever, continuing to drive traffic until the web collapses due to nuclear apocalypse (or whatever).

Fact-check (answers at the back)

1. This chapter is all about:
   a) Getting traffic from Google ❏
   b) Getting traffic from outside Google ❏

2. Press releases are:
   a) Still effective today ❏
   b) Old fashioned ❏
   c) Useless ❏
   d) Nice but too expensive ❏

3. Yahoo Answers and Quora are exactly the same.
   a) True ❏
   b) False ❏

4. Yahoo Answers is more for specific questions about how to do something.
   a) True ❏
   b) False ❏

5. Quora usually requires more thought and care in how you answer than Yahoo Answers.
   a) True ❏
   b) False ❏

6. Guest blogging:
   a) Is the best traffic source imaginable ❏
   b) Is not all it is cracked up to be ❏
   c) Should be outsourced ❏
   d) Both b and c ❏

7. HARO stands for:
   a) Hi are you rolling OK? ❏
   b) Hold already ramping one ❏
   c) Help a reporter out ❏
   d) Handy Arnold rounded over ❏

8. When you start following someone on Twitter you really want to:
   a) Be cool and get to know them first ❏
   b) Spam them with all you got ❏
   c) Get to know them, then spam them ❏
   d) Spam them and all their followers ❏

9. One type of person to follow is:
   a) Experts in your niche ❏
   b) Reporters in your niche ❏
   c) Celebrities that like your niche ❏
   d) All of the above ❏

10. To turn a piece of content viral:
    a) Put it into a viral machine ❏
    b) Turn around three times and wiggle your nose ❏
    c) Be humorous and resonate with your existing audience ❏
    d) Spam people with junk videos of your kids playing on the playground ❏

7 × 7

1 Seven dos of digital marketing

- **Do** make sure you are aiming at the right people. The quality of visitors is more important than the quantity.
- **Do** make engaging content your targeted visitors will want to stay and consume.
- **Do** keep to the highest standards possible in your link building (never *ever* take shortcuts here – always aim to at least 'look' natural).
- **Do** spy on your competition and aim to be better than them in every way.
- **Do** maintain active social accounts and be as social as possible in the places that your target prospects visit (search engines and real people like this). Remember YouTube is a great marketing channel, as well as a source of good links and traffic, so use it as much as possible.
- **Do** PPC right. Make sure you have an action that you are aiming for – visiting your home page doesn't count.
- **Do** constantly be testing, changing and growing. Don't ever just settle for the status quo.

2 Seven don'ts of digital marketing

- **Don't** try to find search engine marketing 'secrets' or 'hacks' – most fail because they are short-term loopholes and can get you penalized by Google.
- **Don't** waste time writing bad or boring content and expect amazing links from 'authorities' to boost your rankings. Invest some time in writing quality content that people will love and want to share.
- **Don't** do anything without some kind of plan and an end game in sight.

- **Don't** penny pinch if you outsource your SEO by using cheaper services in countries like India (as an example), no matter how low the rate. I guarantee 99.9 per cent of them won't know how to do it properly and you'll risk your site with Google.
- **Don't** set up your PPC campaigns and forget about them.
- **Don't** do anything just to be 'different'. Aim to follow time-tested processes in similar niches to your own rather than trying something just because it is new.
- **Don't** set up social accounts and then desert them with no interaction. This turns off customers and search engines.

3 Seven best tools and resources

- Adwords Keyword Planner: https://adwords.google.co.uk/KeywordPlanner
- Majestic SEO for checking out the SEO competition: http://majestic.com
- Email Marketing: http://aweber.com
- Website Analytics Software: http://google.com/analytics
- Outsourcing: http://upwork.com
- Daily reports on how your site is doing in the rankings, plus Adwords intelligence reports on the competition: http://semrush.com
- Building a website from scratch or adding a blog to an existing website: http://wordpress.org

4 Seven things to do next week (if you haven't started yet)

- Choose the niche (if you don't already have a business) you will make a website about.
- Do initial keyword research in Google Keyword Planner to see the keywords you need to be going after (and also to see if they have enough volume to support a business).
- Buy a domain name and secure your webhosting.

- Build your website (I recommend using Wordpress) or organize it to be outsourced.
- Map out your website pages and write the text for each (look at other websites for inspiration, but don't plagiarize).
- Set up all relevant social networking accounts and add them to your Google+ profile.
- Start thinking about ideas for articles to put on your website/blog and commit to a regular publishing schedule.

5 Seven things to do each business day

- Try to write every day – even just a little bit, whether an email or a page on your site. You will be amazed how it adds up over time and makes you a better writer.
- Try to connect with other non-competing business owners via social media and other online resources like LinkedIn. Not only will you learn ways other businesses promote themselves that you can model for your business, but you'll have a support network to vent and bounce ideas off. It can be a tough and lonely job running a business – there's no need to be on your own.
- Check your analytics and see how people are reacting to content as you produce it. Do they come and immediately leave? Or do they stay and visit other pages?
- Set goals for your site in Google Analytics (depending on the main action that you want them to take that leads to money for you) and check if the goals are being reached – if not something is wrong.
- Set up a Google alert to run every day for your business name. In this way you will be able to see as soon as Google detects people talking about you, and you will be able to respond immediately.
- Check any PPC campaigns and see if there are any immediate obvious changes needed.
- Check your social accounts for any activity and respond to any questions or comments.

6 Seven things to do monthly or occasionally

- Check your rankings in Google Webmaster tools. You would think it would be advantageous to do this daily, but it is best not to give much credence to short-term gains or losses but rather look at the big picture.
- Do a full audit of your Adwords campaign and make sure any keyword producing no profit (or not enough profit) is axed.
- Do a 'site:yourwebsite.com' search in Google. Hackers are rampant these days and if they hack you, you might not even know it – they can even post web pages on your site invisible to you. This way you will see them fast.
- Do a full audit of where visitors are landing on your site and where they are going. They might be landing in unexpected places for unexpected reasons.
- Change your goal values in Google Analytics to more accurately reflect how much money each action earns you.
- Check how many people are coming to you via your YouTube videos or social platforms and see if you can identify what made them click. Do more of that.
- Find your most popular pages using Google Analytics and make more pages like them.

7 Seven future digital marketing trends to look out for

- Look for Google to clamp down more and more on spam. Aim for your links to just keep getting more and more 'natural looking' (even if they aren't strictly 100 per cent natural unasked-for links).
- Social signals and links will acquire increasingly more power as Google knows these are tougher to fake.
- Mobile marketing will acquire increasing prominence – make sure you get in on this today.
- Facebook is part of daily life now. Expect for it to only rise in prominence in rankings and marketing in general.

- Reviews will become more influential in rankings. Again Google is looking to really know if a site is good or not and they will look at your star ratings on other local review sites as they figure out which sites give the most accurate picture of a business.
- Interactivity will also be more important. Google is getting better and better at measuring how your visitors interact with your site, and it is increasingly important to make sure your sites are fun and meet your customers' needs.
- Look for unexpected changes and aim to always see them as an opportunity to advance your site; for example, maybe a new way to communicate with your clients will beat email. If it shows potential, at least give it a try.

PART 2
Your Search Marketing Masterclass

Introduction

Contrary to popular belief, SEO and SEM are not too complex for 'mere mortals' to understand and you don't need to spend a fortune on hiring an SEO/SEM expert. I want to strip away as much of the mystique from SEO and SEM as possible, so that you have enough knowledge of all the basics and the terminology to be able to understand the 'techiest' of traffic geeks and even have a conversation with them. We'll uncover the meaning of the jargon and acronyms you need to know, such as pay-per-click advertising (PPC), backlinking, social signals and algorithms.

This masterclass is not a 'magic button' or an immediate fix for any traffic problems you have. If you're looking for a way to get a free, instant, never-ending stream of visitors to your website, all throwing money at you, you're going to be disappointed. You won't find it because it doesn't exist so, if this is what you hoped for, please put this book back and leave it for someone with more realistic expectations.

What this masterclass *will* do for you is teach you how to structure your website to deliver what the search engines are looking for and thus promote it to the world. If you understand the principles in this Part and follow them to their logical completion, you'll see opportunities that even I haven't thought of. I know it may seem far-fetched now, but – trust me – it's true. The web is an ever-evolving thing that changes alarmingly fast but, if you follow the guidelines and principles in this book, you'll never be left with less traffic coming to your site. You can *only* gain from any changes in the future.

CHAPTER 8

An introduction to search engines and SEO

So you have (or want to build) a website. Whether it's a blog, an e-commerce store, an information centre, a niche-specific portal, a company website or any combination thereof, you are probably wondering about the best ways to encourage people to visit your site.

In this chapter you will find out:

- what SEO is
- what the search engines *really* want
- why you need to SEO at all.

We'll then tell you a little about the layout of the web as it stands now and how to get started.

What exactly is SEO?

Simply put, SEO is the practice of optimizing each page on your website so that it will show as high up the list as possible in the search engine results pages (SERPs) for a particular keyword.

A keyword can be an individual word but it is more likely to be a phrase that a person types into a search engine to get a set of results. The phrase 'underwater cat juggling videos' is a keyword just as much as 'where can I find an emergency plumber in Hoboken New Jersey'.

The higher your website's page shows up in the search engine results for a keyword, all things being equal, the more people will click that link to your web page, come to your website and buy your products, ring for a free quote or whatever you determine to be your most wanted action (MWA). It is important to keep your MWA in your mind at all times, as this is the whole point of your traffic generation efforts.

It sounds simple, but the reality is a little more complicated when we consider how to get noticed.

What do search engines want?

What exactly do search engines want? How do they decide what to rank, and where? Do they even really know? Well, yes and no.

Any honest SEO expert out there, if you get them in a back room (and after they have searched you for hidden microphones), will tell you that we really don't know *exactly* what the search engines want. We know what they *say* they want, but the actual formulas each search engine uses (the computer algorithms) for precisely how and where they rank each of the web pages on your site are kept secret, to try to minimize the ability of unscrupulous people to 'game' their results.

Not only are all the ranking formulas for each search engine kept secret, but each search engine also has a different formula, which is changed and refined on almost a daily basis.

What the search engines say they want basically boils down to one thing: user experience. They want their users to have a good experience. This is where *exactly* what they want becomes less relevant. When Jane goes online and types in her search query for 'best cat food recipe', they want her to get just that: a listing of web pages that each contain information directly related to 'best cat food recipe'.

They don't want Jane to find someone who merely saw a good opportunity to make some money and made their site look to engines as if it was the place for 'best cat food recipe' but – when she clicks on it – it offers nothing but poor-quality information covered in advertising banners. (This happens a lot!)

The question you might now be asking yourself is, 'If I write, design and build an amazing site that delivers the perfect user experience and that is all they really want, is SEO necessary?'

Why do SEO at all?

You might think that, if you provide an amazing user experience, the search engines will find you eventually. This may be true, but it is not a guarantee. Being a search engine is like being a person walking into the Dallas Cowboys' stadium at half-time and told to pick the best fan. You may be the best and biggest fan in your heart, but who is the guy going to notice the most? Will it be you, in your T-shirt emblazoned with 'Cowboy's Biggest Fan' up on the back row, or the man in the cowboy outfit and the massive Stetson on the front row, with the flare gun?

Eventually, search engines may be able to check every site as a human would, but that is decades off, and would no doubt require artificial intelligence. Till then, SEO is the only real way to equip yourself with that cowboy get-up and flare gun and so get noticed before your dreams of being chosen as the Cowboys' fan of the day turn to so much dust (or maybe that was just *my* dream...).

So now that we know that we have to do SEO to get noticed by the search engines, we need to understand how this translates into a good user experience.

What's a 'good user experience' to a search engine?

To answer this question, think about it for yourself a second. When you like a page on a website, what do you do?

In our earlier example, what if, instead of finding that junk 'best cat food recipe' page, you found the best site in the entire world for cat food recipes? What would you do? You'd probably bookmark the site, stay there a while, copy some recipes, watch any videos they have and share the website URL on Facebook with all your friends on 'Cat Lover's Anonymous' and that forum at *Cats Forever* magazine.

All of these things show a *very good* user experience. That's what the search engines are looking for from your site and from every page on it. They (the search engines) want your users to have a good user experience with your content, but you won't get many users (in the thousands) unless they can find you and know you exist. This is where SEO comes into its own.

Let's take a moment and focus on you and your business, with this in mind.

What's *your* good user experience?

Now that we know that we need to show the search engines a good user experience, let's consider exactly what that means for you. It depends on what you are trying to accomplish for your website overall and on each of its pages.

- Do you want readers to see your blog?
- Do you want people to buy products from your e-commerce store?
- Are you trying to increase brand awareness for your company?
- Do you want to build an email list of prospects?
- Are you aiming to get leads for your business?
- Are you promoting a cause and requesting donations?

In all the cases above, you require a response from your visitors. This means that each of your web pages needs to be making that action easy for them – even provoking them to make that choice.

If you have an e-commerce store and you SEO it to within an inch of its life but none of your visitors ever buys, what good is it, really? If you create a blog, what would be its point if no one ever looked at it for longer than a few seconds?

The search engines use 'time on site' data as part of their ranking formulas. They look at things such as bounce rate (the percentage rate of users who stay for a few seconds, then return to their search results), how many pages the average visitor goes through, and so on.

If you ignore this factor, you may see your search engine rankings drop over time or, at the very least, watch your competition overtake you in the rankings if they have taken care of it. There is more on this later in this Part.

So now is the time to sit back and think like a visitor who has never been to your site before.

● What would *you* want to see?
● What is most important to you as a user?

This is not necessarily what actually *is* most important but what the user *thinks* is most important for them.

● What sort of graphics do you want?

For instance, if you are targeting professors who probably don't want fancy graphics, you probably shouldn't go for a super whiz-bang animated masterpiece but should choose a more refined, academic style.

You are most likely an expert in what you are trying to promote but, because sometimes it's hard to take a step back, it might be important for you to ask your friends and family. Be sure to get as much feedback as possible from people who are interested in your topic but not experts in it. Discussion forums and Facebook groups are great places to help you get started and give you comments on your efforts.

Researching your competition

Once you know what you want to do and have an idea of what your visitors want, it's time to do a little initial competitive research. (For more advanced methods of doing this, see Chapter 12)

Let's say you have – or want to set up – a website for your insurance company and you want to see what your competition is and how they're marketing themselves.

1 Pick one of your offerings at random, like home insurance. Go to Google and type it in. If you service a certain geographical area, type in "home insurance your city".

2 Now look at how many different results you get. For home insurance hoboken (without the quotation marks), I got about 1,570,000 results.

 TIP *To narrow down your search, type the search term in quotation marks. For "home insurance hoboken:" I get just 26,000 results. This is because the search engines are showing pages focused on those words in that exact order, which is a better indication of your level of competition for that search term.*

3 Take a look at those in the top ten. These ten get about 70 per cent or more of the clicks, depending on the subject and how well it is covered.

4 Click each link and look at what they are doing with their page.
   - Are they focused on getting people signed up to a newsletter?
   - Do they have plenty of content?
   - Do they have a super-slick design or are they minimal in style?
   - Do they give away freebies in exchange for an email address? If so, sign up using a non-work-related email address and see what they do. Keep copies of all emails they send, to give you more ideas.

5 How is the website set up as a whole?
   - Is it a glorified brochure or do they have a tiered website structure with a home page linking to secondary pages?
   - Does there seem to be a constant stream of new information, or is it more static and never changing?
   - Is it a Facebook fan page?

Now that you know what the competition is doing, what can you do to improve on what they are doing? How can you make your site more interactive? You know that the search engines love user feedback, so think of how you can offer more ways for users to give you feedback. Be creative here: there are hundreds of online interactions you can create, so make a note always to be thinking of more.

The landscape of the Internet today

Who holds the keys to search right now? Pretty much the universal answer to that question is Google. The sheer massiveness of Google is mind-boggling. According to Statista, as of December 2021, approximately 85.55 per cent of all search queries worldwide were performed using Google. Bing and Yahoo had just 7 per cent and 2.85 per cent market share respectively. In most individual countries, this market dominance holds true. For instance, as of September 2021, Google has more than 85 per cent of the UK's search engine market share with Bing way back in second place with just 9.61 per cent.

It's a similar situation with most countries, although there are exceptions like Japan (who seem to prefer Yahoo) and China and Russia who have their own local behemoths (Baidu and Yandex). So if you're looking at attracting customers only from your own country, it might be worth a quick check to see what Google's market share is where you are.

Google owns not only 'regular search' but also 'video search' (it owns YouTube, the third most searched site in the world) and 'image search'. It also dominates 'map search' and looking for local businesses. If you look for it online, Google probably has you covered. This is therefore where you should focus your SEO efforts.

TIP

While focusing on optimizing your site for Google, make sure you are also indexed by Bing and Yahoo. Making your site more Google compliant will make your site more Bing compliant, because both are really just looking for the same thing and, with Bing serving up the search results for Yahoo as well as themselves, it cuts down your workload even more.

Summary

In this chapter you learned that SEO does not have to be a mysterious code or formula. It's the key to generating traffic to your site – but not just any traffic: the point of your website is to attract buyers, not just visitors. You have learned what the search engines *really* want – a good user experience – and why you need to SEO. Everything you do should be geared around those two things. If it doesn't make people click or can distract buyers from buying, it should be immediately removed from your site.

We discussed ways to start to research the competition and find out how your competitors attract users to their site. Always do this before you invest in a keyword, to make sure that you can improve on what the competition offers and that you are not wasting your time.

You also learned about the layout of the web as it stands now and why you need to spend your time focusing on optimizing your site for Google.

Fact-check (answers at the back)

1. What does SEO stand for?
   a) Sequenced echo optimization ❑
   b) Search engine orchestra ❑
   c) Search engine optimization ❑
   d) Sending extras out ❑

2. What's the purpose of SEO?
   a) To get a constant stream of visitors to your site ❑
   b) To make your pages profitable ❑
   c) To get your pages scanned ❑
   d) To get your pages noticed by the search engines ❑

3. What do search engines aim to make their search algorithms?
   a) As simple as 1-2-3 ❑
   b) Harder to crack than the National Security Agency (NSA) mainframe ❑
   c) Impossible to analyse completely ❑
   d) Open source to everyone ❑

4. How often do search engines change their criteria?
   a) Constantly and randomly ❑
   b) Every once in a while ❑
   c) Every other week ❑
   d) Every year ❑

5. What do search engines want the most?
   a) Lots of graphics on your site ❑
   b) You to be seen by millions ❑
   c) A good user experience for their searchers ❑
   d) Sites full of advertising ❑

6. If you put a search in quotation marks, what does this make the search engine do?
   a) Look for those exact same words in that same order ❑
   b) Think you are being sarcastic ❑
   c) Do a search for something random ❑
   d) Turn on special SEO powers ❑

7. Which of the following can be a website for an online business?
   a) A blog ❑
   b) A static site ❑
   c) A Facebook fan page ❑
   d) All of the above ❑

8. How much of everything search-related does Google own?
   a) 30 per cent of searches ❑
   b) 40 per cent of all traffic ❑
   c) 50 per cent of the search engine market ❑
   d) Over 65 per cent of everything search-related in the world ❑

9. Who owns YouTube, the third most searched site in the world?
   a) Google ❑
   b) Yahoo ❑
   c) Bing ❑
   d) None of the above ❑

10. What percentage of your valuable search engine friendliness time should you spend with Google?
    a) 50 per cent ❑
    b) 90 per cent ❑
    c) 70 per cent ❑
    d) 100 per cent ❑

CHAPTER 9

Keyword research

In this chapter we will cover the R part of R & D (research and development) for your website. This should always be your first step before you start building any website or web business online, because here is where a business lives or dies. If you already have a website and haven't done this step, it's still possible to do the research and make changes – nothing is carved in stone.

The first part of the research stage involves looking at which keywords (searches) you want to show up for in the search engines/Google. If you don't have traffic, your business dies but – more than that – if you don't get the right *kind* of traffic, your business will also die.

In this chapter you will discover:

- how and where to find out what your potential clients and customers are already searching for
- how to be sure you can get that click from the related search engine results
- what you can do about it if you can't.

What is a keyword?

Keywords are what your potential clients, customers and viewers type into a search engine to get to your site. To take our example from the previous chapter, "best cat food recipe" are the four words that comprise the keyword that the user typed in.

The user may have found the same site after typing in simply 'cat food recipe', 'cat food' or even (though extremely unlikely) 'cat' or 'food recipe'. All these phrases are *separate* keywords. Each one has different and various amounts of competition and a varying number of people who type it in.

For short, I am going to call this the *supply and demand* of the keyword. *Supply* is the amount and power of the competition and *demand* is how many people are looking for it. The supply for 'food recipe' is huge, probably in the tens of millions, as is the word 'cat', because there are untold millions of websites that compete for those words. But would you want to rank for those keywords, even if you could?

Why are keywords important?

In our example, we wrote about the 'best cat food recipe' so, if someone were looking for a 'food recipe', they would be unlikely to read your page and they would be gone in a millisecond. Similarly, if they had typed in the keyword 'cat', the same thing would be likely to happen. Neither of these keywords is focused enough; they're just too broad. The person typing in 'cat' may have just wanted the literal definition of the animal, not your amazing one-in-a-million cat food recipe.

One of the simple truths of SEO is that, generally speaking, the more focused the keyword, the better the quality of visitor you'll receive because they are more targeted. However, you need to bear in mind that the more focused the keyword, generally the lower the number of searches that will be performed each month compared to the broader keywords like 'food recipe' or 'home insurance'.

This means that, if you want large numbers of quality visitors coming to your website every day, you will need to create lots of pages, each targeting one of these highly focused keywords (known in the trade as 'long-tail' keywords).

> ## Long-tail keywords
>
> The term 'long tail' was adapted from an article (and later a book) written by *Wired* magazine's former editor-in-chief Chris Anderson, where he discussed the shift in business away from focusing on a relatively small number of one-size-fits-all products, services and customers and instead servicing a potentially much greater number of products and services targeting specific different customers and niches.
>
> His excellent blog on the subject is here:
>
> http://longtail.typepad.com/the_long_tail/about.html
>
> It hasn't been updated for a while but is still worth reading.

Applying this principle to your keywords means that, instead of trying to compete with millions of other websites for highly competitive keywords, you create a large number of long-tail keywords that are very specific. Each one will give you a smaller number of searches but, taken as a group, they can give you substantial traffic. Long-tail keyword searches now make up around 70 per cent of all keywords entered into Google and the other search engines. There will be more on reading the mind of your clients through their keywords later in this chapter.

Once you know what a keyword is and the types of keywords you need to be focusing on, it's time to dive into creating your own keywords list so that you know which searches you want to show up for.

Generating your initial keyword list

Fortunately for you, Google has provided a free tool that shows you *exactly* the terms people are entering into its search engine and how many approximate searches there are a month: Google's Keyword Planner: https://ads.google.com/home/tools/keyword-planner/

We're going to use your existing website to generate your 'seed' keyword list. If you don't already have a website, pick one of your direct competitors' websites and perform the steps below with it, then repeat the steps for the rest of them.

1 First, take a sheet of paper and across the top write the following headings: **Keyword; Monthly Searches; Competition**.
2 Go to the Google Keyword Planner and click the option 'Search for new keywords using a phrase, website or category'. It should be under the green 'Find new keywords'.
3 In the 'Your landing page' section, enter your website address or that of your first competitor. Try it first as domain. com; if you don't get any results, then try www.domain.com.
4 In the 'Targeting' section, select the appropriate country and language and leave everything else as default. Then click the blue 'Get ideas' button.

 If your product or service has a worldwide audience, set the country and language options in 'Targeting' to 'All locations' and 'All languages'.

5 A short time after you've pressed the 'Get ideas' button you should see a list of keywords that Google believes are relevant to your website grouped together into themes.

If you already have a Google AdWords account and are logged in, it will return up to 800 keywords at a time. If you don't have an account, you will receive only 100 keywords per search, but that's plenty to get you started. By the time you have finished this book, you should have a Google AdWords account.

1 Click the 'Download' button directly under the bar graph to download all the keywords (including their groups) to your computer. If you want to pick and choose, click the 'Keyword ideas' tab under the bar graph, which will remove all the grouping information, and then click the top column heading for *Avg. Monthly Searches* once to order it by largest search

volume at the top descending down the page to the smallest search volume.

2 Now write down all the keywords that are directly relevant to your business and the related number of *Avg. Monthly Searches*.

3 When you're done, take the first keyword, feed it back into Google's keyword tool and generate another list and repeat the procedure. Order the keywords according to *Global* or *Local Monthly Searches* and add any new relevant keywords and their related searches to your list.

4 Repeat this until you run out of keywords to add to your list and then move to the second keyword from your original list, and so on.

5 Next, you take the first keyword and enter it into Google as a regular search within quotation marks (' ') and then note down the number of results Google returns underneath *Competition* on your sheets.

6 Repeat this task for all your keywords. The process may take a few hours, but it is a very important step and shouldn't be ignored. It might be a good idea to assign this task to a staff member if you have someone available.

Once you have the results for your keywords, first you need to decide which of those keywords will be your *primary* keyword. This is the keyword you most want to rank in the search engines for. This keyword will probably have significantly more 'exact match' monthly searches than other keywords and will be difficult to rank for in the beginning but, as you build up your content over time, so you should slowly climb up through the rankings for your primary keyword.

In addition to your primary keyword, you should look at starting with around 50–100 long-tail secondary keywords. Each secondary keyword should have fewer than 50,000 results back from a 'keyword in quotation marks' search. The number of monthly searches for your primary and secondary keywords will depend on your sector and how competitive it is. Use your judgement with the results and keywords for your niche or industry.

These keywords may be based around your particular market or niche or they could be product names or variations on your theme. If your website is for a service business, it's possible that you may not be able to generate that many relevant keywords, so just generate as many as you can.

If you are targeting a local geographical area, you can append your keywords with your location. For example, instead of trying to rank for 'plumbing supplies', you try to rank for terms like 'plumbing supplies Hoboken NJ'.

If you have or want to build an e-commerce webstore, pay particular attention to keywords that look like 'buying keywords'. These may contain words like 'best' or 'cheapest' or 'review', either at the start or the end. For instance, I once heard of someone who had good success adding the words 'in bulk' to his product keywords. He had an Omega 3 supplement for sale and simply targeted keywords like 'Omega 3 supplements in bulk' and ended up getting quite a bit of targeted traffic.

TIP *When using Google's keyword tool, pay attention to how much it costs to buy ads for the keywords you're going after. This will give you even more insight into how much value your website could have.*

If a keyword has a fairly high comparative search volume per month but the average cost per click (CPC) is quite low, it *could* mean that other businesses haven't had much success in converting searchers into paying customers or clients. On the other hand, if a keyword's CPC is high and its search volume is low, it should mean that – even though it doesn't generate a lot of traffic on its own – because advertisers are willing to pay good money to buy an ad for that keyword, they *could* be converting visitors who click those ads into customers. Obviously, we don't know for certain whether either of these ideas is true; we can only guess, using a little logical thinking.

The above technique also works well for information sites because, if you decide to place Google AdSense ads on your pages, this can give you an idea of how much the ads hosted on your pages will pay you.

Competitive ranking analysis

Once you have your initial keyword list, you need to whittle it down to the keywords you think you can rank in the top ten results for each of your keywords. The only way to do this is to analyse each of the top ten URLs ranked by Google for each of your keywords.

Since having to go through and examine the top ten URLs for 50–100 keywords would take a very long time, software is available that will automate this task for you while you get on with other activities (see below), but you need to know what information to look for and use some free tools to help give you that data.

It's estimated that more than 200 factors influence how Google ranks URLs for searches, and these are grouped into **on-page** and **off-page factors**. We cover both types in more detail over the next couple of chapters but, in a nutshell, to increase your chances of ranking:

- 'On-page' factors are the things you can do to your own pages.
- 'Off-page' factors are the things you can do to increase the quality and/or quantity of links pointing to your pages (known as backlinks).

For competitive research purposes, you need to focus on the following factors.

What's the PageRank for the URL in the search results?

PageRank is how Google determines the 'authority' of a specific URL (not just a home page) in its search engine. PageRank is displayed as a numbered scale between 0 and 10, with 10 being given to the most trusted and authoritative sites and pages. This is commonly displayed as PRx, where x is the number.

For example, the BBC News Technology home page has a PageRank of 8 (PR8), which is very, very high because it is deemed by Google to be an 'authority' on the subject of technology. Any content directly or indirectly linked to from that page will eventually inherit some of that PR8 and so that page over time will also gain a certain amount of authority.

Think of a link from a high-PR web page to yours as a 'vote of confidence' on the quality of your content. The more votes of confidence you get from high-authority websites, the more authority *your* pages will get over time and they will eventually rank higher in the results for your keyword.

For years webmasters used PageRank as one of the primary indicators to reverse-engineer ranking high in Google, but after being constantly abused by webspammers, Google has now stopped updating the public PageRank seen on its toolbar and other services.

Google almost certainly still use it internally as part of the core ranking algorithm and, while any public PageRank figure is extremely out of date, it's worth making a mental note of, especially if a URL is PR4 and above.

In Chapter 11 I will go over the two alternatives I use to determine the authority of a website and specific web pages in place of PageRank, but make no mistake: long-term, it is important that you naturally build links from websites Google deems as 'Authorities' regardless of what metrics you use to determine this.

How old is the domain name?

Google confers some ranking 'weight' to domains that are older, as they deem them to have more authority in view of their age, assuming they have content on them. Generally, if there are few older domains ranking for your keyword, you'll need to do a little extra work building more quality (i.e. high-PR) links to your pages to counteract the difference in domain age.

How many links point to the URL and the home page?

If a domain's home page has 'authority' due to a decent PR level and/or many links pointing to it but the page that is ranking for your chosen keyword doesn't have either, then it is almost certainly relying on the 'authority' of the domain as a whole. This means that you might have a chance of outranking it, simply by having more good-quality links than it does. This can sometimes explain why some pages from authority sites like Amazon and Wikipedia rank at the top of search results, even though they have few or no backlinks pointing to them.

Do the page's meta title and meta description contain the keyword?

When we talk about the page's title in SEO terms, we mean the <TITLE></TITLE> HTML meta-tag markup, which you see in the very top of your browser window when you visit a web page. This is also the blue underlined text you click on in each of the items in a search results page.

Google likes to see the keyword in the ranking page's title tag, so include it as close to the beginning of your title as possible, but make sure it reads naturally. Don't just throw it in there or try to stuff your <TITLE> with keywords, as Google has a habit of rewriting them to show something completely different.

> ### Advice from Google
>
> Here's a direct quote from a Google employee:
>
> 'In general, when we run across titles that appear to be sub-optimal, we may choose to rewrite them in the search results. This could happen when the titles are particularly short, shared across large parts of your site or appear to be mostly a collection of keywords.
>
> 'One thing you can do to help prevent this is to make sure that your titles and descriptions are relevant, unique and compelling, without being "stuffed" with too much boiler-plate text across your site.'
>
> 'JohnMu' Google Search Console Support Group (https://bit.ly/3kZT9Xr)

Does the domain contain the keyword?

If you haven't built your website yet or you're planning to build several external websites pointing to your main 'hub', you'll need to consider whether to have the keyword in the domain name of your new website.

One tactic commonly used until fairly recently was to build a site with a domain name that contained the actual keyword in it. For example, if you want to rank for the search term "underwater cat juggling" and you have underwatercatjuggling. com as your domain name, you'll get extra credit from Google for having the keyword in the domain name, known as an 'exact match' domain (EMD).

However, after Google rolled out a major update in September 2012 to 'reduce low-quality "exact match" domains from showing up highly in the search results', many sites' rankings fell through the floor. The update was supposed to target low-quality 'spammy' sites built just to show advertising and not much in the way of decent content, but plenty of high-quality sites also seemed to be penalized. This means that having the keyword in your domain name is a less useful tactic than it was.

Is the keyword in any of the HTML headline tags?

Google uses headline HTML tags (H1, H2, H3, H4, H5, H6) to determine what subjects are covered in which sections of the web page.

1 Only use the H1 element once per web page. That should contain the main keyword, so make it the page's content title.

2 Use H2 elements to break the page into different sections, possibly using secondary or related keywords where they read naturally. Depending on how long your page's content is, you probably won't need more than three or four H2 tags.

3 There are no limits to the number of H2–H6 tags you can use per page, but don't try to keyword stuff them – Google will know and you will feel its wrath.

4 There is usually no need to use H4–H6 tags; H1–H3 are all you should need.

How to get all this information

You can get some data from the free SEOQuake Browser plug-in for Google Chrome and Firefox, from a free account at opensiteexplorer.org and by checking individual pages.

However, if you don't have time to do all this work or an employee you can assign it to, you can use specialist research software that will semi- or fully automate these tasks while you get on with other things. These keyword and competition research tools are:

- Market Samurai
- Open Site Explorer: shows backlink numbers to individual pages and root domains
- SEOMoz
- KeywordBlaze

We discuss these software tools and services in more detail in Chapter 14.

Reading your prospects' minds

At this point, you should be the expert on your niche and passionate about it, and you should know what words your customers are looking for. But do you know what they really want?

You'll remember that you don't want to rank for the keyword 'cat' if you are selling 'cat food' and that we need to think about a good customer experience. This is what comes into play here. For example, the visitor who types in 'Omega 3 in bulk' may be someone who is not just looking for a great deal when buying in bulk but a potential distributor of your product or a store owner who wants to buy your product for their physical store.

As you go through your list of keywords, apply your knowledge of your offering and ask yourself the question, 'What does the person want who types this in?' If it helps, answer that question right next to the main keywords you have chosen with a clear sentence or two. Even if you choose not to do this research stage yourself and prefer to outsource it to a staff member or a third-party outsourcer on odesk.com or elance.com, at least you'll know what needs to be done.

An advanced technique you might use to get better at ESP is to run a survey on your site or Facebook page. Actually asking your customers what they want and think might produce some surprising answers.

Summary

In this chapter you learned how to get started with keyword research by brainstorming and then how to find your niche – what your website will be about – by seeing how much interest it generates. Keep up on this on a monthly basis while always keeping to your core strategy – for example, don't change course to cat supplies if you started at dog supplies.

Even if your keywords start looking better, you will lose time and credibility in Google's eyes if you change your site too much. If you have the time and money, just start a new site and outsource, if you find a good opportunity.

You also discovered the magic of long-tail keywords and how they can help you win more visitors and potential customers. You never really know when these will show up, so make sure that they are actually searched for in some fashion before optimizing for them.

You also started to become an ESP specialist, seeing what your potential clients are looking for when they type in what they do.

Fact-check (answers at the back)

1. What are keywords?
   a) Curiously shaped letters used to open locks ❑
   b) What a customer types in a search engine to find your site ❑
   c) Islands in the south of Florida ❑
   d) Words with power ❑

2. What does brainstorming help you do?
   a) Find what you are an expert at ❑
   b) Fine-tune your keywords ❑
   c) Learn more about your niche ❑
   d) All of the above ❑

3. What are two free tools for SEO work?
   a) AdWords keyword tool and SEOQuake ❑
   b) KeywordBlaze and SEO Fox ❑
   c) SEO Toolbox and Keywords for You ❑
   d) Market Samurai and SEOMoz ❑

4. How should you describe the keyword research process?
   a) Quick and easy ❑
   b) Fun and fast ❑
   c) Slow but rewarding ❑
   d) A good way to spend Friday night ❑

5. What does a 'niche' mean?
   a) A treasure ❑
   b) Your area of expertise and profitability ❑
   c) A static web page ❑
   d) The area of your website set aside for ads ❑

6. What does finding your keyword niche depend on?
   a) Your style ❑
   b) Your vision for your site ❑
   c) What you want to talk about ❑
   d) Finding enough interest and keywords that match your area of expertise ❑

7. What are long-tail keywords?
   a) High-demand short-length keywords ❑
   b) Low-demand and long-length keywords that contain a high-demand keyword ❑
   c) High-demand but long-length keywords ❑
   d) Low-supply and low-demand keywords ❑

8. Which of these are good words to use in buyer keywords?
   a) Best; in bulk ❑
   b) World; new ❑
   c) Style; amazing ❑
   d) Class; series ❑

9. How can you put a possible value on your efforts for an information site?
   a) By reading about your niche ❑
   b) By watching the news and seeing interest in your niche ❑
   c) By using the AdWords keyword tool ❑
   d) By signing up for a Google account and looking at the estimated costs of buying keywords that you will rank for ❑

10. What does reading your customers' thoughts mean?

a) Having a form of ESP ❏
b) Running a survey ❏
c) Reading about your niche ❏
d) Studying the keywords that will find you and asking yourself what users want when typing them in ❏

CHAPTER 10

On-page optimization

Many people don't take the time to do any research. They put up a website and expect a constant stream of traffic to magically appear. This *never* happens, so please don't expect it. Instead, think about on-page optimization, which covers what you can do on the pages of the website itself.

You already know how to generate an initial keyword list and how to whittle it down to the keywords that will give you a chance of ranking in the top ten. You even know the software options that can automate this work. In this chapter we'll cover the development part of R&D. This will give you a solid start that many of your competitors won't have and the ability to rank much faster.

You will learn about:

- all the tweaks you can do to the pages on your site to increase your chances of ranking
- your *on-page criteria*; this means that, after you get Google's attention and they look at you, Google knows exactly what you are about.

HTML

Just as with SEO, this four-letter acronym/word may fill you with dread, but the term – just like SEO – doesn't have to be scary.

HTML means HyperText (single word) Markup Language. This is the language that your page is written in. Unless you are building your website from the ground up yourself, this is probably all you really need to know about it. If, like most people, you are using a CMS (content management system) such as WordPress to build your website, putting your content online is no more complicated than making a Word document.

I strongly recommend this CMS option for building a website. After all, you probably couldn't strip your car's engine down and rebuild it – but that doesn't stop you driving it perfectly well. There are probably many thousands of free or low-cost website templates out there for you to find, on wordpress.org among many others. Don't worry about becoming 'cookie cutter' or bland: all of them are pretty flexible and can be customized cheaply by any decent website designer to the point that they become uniquely you.

As you build your site, you will need to consider various elements of SEO, including:

- your home page's title tag
- meta tags and link tags.

Your home page's title tag

The **title** on a web page is the single most important on-page SEO factor. Google uses this piece of information first, to determine the theme of that page and the title on your website's home page, and then to determine the overall theme of your website. So it's pretty important.

If you view the source of a web page, the title tag towards the top of the HTML markup source will look something like this:

```
<HEAD>
<TITLE>example of the title tag for a web page</TITLE>
</HEAD>
```

Best practice for the title tag is to use a format like:

[BRAND/COMPANY] – Primary keyword – Secondary keyword

or

Primary keyword – Secondary keyword | [BRAND/COMPANY]

Your home page should contain your primary keyword (the keyword you most want to rank for out of all of your keywords – normally the one with the highest number of searches) and one of your secondary keywords. For interior content web pages, the primary keyword should be the keyword the page's topic is focused on and a naturally occurring secondary keyword.

If you have an e-commerce store with a lot of products for sale or you're a service provider offering many different categories of service, then you could also create a 'landing page' for each category to help direct people to the appropriate product or service they might be looking for.

For example, if you had an e-commerce store selling dog-grooming supplies, you might have the following categories:

- Dog brushes
- Puppy brushes
- Dog scissors
- Dog shampoos

Each of these terms would be the primary keyword for the category landing page, which might have a title like 'Dog shampoos | cleenadogg.com'.

You could show your expertise and optimize the customer's experience even more by having some content about the different types of dog shampoo available and the good and bad points to look out for. Then you might break down your categories even further:

- Organic dog shampoos | cleenadogg.com
- Dog shampoos for long-haired dogs | cleenadogg.com
- Dog shampoos for short-haired dogs | cleenadogg.com

You may have some ideas about how to structure your website from the keyword research you did yesterday. Were there any obvious search queries that might give you ideas for content pages? For example, if there were a lot of searches each month for 'organic dog shampoo', it might be worth putting together a category or sub-category page on the subject. The same goes for service providers; structure your website into categories with relevant and unique title tags and content for each page.

TIP

Remember to keep your TITLE tags to less than 70 charac-ters, as that's the maximum Google will display in its results.

Why add a blog?

In addition to organizing all your static (mainly never-changing) content and pages on your website, al-most all websites can benefit from the installation of a blog. Your blog is where you post your latest news, infor-mation, pages, new products, reviews, demonstrations, thoughts related to your business, etc.

Blogs started out as a way for people to write an online journal but they are now a core strategy in e-commerce, to show Google and the other search engines that you have an active and dynamic website and that they need to keep coming back to check for the latest information you've posted.

Everybody wins when you have a constantly updating blog on your site:

● The customer wins because they become more educated and informed about the products and services they might need.

● The search engines win because they are filled with up-to-the-minute information to show people who are searching for it (as well as making money when people click the ads to the right of your 'free' organic results).

● You, the business owner, win because you have more content indexed by the search engines, increasing the chance of someone visiting your website and eventually becoming a customer or client.

HTML meta and link tags

Other HTML elements we can tweak to improve your on-page ranking factors are meta tags and link tags for each page and category. The meta-tags section contains entries like the meta description and meta keywords. This isn't very complicated as Google only really pays attention to a few of these tags, as detailed below.

Meta description

Google pays attention to this as, most of the time when Google scans a web page to be included in its index database, if there is a meta description tag in the HTML source, they will use it as the description that shows up in the search results underneath the page title.

Every web page should have a unique meta description that contains your page's primary keyword as close to the beginning as possible (while still sounding natural) and it also has to try to encourage the searcher to click through to your page – all in 160 characters or fewer (the maximum Google will display).

An example would be:
<META NAME="DESCRIPTION" CONTENT='Looking for an organic dog shampoo that doesn't contain any harmful parabens? Click to see the top five here...'>

(You can ignore the META KEYWORDS tag as Google, Yahoo and Bing don't use it.)

Meta robots

These 'meta robot' tags allow you to specify which individual pages you want the search engine 'bots' (or 'spiders') to index and follow links from and which links and pages to ignore. Not all search engines abide by these tags, but Google, Yahoo and Bing do, as do most reputable smaller search engines.

Like the other meta tags, the robots tag goes between your <head> and </head> markup code.

The commands you can use are:

- "INDEX" (you may index this web page in your search engine)
- "FOLLOW" (you may follow any of the links on this web page)
- "NOINDEX" (do not index this web page)
- "NOFOLLOW" (do not follow any of the links on this web page).

(Google will index and follow links on a web page by default so, strictly speaking, there's no need to use the INDEX and FOLLOW commands.)

You can combine these tags as follows:

`<META NAME="ROBOTS" CONTENT="NOINDEX,NOFOLLOW">`

This translates to 'Do not index this web page or follow any of the links on this page.'

If you want Google to obey specific commands, change the META name from ROBOTS to GOOGLEBOT, so Google-only commands would be written as:

`<META NAME="GOOGLEBOT" CONTENT="NOINDEX,NOFOLLOW">`

Additional Google-only commands you can specify with META "GOOGLEBOT" are:

- "NOARCHIVE" (you may not create a cached copy of this page to be accessible from the search results)
- "NOSNIPPET" (do not display a description below the page in the search results and also do not cache a copy of the page)
- "NOODP" This blocks Google from looking for any available description of the page from the Open Directory Project (http://dmoz.org) and using it in its search results.
- "NONE" This is the same as "NOINDEX,NOFOLLOW".

Duplicate content and canonical link elements

One of the biggest SEO no-nos, especially for Google, is 'duplicate content'. Most people who deal with SEO think of duplicate content as two copies of the same web page on the same website, but actually this isn't the case.

For a 'bot', a web page is any unique URL it happens to come across, so potentially these two pages:

- http://underwatercatjuggling.com/siamesesnorkelling.html
- http://underwatercatjuggling.com/siamesesnorkelling.html?affiliate=fyusfys

are treated as two separate, unique pages on your website, even though they are really the same page, with the latter having an affiliate's promotional tracking code added to the end of it.

However, before Google's major Panda update of 2011, Google would just dump what it deemed to be a piece of duplicate content on your site into its 'supplemental index', thus, in effect, removing any ranking ability or power from that page. Now, post-Panda, duplicate content can have a negative effect on what Google sees as your site's overall 'quality' and 'authority' in the index. If Google thinks it's finding too much duplicate content on your site, you might find other pages on your site also losing ranking or, in extreme circumstances, dropping out of Google's index altogether.

Fortunately, this potentially serious issue is easily remedied by using the link canonical element, which tells Google the canonical – or preferred – URL of the web page added into the <HEAD></HEAD> section of your web page's HTML code:

<LINK REL="CANONICAL" HREF="http://www.yourdomain.com/page.html" />

In addition to letting Google know the preferred URL to use for each web page, you also need to let them know your preferred choice of formatting for your domain name – either with or without the 'www' at the beginning. To do this, you need first to sign up for a Google Search Console tools account, if you don't already have one, at:

https://search.google.com/search-console

If you already have a Google or Gmail account, log into it and then go to this URL. Once in there, follow the instructions on this page:

https://support.google.com/webmasters/answer/9370220?hl=en

(Your best bet is to hand this job to your preferred outsourcer.)

Primary keyword in page URL, or permalink

Every page you create needs a unique URL. If you're creating your website using individual HTML web pages, this is the filename of the page – for example, 'siamese-snorkelling. html'.

When you use a content management system like WordPress to create your website content, each page is generated from a combination of content stored in its database while the design of the site is stored in separate 'template' or 'theme' files. Each of these 'pages' has a unique URL called a permalink, which generally doesn't have the file extension '.html' at the end.

So, for example, the Siamese Snorkelling page created in a CMS like WordPress would probably have a URL like http://yourdomain.com/siamese-snorkelling. For SEO purposes, they are the same and you should use the web page's primary keyword as the filename or the permalink.

On-page content

If you don't narrow down your content so that you have clear criteria for each page, Google gets confused and you'll end up ranking poorly or not at all. If you don't want this to happen to you, follow the guidance in this chapter to the letter.

You can consider the various elements of your on-page content by asking yourself the following questions about it.

How long should the page be?

The simple answer to this is 'as long as it needs to be'. This may seem to be an evasive answer, but it's true. For example, if you have content on a category landing page for 'organic dog shampoo', the page probably doesn't need to be that long – maybe 400–500 words. If it's more of an article page, talking about 'How to avoid the seven most common mistakes when training your German Shepherd' or sales copy on a product's page on an e-commerce website, then make the length as long as it needs to be to cover everything you want to cover. On the whole, Google likes longer content, provided it's relevant to the page's subject.

What on-page tricks will boost my chances of ranking?

1 **Upload a video to your YouTube channel.**
This should be focused around the same primary keyword as your page and then embedded into the page using the code YouTube gives you. The video could be a demonstration of a product, a spoken version of the text on the page or you talking in more detail about one part of the content.

> # Google and YouTube
>
> Google *loves* video and especially loves it when you embed video from YouTube. The number of times a video is embedded and the number of views it gets are two of the main ranking factors for the video to show up in YouTube searches, which are separate from Google's main search engines. So you can kill two birds with one stone!

2 **Create an account on Scribd.com and upload PDF documents to it.**
You can embed these or link them to your pages where relevant. The Scribd.com home page has a PageRank of 8, so it's fair to say that Google loves Scribd. Every document has its own page on Scribd, and so your document page will inherit a tiny fraction of the Scribd PageRank after it's trickled down through the website, so it might also end up ranking for your primary or secondary keywords, depending on how competitive they are.
PDFs could be usage and configuration instructions for a product, a partial transcript of the video on your page with a link to the page at the end, recipes with your product as the star, tips and tricks and so on.

3 Upload a slideshow presentation to Slideshare.net

If you are a service provider and/or consultant to the B2B (Business-to-Business) sector, then I would definitely recommend creating slideshow presentations (using PowerPoint or Keynote), uploading them to Slideshare.net and then embedding them on to a page on your website. Google loves Slideshare.net (now owned by LinkedIn) - the homepage is PR8 at last update and individual presentation URLs are able to show up in Google results. When you embed slideshows on your own website, you'll also get a small amount of the authority 'juice' passed to your website to help bump your rankings.

TIP *To turbo-charge these three tips, get social signals like Tweets, Likes, Shares, etc. to each resource on your website and watch your rankings climb over time.*

What should the keyword density be?

This is the number of times a keyword is mentioned on a web page, expressed as a percentage of total word count. If you had 1,000 words on a web page and your keyword was used 10 times, your keyword density would be 1 per cent.

Google Panda – an overview

Google rolled out its first Panda update in February 2011 and is designed to combat websites with little or no quality content, duplicated content or containing over-optimized pages using dubious techniques like aggressively keyword spamming a page's primary keyword too many times.

Before Google would just penalize the page's URL but now too many low-quality pages on a website will result in a negative 'score' for the site as a whole and you can expect to see lower rankings for any web pages on a website.

For the first couple of years updates were issued monthly, but now they are gradually added into Google's algorithm over time, so huge troughs and spikes are less likely to happen.

Years ago, you could rank highly in Google just by adding dozens of keywords to the bottom of each web page, changing the font and colours so they were invisible or virtually invisible to the visitor. Do not even think about trying to do this. It hasn't been advisable to use this technique for several years now, but since Google's Panda update it has been almost suicide to try it.

Although Google doesn't specifically track and monitor the keyword density on a web page, they do track and monitor other related factors. What's important is that you use your keywords naturally (for the users) and you don't use them too often (for both the users and the search engines).

How much is too much? Lots of opinions are out there; I recommend erring on the low side and staying under 2 per cent. Follow that and also bear in mind that, if you read through your page and you feel that it might be too much, the engines will probably feel the same.

What about headline tags (the H1–H6 tags)?

As discussed yesterday when we were researching your competition, these HTML heading tags are what the engines look for to see what is most important in a page's content (you can find these in the heading section of any legitimate CMS). H1 defines the most important heading, while H6 defines the least important.

- **H1** is only for the title right at the top of the page and will contain your main keyword. (You can probably just use the page title again.)
- **H2** is for your main sub-categories on the page. One should contain your main keyword and the others should contain the other naturally related keywords. This is not a hard-and-fast rule, though; only do it if it flows naturally.
- **H3** should be only for subheadings under H2 tags or for other points of interest, links, etc. It should be used sparingly.

These three are easy to add to your pages and, because they create your pages' structure, they help search engines categorize your pages more efficiently, which helps improve your rankings. To keep things simple, you don't need to use the H4–H6 tags; it can get a little confusing if you do try to use them.

What about images and videos?

Use these wherever possible. They will give you extra points, especially the images, because you can even get extra traffic from them in Google and Yahoo.

Rules for images

● Your image should have the name of what it is. It's not helpful to have a name like DSC-394908, which is no use to Google. So you should name it properly as, say, 'Dog-hair-clippers.jpg' or, better still, 'dog-hair-clippers-for-long-haired-dogs.jpg'. This can sneak in your long-tail keyword where only the search engine notices it, and keep it 'legal'.

● Add an 'ALT' tag that has the same text as the filename. An 'ALT' tag is written like this in HTML:

<IMG src=".../images/dog-hair-clippers-for-long-haired-dogs.jpg" alt="Dog Hair Clippers For Long-haired Dogs">

Most CMS programs will let you add this in when you add the image. If you have multiple images on a page, do not name or ALT *all* the images with the same keyword – Google classes this as 'webspam' and therefore bad.

Rules for videos

● Make sure it is a YouTube video (Google loves them because they own them).
● On YouTube, it needs to be set to a public video.
● Before you upload the video, change its filename to match your target keyword, so something like: home-insurance-hoboken-nj.mp4
● On Microsoft Windows, right-click the video, select Properties and then Details. Put the target keyword in Title, a secondary related keyword in Subtitle, use both again in Tags and in Comments include a short description including both keywords again.

- The video title should also contain your long tail as well as the description in the video itself loaded on YouTube.
- Do not make it autoplay; make the user click it to play (user interaction is a ranking factor on YouTube, albeit probably a small one as it is a factor that is potentially easy to 'game').

Things not to do

1 Do not try to trick 'the Google' in any way. Spammy tactics will usually backfire.

2 If you decide to outsource your SEO campaigns to a third party, don't believe anyone who says they can get you guaranteed first-page rankings for all your keywords. All they will do is take your money and deliver little or nothing in return. Nobody can guarantee to get a web page in the top ten results for a keyword because they don't own Google, Yahoo, Bing or any other search engine.

3 When optimizing your content, don't use:

- **frames:** this looks old-fashioned, ugly and unprofessional – so don't do it
- **Flash:** Google and the other search engines cannot properly scan a website built with Adobe's Flash, so it's a waste of time
- **hidden keywords** (as discussed earlier): Google's Penguin update has pretty much destroyed this strategy, anyway.

LSI: is it important?

LSI, or Latent Semantic Indexing, is a process Google uses to discover words and phrases that are related to each other and the context of the document they are in, to help decide whether a page should rank for a particular keyword. Google does this programmatically with specialist software and huge server power.

From your perspective as a website owner, all you need to do is make sure you have additional keywords on the page that are related to the page's primary keyword. For example, the keyword 'broken dentures' might generate the following related keywords using LSI: dentist, tooth, fix, denture repair, cosmetic dentistry, denture repair kit, emergency dentist. You can see that all the words are related to the original term.

Don't worry too much about trying to include a certain number of LSI-related keywords in your page's content. Just add something when it's relevant and when it would naturally appear. Don't try to force a keyword in there just for the sake of it. Be natural and real in your content and you will have no problems with Google. Try to trick them and… well, you already know what happens then…

Technical considerations

It's also important to take into account the following technical considerations when looking at on-page optimization:

- your site loading speed
- your file sizes
- caching
- your IP address.

Maximize your site loading speed

One important ranking factor that few people know about is the time it takes for a web page to load in a browser. Since Google wants the best experience possible for visitors, it cares about this and makes it a direct factor in its ranking formula.

According to Google's own research, the average time it take a webpage to load on a mobile device is 22 seconds, however 53 per cent of visitors will abandon a website if it takes more than three seconds to load on a mobile device (source: https://www.thinkwithgoogle.com/intl/en-gb/marketing-strategies/app-and-mobile/mobile-page-speed-new-industry-benchmarks/).

The three best ways to optimize your site's loading speed are as follows:

- Make sure you're running on the fastest server possible within your budget.
- Minimize the sizes of web pages, images and other related files on your site.
- Use caching wherever possible, if you are using a CMS or other database-driven website system.

Web hosting is now extremely cheap in comparison with paying shop rents and business rates, so don't penny-pinch. You can get great super-fast hosting from as little as £5 ($8) a month from a simple shared hosting account, right up to £500 ($800) a month for a fully maintained server just for your website.

It can be difficult to determine exactly what level of hosting your website requires, especially when most basic shared hosting packages can come with what looks like more bandwidth resources than you'll ever need. In web-hosting parlance, bandwidth (sometimes called data transfer) is the amount of data in megabytes (or sometimes terabytes) your website can serve to your visitors per month. That's for every web page, every image and every single file on your website.

Even though basic hosting packages can come with quite substantial-looking bandwidth allocations, what they don't cover is the number of visitors they can handle at the same time. I learned this lesson over time when one of my websites became extremely popular, to the point where today it attracts nearly 1,000 visitors an hour, every hour. I had to upgrade my server's power rapidly to stop it from gradually slowing down, and then freezing and having to be rebooted every day.

If this had kept happening every time Google came back to scan my site, I would almost certainly have lost some of my hard-earned rankings and income.

Minimize your file sizes

Likewise, do whatever you can to minimize the sizes of all the files on your site, particularly images. Be aware that simply resizing a large image down so it's smaller on the page doesn't make it any quicker to load. If you've got high-quality images, get an in-house graphic person (or external outsourcer) to run them through Photoshop and create web-friendly versions of them.

By simply using default settings, you can easily reduce large, high-quality image files and resize them down so that they fit nicely on a web page with a final file size that's tiny in comparison to the original, and with barely a noticeable difference in quality. You'll be surprised how much of an increase in speed you can achieve when you optimize everything.

Make sure that your coding meets W3C standards. This is not necessarily a ranking factor but it can help Google index your information that much faster.

You can find a great validation checker here: http://validator.w3.org/

Use caching

Caching works particularly well if you have a database-driven site that generates pages 'on the fly', rather than having a site consisting of static HTML pages. With a database-driven site – for example, one made with a content management system like WordPress – every time a visitor requests to display a certain page, the CMS has to go through all the procedures needed to create that page. So it has to connect with the database, search for the required content, pull the content out, locate the page template and render the completed page.

This all takes time and server resources, which doesn't help you if you have a lot of people visiting your site at the same time and/or an underpowered server. A far better idea is to see if you can set up a static version of your page and display that instead. WordPress can do this, via a free plug-in called W3 Total Cache, and other CMS systems like Joomla give you the option to do this as well.

If you're not sure, speak to your tech person to see if it's possible on your system.

Have a unique IP address

Your IP address is the string of numbers separated by periods that identify a computer on a network, in this case the Internet.

On the Internet this becomes slightly more complicated if you have a shared web-hosting account, because there may be many dozens or hundreds of websites that are assigned the same IP address.

Ideally, you should spend a little more per month and get a unique IP address. There are two main reasons why this is a good idea:

1 A website you share an IP address with may be aggressively doing bad SEO. While there's no proof that Google would punish all websites on that IP address, for the sake of an extra few dollars or pounds you can protect yourself from this possibility.
2 If you're thinking about setting up secure e-commerce facilities directly on your website, you'll need a unique IP address assigned to your website before you purchase your secure certificate.

Content reorganization

We've already talked about the best ways to organize your information on your website. If you have an existing website with a structure that you want to change, you need to make sure you have some search engine redirects in place to tell Google and the other search engines where your new pages are. You can find more information on redirects here: http://www.webconfs.com/how-to-redirect-a-webpage.php
(The main redirect I use is a 301 – a permanent redirect.)

Get your robot director going

This is known as a robots.txt file. This tells the search engine bots where to go and to differentiate the important things from the unimportant. Some CMS programs generate this automatically. To read more about robots.txt files, go here: http://www.robotstxt.org

If your site doesn't have one, or your CMS doesn't generate one, here's a free online robots.txt generator: http://tools.seobook.com/robots-txt/generator/

Send your sitemap to the search engines

After you have built and launched your site, you want to make it as easy as possible for Google and Bing to come and scan all the pages on your website, so you need to create and submit a sitemap to them. (Yahoo no longer has its own algorithm and only uses Bing; it is now pretty much just a news portal with a Bing search box.)

Some content management systems are able automatically to generate a sitemap, either directly or with the use of a plug-in. For WordPress users, I recommend the free WordPress SEO plug-in by Yoast:
https://wordpress.org/plugins/wordpress-seo/

If your website cannot automatically generate its own sitemap, Google has kindly created a free online tool to help you generate a sitemap for you:
http://code.google.com/p/googlesitemapgenerator/

It hasn't been updated in a while so you may need your tech guy to test it out to see if it works. It will also need to be loaded on your site and refreshed frequently if it is not automated. Google checks your page frequently, and that is the first place it goes.

For websites that I build that do not have built-in sitemap generation, I use a paid software program from https://www. xml-sitemaps.com which hooks into my webhosting's 'cron' to automatically scan and index all the pages on the site, create the updated sitemap file and then ping Google, Bing and Yahoo with the new info – all without me doing anything.

This script is cheap and very easy to set up – your tech guy should have it up and running in 10 minutes or less.

Once you are done, go here to submit it to Google:

● http://google.com/webmasters

and then here for Bing:

● http://www.bing.com/toolbox/webmaster/

Be sure to update your sitemap every time something changes on your site or, if that's too inconvenient, just do it once every week or two. Don't overdo it: the search engines don't like it and you'll just look like that kid in your year at school who was always desperate for attention – 'Look at me, look at me!'

Summary

In this chapter you learned how to make your pages ready for Google to have a look and, when they look, to like what they see. You now know how to optimize your pages for keywords. Keep your site structure simple (two or three tiers) and remember to put your keywords in everything, from the domain name to the fine print, but without overdoing it.

It cannot be over-emphasized that it's vital to make your site interactive. Embed YouTube videos, good content, places to comment and leave feedback, as well as product review sections and other features all over the place for your customers to enjoy.

In the next chapter, we are going to look at off-page ranking factors, which is the next area of SEO to tackle once you are happy with your on-page factors.

Fact-check (answers at the back)

1. What does HTML stand for?
   a) Hyper Text Management Language ❏
   b) HyperText Markup Language ❏
   c) High Text Meta Links ❏
   d) Human Text Markup Language ❏

2. For domain name SEO, what should you aim to do?
   a) Always think of something cool and unique ❏
   b) Put in some random numbers and letters ❏
   c) Concentrate on branding rather than trying to put keywords in it ❏
   d) Aim to be the next Google ❏

3. Titles on a home page should optimize for no more than how many keywords?
   a) One ❏
   b) Two ❏
   c) Three ❏
   d) Four ❏

4. How many keywords should you optimize all the other titles for?
   a) One ❏
   b) Two ❏
   c) Three ❏
   d) Four ❏

5. Which H tags are not really needed?
   a) H1 ❏
   b) H2 ❏
   c) H3 ❏
   d) H4–6 ❏

6. What kind of keyword should images and videos have?
   a) None – they don't need keywords in them ❏
   b) They should be full of the main keyword ❏
   c) They should be focused on a related long-tail keyword ❏
   d) They should always be random numbers and letters ❏

7. How useful are frames, Flash and hidden keywords?
   a) Fairly useful but not essential ❏
   b) Vital ❏
   c) Only if you have time to do them ❏
   d) A bad idea, always ❏

8. What is LSI?
   a) Probably a red herring ❏
   b) Unimportant ❏
   c) Useless to try and guess ❏
   d) How Google finds related keywords to help decide the topic of a page ❏

9. Why is page load time a ranking factor used by Google?
   a) They want the best experience possible for visitors ❏
   b) People will visit a website less often if it's slower than a competitor's ❏
   c) They want to make it as difficult as possible for you to get into the top ten ❏
   d) They want you to spend more money on your server ❏

10. How often should you resubmit your sitemap to Google and Bing?
a) Every day ☐
b) Every time something changes on your site ☐
c) Once a year ☐
d) Never ☐

CHAPTER 11

Off-page optimization

You now know how to build and structure your website to get the maximum SEO benefit from it, so all you need now are visitors. In this chapter, you will learn how to increase the chances of ranking even further, by creating high-quality links that point back to pages on your site.

You've already considered the kinds of things you do when you find a website you like, and now you'll find out how to apply those factors to your own site. It really all comes down to how much people like you and how much they show that love to you, and in this chapter we're going to be talking in detail about:

- backlinks and external PageRank, and how to examine and improve your backlink profile
- a major change, called AuthorRank, that will probably alter SEO as we know it and how you can start positioning yourself to take advantage of it now.

Why are backlinks important?

As mentioned in Chapter 9, backlinks are links from a page on someone else's website to a page on your site. They are normally shown as blue, underlined text, although they may be another colour and not underlined. But most webmasters now stick to the de facto standard of blue and underlined.

Images can also be made into hyperlinks that can take you somewhere else when clicked.

Backlinks are important when it comes to SEO because they are at the core of how Google decides to rank individual web pages for keyword-related searches. It measures this using a system called PageRank.

What is PageRank?

As mentioned in Chapter 9, PageRank is Google's method of determining how trustworthy and authoritarian the content is on a page.

The higher the page's PageRank, the more trustworthy Google treats it. So if you get have a high PR web page linking to one of your web pages, some of that PR will be passed on to your web page and Google will (all things being equal) begin to treat it as an authority on your page's topic. It will begin to use that as a factor to possibly rank the page for the primary keyword.

 Remember: PageRank is just one of more than 200 factors Google uses to determine the ranking of a page for a keyword. Getting high PR backlinks to your web page on its own is no guarantee you will rank ever for a keyword, but common sense will tell you, it certainly won't hurt.

If you think about it, it makes sense that Google would see this as a good thing, as high (trusted) PR links pointing to another page is a 'vote of confidence' that the information on the page is good and relevant and something visitors might find useful.

But getting these high PR backlinks isn't always easy and so what happened was some marketers and SEO people would switch quality for quantity. They would use automated software and cheap outsourcers in India and the Philippines to blast hundreds and thousands of low-quality links (like blog comments, links in web 2.0 profile pages and in discussion forum signatures) and ended up ranking lots of low-quality sites in Google in the top ten for their keywords.

But over the last few years, Google has been on the attack to eliminate these 'webspam' techniques from its index and culminated recently in two major updates:

1 The Google Penguin 'Penalty' (discussed shortly)
2 Public PageRank metric updating stopped in December 2013.

While we can be certain that Google is still using PR internally as part of its ranking methodology, website owners can no longer use PR as a reliable indicator of authority or quality. Fortunately, there are excellent alternatives to the PageRank metric:

● TrustFlow and CitationFlow by Majestic.com
  Excellent training videos here: https://goo.gl/DNj9p1
● MozTrust, MozRank, Domain Authority and Page Authority by Moz.com
  https://moz.com/learn/seo/domain-authority
  https://moz.com/learn/seo/page-authority
  https://moz.com/learn/seo/moztrust
  https://moz.com/learn/seo/mozrank
● ARank (AR) by Ahrefs.com
  https://help.ahrefs.com

Moz's Domain/Page Authority is probably most popular but Majestic's TrustFlow/CitationFlow is generally thought to be more accurate and less likely to be 'tricked' into higher values with low-quality URLs.

I like to err on the side of caution so I stick with Majestic's metrics and I will be using Majestic's system to perform analyses in this section of the book.

Examining your backlink profile

As the name suggests, your backlink profile is the overall picture of all of the backlinks pointing to all your pages on your site.
   To generate your backlink profile:

1 Sign up for a Silver-level account with Majestic.com
2 Enter your homepage URL (without http://www), select 'Root Domain' from the dropdown menu and click the orange 'Search' button to start the analysis.

The Summary screen (which you see first) will give you the big picture overview with lots of data. When looking at your backlink profile there are several things to consider: link diversity, unnatural anchor text profile, low-quality links, relevant links and link velocity. You also need to look at when to use rel='nofollow' and at other linking no-nos.

   I realize that all sounds a bit 'jargony' and techie, but don't panic – we'll go through it all now in more detail.

Link diversity

Ideally, you should have a large variety of different types of link pointing back to each URL on your site. No one type of link should have a significantly higher percentage compared with the others, especially with link types Google can class as 'spammy', such as links from forum profiles and blog comments.

Click the 'Backlink' tab in the horizontal menu and then click the 'Hide deleted backlinks' button.

This will show all the links pointing to your homepage that Majestic has logged in its database.

Scroll through the list to see where your links are coming from. If you seem to have significantly more of link types that Google might deem as spammy, you could try contacting the webmaster of the link pointing to you to see if they would remove it, make it 'no-follow' or try to increase the percentage of your other link types so they even out across all your link profile.

Unnatural anchor text profile

While you want a diverse 'footprint' of link types pointing to your website pages, you shouldn't also have a large number of links using the same anchor text pointing to your pages. This is one of the main 'over-optimization' factors Google stamped on with its size-11 steel-toe-capped boots.

On the Summary page you will see a simple pie-chart graph showing the anchor text profile for your homepage. What you're looking for is a nice fairly even spread of different anchor text wording across all the links.

I personally like to keep each anchor text percentage on the low side, around 6 or 7 per cent, and, while I do use primary and secondary keywords linking to the relevant pages, I also use anchor text that doesn't contain any of my keywords – so anchor text like:

- [www.mydomain.com]
- [click here]
- [check this out]
- [website]
- [My Company Name]

Click the 'Anchor text' tab in Majestic and you'll be able to see exactly where your links are coming from and the text they are using (if any). You'll be able to see instantly if there are any links with anchor text that isn't relevant at all and then you can decide what action to take.

My personal 'red flags' are links from domains with a TrustFlow and CitationFlow that are under 10 and whose Topical TrustFlow (discussed shortly) isn't remotely close to my website. To confirm this, I will manually check the referring link to see if it's legit or spammy.

> * Domain authority is Open Site Explorer's best guess as to how well (or not) a website will rank in Google's search engine rankings. It is generally seen by the SEO industry as comparable to PageRank.

Link spam (low-quality links)

If you've been doing manual backlink building, the chances are that you won't run into this problem. The most common cause of having large numbers of low-quality links pointing to pages on your site is using automated software or cheap outsourced labour. Using these methods, it's possible to generate hundreds, thousands or even tens of thousands of low-quality links. If that's something you have done in the past, it's unlikely that you'll have the time or resources to remove these links. You therefore need to start manually building high-quality, relevant links from authority sites in your niche or sector, to mitigate the effects of the bad links.

See this post for 17 different types of link spam to avoid using:

http://www.seomoz.org/blog/17-types-of-link-spam-to-avoid

Link relevance

It's common sense that it's more likely for a site on a certain topic (let's say Harley Davidson motorcycles) to be linked to by other relevant sites (those that talk about Harleys, motorcycles in general, the history of Hell's Angels, etc.). Of course, you do get the odd one or two links that might not seem obvious at first glance (like a link from the owner of an orange grove on his bio to a page that has a picture of his first Harley), but on the whole the vast majority of links pointing to a page should come from pages deemed by Google to be 'on theme' – in other words, related to the subject on the page and the site in general.

We don't know exactly how Google determines relevance, but we can assume that it uses a combination of:

● TITLE tag
● H1 and H2 headline HTML tags
● the text surrounding the link if it's in the main page content
● the overall topic of the page.

Your aim is to make sure that most links pointing to each page on your website are related, by content and by subject.

Fortunately for us, Majestic does that for us thanks to its Primary Topical TrustFlow metric. In a nutshell, this is the 'theme category' of each link that points to your website.

When you click the 'Anchor text' tab you will see the estimated Primary Topical TrustFlow of all the links pointing to your homepage organized by the different anchor text.

If you click the Referring Domains or Total External Backlinks figure next to the related anchor text, it will display all the domains and URLs and show their Topical TrustFlow (their 'theme'). The aim here is to have as high a percentage of closely matching 'themed' links as possible.

Direct from Google

'Your site's ranking in Google search results is partly based on analysis of those sites that link to you. The quantity, quality, and relevance [my emphasis] of links influence your ranking. The sites that link to you can provide context about the subject matter of your site, and can indicate its quality and popularity.'

http://support.google.com/webmasters/bin/answer.py?hl=en&answer=66356

Link velocity

Link velocity is just a fancy way of describing how fast you build links to your web pages.

In the days when Google couldn't index and rank pages at the speed it does now, if it detected large numbers of links suddenly appearing to a fairly new site (less than six months old), it would 'sandbox' the site to the bottom of its index until it determined the validity of the links pointing to the various pages. It would then rank each page accordingly, which could take as long as 18 months.

Getting large numbers of links pointing back to your pages in a comparatively short time *can* be a flag for Google, especially if your website is new. However, the key here is the quality of links you get and the age and PageRank of your website. If your website suddenly gets tens of thousands of low-quality, spam-type links in a short time, then Google, rightly, will smell a rat.

If, on the other hand, your website is mentioned on the news and you suddenly get tens of thousands of links from reputable websites within a short period, the chances are that you won't be penalized. In addition, if your website is well established and has a high PageRank, the less likely it is that you would be flagged as a potential webspammer, should you get a sudden influx of links in a short time.

Rel='nofollow'

'Nofollow' works in the same way as it does for the 'nofollow' instruction in the meta robots tag discussed yesterday, except that rel='nofollow' allows you to specify exactly which links you wish Google to ignore:

<a href='aboutme.html' rel='nofollow'>About Me</a>

When a link is formatted to be nofollow, Google will not index it, follow where it goes or pass any PageRank through to it (as long as no one else is linking to that page without the rel='nofollow' or a link to that page is in a sitemap.)

There are two reasons to 'nofollow' a link:

1 If someone has paid for a text advertisement on your website, it's against Google's webmaster guidelines to buy or sell links that pass PageRank (see Other linking no-nos, below).
2 The content is untrusted. For instance, if you run a popular blog with high PageRank and you get lots of people commenting, you may want to prevent spammers from trying to automate their blog comments in the hope of getting lots of PR power from you without contributing anything useful.

As mentioned previously PageRank hasn't been updated in quite some time, so while you won't find many vendors making a big deal out of selling links on a 'high PR' website, the same principle applies to webmasters selling links on domains with a high Domain Authority or TrustFlow/CitationFlow.

In other words, ensure that any text advertisement you sell that is on your website is a rel='nofollow'.

Other linking no-nos

Again, direct from the same page as above from Google, the following are examples of link schemes that can negatively impact a site's ranking in search results:

- **Buying or selling links for the specific purpose of manipulating rankings** This includes exchanging money for links, or posts that contain links; exchanging goods or services for links; or sending someone a 'free' product in exchange for them writing about it and including a link.
- **Excessive link exchanging** ('Link to me and I'll link to you.')
- **Linking to web spammers** or unrelated sites with the intent to manipulate PageRank
- **Building partner pages** exclusively for the sake of cross-linking
- **Using automated programs** or services to create links to your site

Don't be tempted to do any of this type of linking. You might be lucky and it might work for a while, but eventually your luck will run out and your rankings, and possibly your revenue, will drop.

Case study: A drop in the rankings

In 2011 the website for J. C. Penny, the US retailing giant, was the target of an investigation by the *New York Times*, who were amazed at how well it was doing in Google's rankings. It turned out that the SEO company it had hired seemed to have used tactics that contravened Google's webmaster's guidelines and, for a short while, the J. C. Penny website was nowhere to be found in Google after 'manual action was taken'.

http://www.nytimes.com/2011/02/13/business/13search.html

Eventually, J. C. Penny was back in Google, but it must have been a frantic, painful time for the management team, not to mention expensive in hiring another, more reputable SEO firm to fix those errors, and it probably did the company some branding damage too.

Don't make the same mistake!

AuthorRank: a seismic shift in SEO

Until now, we've discussed PageRank, which Google uses to determine the authority of a page based on the quality and relevance of the links pointing to it. Google has now introduced another measurement of authority, called AuthorRank. Unlike PageRank, which applies a quality value to individual links pointing to a page, AuthorRank monitors the number of times your content is tweeted and retweeted on Twitter, liked and shared on Facebook and generally spread around the social networks. AuthorRank applies the value to *you*, the author.

The more you create unique, high-quality, interesting content and the more this is spread by relevant, authoritative people, the more Google deems you to be an authority in your field, your sector, your niche. And the more authority you have, the more quickly you will move up the ranks in Google's index.

Everything you have learned so far in this book is still important (creating a good user experience, making the user want to share your page, search around, like you and post your page in other places, etc.) but you also need to start telling Google you're an expert in your field as well. To do this, you need to:

- get a Google+ account
- link everything you can to it, including your website and/or blog, and share all your articles, etc.
- make a lot of friends on there and share back and forth as much as possible
- use your Google account to log in everywhere you go, if possible
- make a point of linking everything possible to your name, i.e. sign them always with the same name from your Google+
- use the same photo all the time.

Do all of these steps, and more if you can think of them. Essentially, make it so that Google can track the content you create and see how it does. If you are creating good content, this will turn into a good thing for you because you will be prepared when others aren't.

Make the most of AuthorRank

To make the most of AuthorRank, make your content as good as you can and link it to your name and reputation as much as possible. This will give you good AuthorRank and, in time, all this excellent quality content passed around by bigwigs in your industry, sector or niche will link back to your site and – because you did it all under one name – it will definitely be a factor in ranking in the future, sooner rather than later.

AuthorRank also ties into the idea of Google directly monitoring the likes, shares, retweets, etc., that a page gets, so the more of these social signals that are pointing to a URL, the higher the chances are that it will rank, in combination with the other ranking factors.

There's no hard, definitive proof that Google is doing this but, if we apply a little common sense and think about how influential social networks like Facebook, Twitter, LinkedIn, Instagram and Google+ are quickly becoming, it seems very likely.

Here's an excellent blogpost on the subject of social signals and also AuthorRank:
http://www.seomoz.org/blog/your-guide-to-social-signals-for-seo

TIP *Go out and get links, but aim for quality not quantity, and don't take short cuts. Do start thinking about AuthorRank and your social 'footprint'.*

Summary

In this chapter we have talked about what back-links are and why they are important for your site. You learned what good and bad links look like, where not to put your links and how to give the user a good experience when they click on that link. A good link is one to another page containing keywords related to your keywords, from a good, high-authority site. YouTube is a great example of where you can make these links yourself.

You have also learned about the significance of AuthorRank and the social signals that arise from your social networks. You now need to start preparing for them both, just to be safe. So get yourself a Google+ account and get active with Facebook – whether you like them or not.

Fact-check (answers at the back)

1. What are backlinks?
a) Connections at the back of your computer ❏
b) The back pages of your website ❏
c) Where website codes are stored ❏
d) Links to your website from other sites ❏

2. How important are backlinks for SEO?
a) You need lots of backlinks from all over the web to rank in Search ❏
b) You need only high-quality, relevant backlinks ❏
c) You need to get as many links as possible as quickly as possible ❏
d) Only if you use automated programs to get them ❏

3. When it comes to links, what wins over what every time?
a) Quantity over quality ❏
b) Quality over quantity ❏
c) Authority over relevance ❏
d) Automated programs over fashion ❏

4. How important is it to buy links?
a) Very important ❏
b) You should never do it ❏
c) OK in moderation ❏
d) Google doesn't care ❏

5. How important is it to get links on a similar page to yours, after asking the owner of the site?
a) Essential ❏
b) Bad ❏
c) Google doesn't care ❏
d) OK in moderation ❏

6. According to Google, what is your site's ranking in its results based on the analysis of?
a) The quantity of links pointing to you ❏
b) The quality of links pointing to you ❏
c) The speed you acquire the links pointing to you ❏
d) The relevance of links pointing to you ❏

7. Getting a large number of links very quickly to your site is:
a) A core part of your SEO strategy ❏
b) Very bad and never to be attempted ❏
c) OK, providing that they are quality links from reputable websites and your website has enough age and PageRank ❏
d) A way to move up the rankings ❏

8. What does rel='nofollow' mean in an HTML hyperlink?
a) It tells the search engines you don't understand something ❏
b) Don't follow the link or pass PageRank to the destination ❏
c) Ignore all the links on the current page ❏
d) The link is highly trusted ❏

9. How should you make the most of AuthorRank?
a) By making your content as good as you can ❑
b) By using the same photo all the time ❑
c) By writing a blog about it ❑
d) By telling everyone in your address book about it ❑

10. What are the key lessons in off-page optimization?
a) Get quality not quantity links ❑
b) Set up an account on Google+ to take advantage of AuthorRank ❑
c) Creating great content and linking it to your reputation will help make you an authority and probably rank higher in Google in the future ❑
d) All of the above ❑

CHAPTER 12

Getting other traffic sources to your website

Once you have got your website up and started getting traffic from the search engines, you'll realize that it comes as just a trickle to begin with. However, there are more ways to get traffic to your site beyond mighty Google.

These other tried-and-tested methods involve using three major sites that you will have heard about; they each deserve a separate book to themselves. These sites are none other than YouTube, Amazon and Facebook. They are all behemoths, up there with Google. YouTube is the third most visited site in the world and, to all intents and purposes, the second biggest search engine (over Bing), Amazon is the largest online retailer and Facebook is the largest and most visited non-search engine site in the world.

Fortunately for us, they cost nothing or very little for you to leverage them. In this chapter you'll learn some basic dos and don'ts and ways to get started.

YouTube

YouTube, the second biggest 'search engine' after Google, is also owned by Google. This means that videos put on YouTube instantly get more Google 'love' than any other video service and often end up in the top ten of Google quickly, with little effort. Putting your link in the video's description will certainly not hurt your SEO efforts either.

Almost any business in the world could benefit from several YouTube videos, so it is worth paying attention and working out how your business could take advantage of this opportunity.

If you have a webstore, you could use YouTube to show:

● videos that feature your products
● how-to videos on your products
● video reviews of products you sell
● your major marketing campaigns
● fun videos featuring your products indirectly.

 If you get a good writer and fun material for your YouTube video, it could well go viral, which would be pure commercial gold for your business.

If you have an informational niche site, you could post:

● informational videos
● how-to videos surrounding your niche
● interviews with experts in your niche
● testimonials from readers/users.

If you run professional services, you could post:

● interactive videos about your services
● client testimonials
● interviews that you have given to other related businesses.

If you offer local services, you could post:

● videos of your staff, so that customers can 'meet' the person who will come and paint their ceiling or check their drain
● solutions to simple problems to demonstrate your expertise

- videos of local events, featuring your business as an ad at the front.

These are just a few examples of what's possible; the list is endless. You could even simply make a visual or an audio file, or post still pictures of participants and have an interview playing in the background.

Making the most of YouTube

Some videos get a lot of views, but that does not mean they get a lot of people clicking on your site to find out more. To make it more likely that one of your videos is successful, use all the resources you have available, bearing in mind the following top tips.

Make lots of videos

You never know what will go viral and what won't. Certain videos will be picked up and someone with a big following might tweet it, and on and on it can go.

Aim for quality

Make sure that you put in the effort to make a good-quality video. Use good music, fade-ins and -outs, a lead-in screen with your website address and credits with your web address as well.

There's no need to get the best equipment in the world, but at least use something better than your webcam. The prices of high-definition camcorders (1080p HD) have dropped a lot during the last few years to the point where they are very affordable and if you have a fairly modern smartphone that will probably also be capable of recording video in HD so, if you're lucky, all you'll need is a tripod to keep your phone steady. And, thanks to royalty-free music and the availability of graphics packages and marketplaces, you can get amazing results while spending only a fraction of what you used to have to spend.

I can recommend the following sites on the Envato network:

- audiojungle.net (*stock music and audio*)
- videohive.net (*motion graphics*)
- graphicriver.net (*graphics, vectors and print*)
- photodune.net (*stock photography*)

Alternatively, just search on Google using some of the italicized terms above.

Do not shy away from controversy

Do you have a product that works better than a competitor's? Can you demonstrate better/faster/cheaper results from your service compared with other companies? If so, create a video of the showdown, but do it with class. You can then target your competitor's keywords as well!

Make sure that you have accurate hard data and facts to back up your claims. If you don't, not only will you not convince most of your customers of what you have to say, but you could also find yourself with a libel or defamation lawsuit from your competitors.

Even if your product or service isn't in itself controversial, you might still be able to link it with a controversial topic, where you argue the case for one side of the argument. If you can find someone from the opposing side willing to discuss the issue with you, you could record yourselves talking on Zoom and then make it available to watch.

● https://zoom.us/ ← *free video and audio calls over the Internet*
● http://www.pamela.biz/en/shop/pamela_call_recorder/ ← *Pamela Software Skype Call Recorder*

Don't discuss religion or politics, unless you are a political or religious site. It may be something that is affecting your business, but mentioning it will immediately turn off half your customers.

Remember that the best videos are fun videos

This point beats all the rest hands down. If you really want something viral, it needs to have a bit of fun in it. This doesn't mean that all your videos need to be fun (a mix of commercial, fun and informational could hit the ticket). But at least some of them have to be fun. If you can't think funny (or at least not funny for everyone), hire a writer from Upwork.com.

Put your keywords everywhere

This will help the site and page you are linking to immensely. Do not forget the strategy of deep linking. If you want to promote a dog brush you sell on your website and you make a dog brush video with dog-brush-related keyword tags, title and words in the description, don't add a link in the description to your home page; link it directly to the page on your website that is talking about dog brushes.

Follow the advice given in Chapter 9 regarding keyword stuffing. Just make it look natural.

Drive links to your video

As well as linking directly back to pages on your website, it can also benefit you to create a linking campaign for each of your keyword-targeted YouTube videos. There are two main reasons for this:

- Since YouTube is technically the second largest search engine, it's possible to get traffic just by ranking for your keyword on YouTube.
- We know that Google loves videos, and a high-ranking YouTube video is more likely (although not guaranteed) to rank high in the related main Google search index.

Amazon

According to web stats company SimilarWeb, Amazon is the world's largest online retailer and the twelfth-most trafficked website in the world. You probably already know that it sells everything – from books to treadmills, engagement rings to flooring – in vast quantities (total worldwide sales during Q4 2021 were $137.4 billion – an increase of 9 per cent during the same period in 2020). (Sources: https://www.similarweb.com/website/amazon.com/#overview; https://ir.aboutamazon.com/news-release/news-release-details/2022/Amazon.com-Announces-Fourth-Quarter-Results/default.aspx)

You could argue that Amazon and other very large commercial websites are in some ways more important than sites like Google, YouTube and Bing. While these three are made up of *searchers* looking for information, maybe before they make a buying decision, Amazon is populated by *buyers*. It's not a search engine; it's literally a buying engine.

If you're a retailer, using Amazon for research is an excellent way to find out about the hot products you should be selling. Just type in a keyword or go to a category, bring up the listing and organize by best-selling/popularity.

Harnessing the power of Amazon

How can you harness the power of Amazon for your own website and business? One obvious way is to write a book giving valuable advice, hints, tips and tricks about your area of expertise. Nothing shouts 'expert' more than having a book for sale on Amazon and it can be used to benefit any type of business, whether it's an e-commerce store, an informational site or a service provider.

E-commerce stores

You could write an instructional guide linked to your products, and include the use of specific products in your store. In the resources section of your guide, you can link back to the product page(s) on your site.

As an example, let's say you have your dog-grooming online store and you want to sell more of your Splentastic 3000 Grooming System. Your idea might be to create a series of books showing people how to groom various breeds of animal. How do you find out whether there is a market for your idea?

1 Go to the top of any page on Amazon and begin typing in the search box and see what comes up. For example, if you start typing "How to groom a..." Amazon will suggest some search terms people have used, one of which is "How to groom a Yorkie" (Yorkshire Terrier).
2 If you then go to the Google keyword tool and type in "How to groom a Yorkie", you'll find 880 exact match searches for that term. This means that nearly 1,000 people a month, all over the world, are looking for that information. There are plenty of similar search terms that you would have a good chance of ranking your Amazon product page for.

3 If typing that search term into Google brings up no Amazon listings in Google's results and typing it into Amazon brings up only three books, you know that there's a gap in the market.

After writing any book, you can then create an author page on Amazon. Not only does this increase your standing and trustworthiness, but it also lets you link your website or blog to that page. One-way backlinks from super-duper authority site equal SEO gold!

Informational sites

Writing a book focused around your niche or sector is especially good for teaching new people time- and money-saving tips, tricks and techniques, and you can use that book to gain interested visitors to your site. Follow the steps above for research and use the same technique for linking your author page to your website or blog.

Professional/service providers

There is no better form of business card for a professional or service provider than a book. How much more receptive and interested do you think a prospective customer or client would be if, instead of you handing them a business card, you gave them a copy of your book with your phone number in it? Do you think they'd see you as an expert and be more likely to hire you?

If you don't know how to write or put a book together, you can outsource the job; see Chapter 14.

To get into Amazon, take the following steps.

1 Sign up for an account on Amazon (if you don't have one already) and then go to http://kdp.amazon.com and http://createspace.com and sign up for an account on each of them.
   - Createspace (owned by Amazon) allows you to self-publish and sell physical books that are printed and delivered by Amazon.
   - KDP (Kindle Direct Publishing) allows you to digitally publish and sell your book in Amazon's Kindle store.
2 Take your book, reformat it for the Kindle (you can also outsource this job and it will definitely save you a world of hassle) and upload it to your KDP account.

You are now published on Amazon! Now you just have to get the word out.

You can SEO your Amazon physical and Kindle book pages, which shouldn't be too difficult since your book title (ideally) contains a keyword. You can also create a backlinking campaign for your pages by getting some friends to buy your book and have them give you reviews.

The key strategy with using books as a marketing tool is *not* to aim to get rich from book sales; any money you make from them is a bonus. The primary use for books is as your business card – as a way for prospects to perceive you as an expert.

There isn't the space here to go into everything to do with specific marketing tactics with a book, but it is important to make sure you link your website to your Amazon author page as well as your YouTube videos and your Facebook page.

Facebook

Facebook is the Internet's third-most visited site, with 3.64 billion monthly active users (Statista, Q1 2022) equating to very nearly half the world's population.

This is why you need to be on Facebook. Regardless of how you might feel about it and about privacy issues, if you are a business (and especially if you sell products and services to private individuals), you need to go where the people are – and that means Facebook.

Get yourself a Page, if you don't already have one. You don't have to share this with everyone, though you probably do want to start getting more 'social'; remember AuthorRank and the social signals discussed yesterday.

Get some of your friends to like your page. If you don't have a lot of friends, run a quick Facebook PPC campaign to get yourself some likes, which will help other people to like you once they see that other people have.

When you create your Facebook page, take the following steps to link it with your book:

1 Select Brand/product > website, then enter the name of your book.
2 Upload a picture of the book cover as the page's profile image.

3 Fill in the various sections, adding your main website URL and the Amazon page URL, and then follow the instructions in the pop-up boxes.
4 After doing all that, click the 'Edit page' button to go back into your page's settings to see whether you've missed anything.

Making the most of your Facebook page

The don'ts	
In the timeline layout, don't put any of these in your profile image or cover photo:	• contact information (even your phone number) • price or purchase information.
For posting on your timeline, don't:	• keep posting the same thing over and over again (this will get you unliked really fast) • post only offers and repeated calls to action (such as 'go here to find out about our amazing offer').
For your cover photo and main image, don't:	• just use stock photos bought from some random stock image site (Facebook needs to be personal and that is not being personal).

The dos	
Always be engaging with your posts. The three posts that get the most engagement are as follows:	• pictures (fun and funny, or shocking and that make you think, depending on your page, of course) • videos (people watch these and love to comment on them) • questions (these have to be well thought out and in line with your website).
When someone writes to you, write back.	• If they answer your question, say thanks and also start a conversation. You will be amazed how fast your page can grow if you take the time to do this.
Be real!	• Don't just say 'Thank you for your post'; comment on the other person's photo or directly address them in some other fashion (or at least have a real person who represents you; see Outsourcing)
Use the apps to connect your other social content to your page. Make sure you put these first and foremost on your page, right under the cover image. The three you must have are:	• YouTube app (puts your YouTube videos in the spotlight) • RSS Graffiti (puts your RSS feed in the spotlight and, by extension, your website) • Fan of the week app (this encourages interactions).

The dos	
If you have a business that has been around for a while:	• fill in the timeline with your history and milestones by using Facebook's backdating ability • add positive facts such as any awards you received or major clients you landed • use as many images as you can muster. This can show your story in an engaging way that will have people liking and getting to know you; people buy from people they know and trust.

And finally, make sure that you add a 'CTA' (Call-To-Action) button to your Facebook page by clicking the 'Create CTA' button at the top of the page. Facebook has apparently relaxed its cover image rules so you now put an arrow on your cover image pointing to the 'CTA' button.

Professional marketer tips

Don't just make one fan page. If you have goods, services or books on Amazon, make a fan page for each of them as well. Use your main fan page to 'like' those pages (and vice versa) and have them all deep-link to your main website to get the maximum linkages for your efforts.

To connect your Amazon book and Facebook the most, create a link in your book directly to an opt-in app on your book's or your company's Facebook. Give visitors a good reason to do this, like offering a free white paper, report or an exclusive discount, and watch as the buyers of your books become customers for life.

Summary

In this chapter you learned that Google isn't everything and that there are other ways to get traffic to start coming to your website. By using YouTube, Facebook and Amazon, you can increase interaction and see traffic growth to your site. Just make sure that you are able to be 'real', be yourself and follow the guidelines of these big social and traffic engines.

You can build on the advice given in this chapter to discover the best ways to position yourself to start getting traffic through these giants. So get creative and explore these places. Look at other YouTube videos, Facebook pages and books on Amazon, and feel free to borrow other people's ideas and improve on them!

Also be sure to see what people like. Take note of how many people like a page as opposed to those who dislike it, the reviews a book gets and the interactions of an obviously successful Facebook page.

Fact-check (answers at the back)

1. Apart from Google, what other traffic sources are there?
   a) YouTube ❑
   b) Facebook ❑
   c) Amazon ❑
   d) All of the above ❑

2. How big is YouTube in terms of site visits?
   a) Smaller than Bing ❑
   b) Smaller than Amazon ❑
   c) Bigger than Facebook ❑
   d) Bigger than everyone except Google and Facebook ❑

3. What is YouTube ideal for?
   a) Stores ❑
   b) Informational niche sites ❑
   c) Professional services ❑
   d) All of the above ❑

4. Why should you make lots of YouTube videos?
   a) Videos put on YouTube instantly get more Google 'love' than any other video service and often end up in the top ten of Google quickly ❑
   b) They'll make your site look more attractive ❑
   c) You never know what might go viral ❑
   d) Visitors love them ❑

5. Why should you not shy away from controversy when it comes to YouTube videos?
   a) Because it'll catch people's attention and show up your competitors ❑
   b) Because it'll generate publicity and possibly a lawsuit ❑
   c) Because anything goes ❑
   d) Because you'll get more links ❑

6. What are Amazon Kindle books good for?
   a) Professional services ❑
   b) Local businesses ❑
   c) Informational sites ❑
   d) All of the above ❑

7. What is Facebook good for?
   a) Giving out contact information ❑
   b) Giving out purchase information ❑
   c) Links to your main website ❑
   d) Posting the same thing over and over again ❑

8. What should you *not* do on Facebook?
   a) Comment on other people's photos ❑
   b) Use a stock photo as your profile image ❑
   c) Start a conversation ❑
   d) Use as many images as possible ❑

9. Is it good to put a call to action in your cover photo?
   a) Yes, if the action is good ❑
   b) No – it might get you banned ❑
   c) Sometimes, if you have time ❑
   d) What's a call to action? ❑

10. In everything 'social', the most important thing is to be:
    a) Smart ❑
    b) Sneaky ❑
    c) Real ❑
    d) Likeable to everyone ❑

CHAPTER 13

Pay-per-click traffic: making it work for you

The purpose of this Part is to get you not to rely just on what you are doing today but to have a strategy for the future. In this chapter you will learn how advertising on the Internet can benefit you. This is where you pay money for your visitors, using a method called PPC (pay per click).

Of course, you want traffic that, as far as possible, is free and comes to you naturally, but there are several reasons why PPC should figure in your overall site strategy – at least in the beginning. It's therefore worth discussing here the reasons for doing PPC marketing, so that you don't waste a single penny or minute of your time with it unnecessarily.

In this chapter we'll discuss:

- what PPC marketing is and how it works
- the major players in this arena
- the pros and cons of marketing this way
- the potential costs
- the six situations when you should use this marketing method
- how to set up your successful campaign.

What is pay-per-click marketing?

Pay-per-click (PPC) marketing is a method of advertising on the Internet that is used to direct traffic to websites. Pay-per-click ads usually appear in a coloured box on search results pages, separate from the regular search results. The advertisers pay the publisher (usually a website owner) every time the ad is clicked.

With search engines, advertisers typically bid on keyword phrases relevant to their target market. Content sites commonly charge a fixed price per click rather than using a bidding system. PPC 'display' advertisements, also known as banner ads, are shown on websites or in search engine results with related content that have agreed to show ads.

It should come as no surprise that Google is first on this list. Search and PPC ads are the primary way Google makes its money. When someone types in a keyword, the first two listings on the results page are for ads and all the links on the right-hand side of the page are links to ads. This is Google's Search Network.

Google also has its ads on millions of web pages across the web. This is Google's Display Network. Website owners can apply to Google to have these ads on their web pages via their AdSense program and it's a legitimate way to help monetize a website.

You can learn more about Google's ad networks here: http://adwords.google.com

There are other players in PPC, like Yahoo/Bing, whose ads follow pretty much the same rules as Google, and other, smaller players, but Facebook and Google are where you should focus your effort if you choose this path. To reach the most people fast, it makes sense to use the organizations with the biggest reach.

How does PPC marketing work?

There are two main types of PPC marketing: keyword related and psychographically related. Keyword related is how Google does it in their Search Network. You bid on which keywords your ad will show up on the right-hand side of the search results and you pay the website owner every time your ad is clicked.

PPC and Google

Google is the biggest provider of PPC ads, and you can find out the average cost per click (CPC) for each keyword using either the Google keyword tool or Google's traffic estimator tool (accessible only from within a paid AdWords account). The price you pay is a combination of the amount of competition there is for the keyword and how popular your ad is.

In my PPC campaign, the more times my ad is clicked, the more Google rewards me by – ever so slowly – nudging me up the paid ad rankings. Thus, if my ad was initially placed fourth and ended up getting more clicks than the ads in third, second and first place, it's possible that my ad will jump the queue into first place and, not only that, I'll still be paying the same figure as I was in fourth place.

Once again, Google rewards relevance with ranking and, since ads in first place generally get more clicks than ads in a lower position, you'll get more traffic coming to your website.

Google's Display Network works in a different way:

1 With the Search Network, you're limited to using only text ads. But, because the Display Network is made up of external websites, you can use a text ad, a banner image ad or a video ad.
2 You don't bid on keywords shown up from a search. Instead, you bid to show your ad on pages Google deems relevant to a keyword.

With the Display Network, you can pay either CPC or CPM (cost per mille, the cost per 1,000 impressions – so, when Google shows your ad 1,000 times, you pay the same, regardless of whether your ads are clicked or not).

PPC and Facebook

The second big player here is Facebook. Instead of targeting what people are searching for, you can target people according to their demographic (their age, their sex, etc.) and their psychographic (behavioural) information (e.g. the TV shows, films and products they like).

Although you can also do demographic targeting in Google, it's nowhere near as detailed as it is in Facebook, because Google simply doesn't have the data. (This is possibly another reason why Google+ was created.) The problem here is that some people don't realize that Facebook has ads. When I mentioned to my mother recently that I was running ads on Facebook, she said, 'Really? Do they have those? Where are they?' so be aware that 'ad blindness' can be an issue.

The advantages of PPC

Using PPC marketing has four main advantages:

- You know people will probably be interested in what you're offering. They went through the trouble and risk of clicking on your ad, so they probably are pretty interested to see what's on the other side.
- You can focus down to the detail for your visitors.
  If you want a specific customer – people from North Dakota who like bubble gum and rock and roll, say – you can definitely find them with Facebook. Google is not quite so refined.
- You can know with almost complete certainty that you will get traffic.
- With a fixed daily budget you know that (once your campaigns are optimized) you will receive a steady, consistent stream of targeted visitors to your offers.

When they're on the ball, Google and Facebook can approve an ad very quickly. I've personally had ads approved and live in as little as ten minutes.

The drawbacks of PPC

The main drawbacks of PPC are the cost and the time required for research and tracking.

1 **Costs per click are rising generally and can be unnaturally high.**

To reduce costs, you will need to do proper research and point your ads to a specific page (the landing page) on your site, not your home page. Both Facebook and Google are now public companies, answering to shareholders and having to go out of their way to make sure they are profitable. That means that they must extract as much money as possible from advertisers.

Landing page testing

PPC works really well if you're doing any type of landing page testing, as you can find out pretty quickly which landing page is working best.

Keep in mind, though, that you should aim to generate around 200 visitors a day to one or other of your landing page test URLs, so you can find out quickly which page is the best. Then pause this campaign until you need it again, to test the next landing page design against your current champion.

Make sure you set your daily budget high enough to get those 200+ daily visitors.

PPCs can range from anywhere between a few pennies or cents to £30.00 ($50) *per click,* and sometimes more. It all depends on the market and the keywords being bid on. So you really have to do your research into every word you are bidding for to make sure you are getting the amount you can afford. Even this can get really expensive, really fast.

Luckily, both Google and Facebook allow you to set a daily budget limit, so you shouldn't have to sell a kidney or your firstborn to pay your PPC bill. But that daily limit needs to take into account the number of clicks you want sending people to your website.

2 It requires a lot of research and tracking.

Some keywords may be expensive, but they might end up converting less well than other cheaper keywords for you, or vice versa. This is why you need to do research, combined with a lot of tracking. Tracking is where you see where the traffic is coming from and how well it converts (how much they do what you want them to). Compare them to other keywords and narrow down exactly what you need.

When to do PPC

If you're just starting out with a new business and website, you won't have any data to tell you how much to spend on PPC, so just concentrate at this stage on coming up with a compelling offer with a great price. Make a great-looking site and direct traffic to a landing page that presents your offer well (more on landing pages below), and then you will find out whether anyone is interested enough to buy.

Keep track of your results and, as you discover over time how long customers stay with you, you'll be able gradually to increase your spending to acquire new customers.

 Don't ever do PPC simply to get visitors to your home page. If you are going to put together a PPC campaign that has any kind of effectiveness, you'll need to make sure that your visitors will have a real reason and purpose for visiting.

Subscription services

You can use a subscription service if you have a product that is purchased by monthly paid subscription, a service to which customers will be loyal or a high-converting, high-value item that hasn't cost you a lot of money. One example of this might be an online business writing press releases for companies, where you have a service supplying a certain amount of material per month, or when you know that, when you write for companies, they tend to stick with you because you do such a good job.

Either way, depending on how much you charge, you now have an idea of how much you can afford to spend to get one customer. This is called the client lifetime value. So, if you charge £49.95 a month for your subscription and you know that a customer will stay with you for an average of 12 months, then the lifetime value of that customer is 12 × £49.95 = £599.40.

Why is this important? When you know how much each customer is worth to you, you can figure out how much you're prepared to spend to acquire each new customer.

High-value items

PPC is also worth doing if you have a high-value or 'big-ticket' item. For example, say you specialize in selling classic Ferraris, and the average profit on each car you sell is at least £7,000 ($10,000). If it costs you 70p ($1) per click to get people to your website and if one out of every 500 visitors buys a car, it might have cost you £350 ($500) to get that new customer, but you still made £6,650 ($9,500) gross profit and you now have them in your customer database, where you can follow up with additional offers for almost no cost.

Social experimentation

PPC could also work in the short term if you need to get a number of people on whom to try out your ideas and see whether they would be worth developing. It's a form of social experimentation as well as an effective marketing method.

For instance, say you are writing an Amazon e-book and you want to know whether people are interested in your subject of hang-gliding in the Andes Mountains. You could put together a little campaign that targets hang-gliding and Andes mountain-related keywords with its title 'Hang-Glide The Andes Mountains?' You can then judge the level of interest by how readily people click on the ad.

You could also put on the landing page a place for people to ask their most burning questions about hang-gliding in the Andes Mountains. Their input will tell you exactly what they will want to see in your book (that isn't even ready yet) and also give you a list of people to email when your book is ready, for a quick burst of sales.

The same theory applies to product retailers and service providers. If people ask the same range of questions before they purchase what you're offering, put up a frequently asked questions (FAQ) page answering them.

Book titles

PPC can also work if you are writing a book and are wondering what the most effective title would be. Take the best ones you have thought of and put them side by side in a PPC campaign. The one that gets the most clicks with the best conversion rate wins! Then, as with social experimentation, you can ask the people who responded what they want to know and get their email addresses.

Niche products

You can also use PPC if you have a small niche product, to get subscribers to your newsletter or RSS feed. This is where you can use the fact that you are a small site to your advantage. I heard about someone who once did a small PPC campaign to their niche bulldog website. It had one focus: getting newsletter subscribers. They spent £20 but ended up with 100 subscribers, several comments on how nice their site was and even a couple of sales.

Facebook sites

As mentioned earlier in the discussion of social media, it is sometimes good to get those first few fans with a quick campaign to target people who will be interested in your page in the first place. For more social media strategies, see below.

PPC advertising strategies

Now you know what you'll focus on, follow these steps on how to set up your PPC ad campaigns.

1 **Watch the relevant tutorial videos.**

These are provided by Google and Bing to show you the *mechanics* of creating campaigns and ad groups:

2 Plan the structure of your campaigns.

Think about how you'll structure your campaigns on the Google and Bing search networks. The most common way is to use the 'long-tail keyword' approach by creating multiple ad groups, each revolving around a main root keyword and having similar keywords in the same group.

If we go back to the dog-grooming example, and I type in the keyword "dog grooming" into Google's keyword tool, I'll get a series of keywords all grouped together by theme, as follows:

Kit	Tubs	Clippers
Dog-grooming kit	Dog-grooming tubs	Dog-grooming clippers
Dog-grooming starter kit	Dog-grooming tub	Best dog-grooming clippers
Grooming kits for dogs	Dog-grooming bath tubs	Dog-grooming clippers reviews
Dog-grooming kits for sale	Dog washtub	Wahl dog-grooming clippers
Dog-grooming kits	Dog-grooming tubs for sale	Clippers for dog grooming
	Used dog-grooming tubs	Dog-grooming clippers australia
	Dog bathtub	Best dog clippers
	Dog-grooming baths	Dog-grooming clippers for sale
		Clippers dog grooming
		Dog-grooming clippers uk

3 Transfer your chosen keywords and ad groups to an existing campaign.

Once you've selected the keywords and ad groups you want to use, you can transfer them into an existing campaign in your Google AdWords account (if you're already logged in) with a couple of mouse clicks, by selecting the 'Add to account' button. Bing's process isn't quite as refined as Google's, so what I generally do is use exactly the same keywords and ad grouping in Bing.

If you use the free Google AdWords Editor and Bing Ads Editor software programs, you can easily export your Google campaigns and import them into Bing quickly and easily. Just search in Google for "Bing Ads Editor" and "Google AdWords Editor" to get the download links.

Some dos and don'ts

Do:

✔ **set a daily amount you can afford**
Even if it doesn't convert at all, never spend more money than you have budgeted for.

✔ **have an open mind and test out different headlines and bodies of your ads**
See which work out and which don't (this will sometimes be the exact opposite of what you think will happen).

✔ **focus on the *exact* keywords that you want to get clicks on**
The more specific they are, the cheaper and more effective the clicks become.

✔ **point your ad to the right page**
Wherever possible, point an ad to a landing page on your website that is related to your ad.

✔ **always try and get at least an email address for your efforts**

✔ **follow Google's guidelines to the letter.**

Don't:

✗ **make the click go to a one-page website**
This will never be approved by Google and is increasingly not being approved by Facebook. Instead, have it focused on a landing page somewhere in your site where the focus is on what you want them to do.

✗ **make the click go to a page where you can get visitors to click another ad**
This is known as 'arbitrage' and will eventually result in you having your Google AdWords account banned.

✗ **make low-quality landing pages that are not directly relevant to the ad text**
For more information on best practices for landing pages, refer to this guide by Google: http://bit.ly/ReH2nd

✗ **write headlines or body text just to get clicks.**
Clicks are not the point; the point is to get the right people – those who are already interested in what they will get on the other side of your ad.

PPC strategies for Facebook

As mentioned before, Meta is a different beast from Google in that there are no keywords, as such, to bid to show your ad for. Instead, you need to target people according to demographics or psychographics – people who are interested in certain subjects, located in a certain geographical area, went to a particular college or university, or another type of indicator.

Meta (Facebook) has changed which interests and indicators you are permitted to use many times since this book was first published and so what I would recommend first before you begin any advertising campaign, is to read their advertising Terms and Conditions: https://www.facebook.com/business/direct_terms_ads_en.php

There are a number of additional steps within your Ad Account to set things up correctly, thanks to Apple's IOS 14.5 update, so I recommend searching YouTube using a phrase like:

how to set up facebook ad account [whatever year you're reading this]

Now assuming you have read the T&Cs and you have your Ad Account setup, here's a strategy that's known to work well.

First create a Conversion campaign, since you probably want to make sales or generate leads.

1 Create a list of very broad interests related to your product or service. These should be ideally over 1 million people in size. You can find these by setting up a test ad in your Ad Manager and using the Suggestions tool in the Adset section.
2 For your first ad, create a very simple text and image one using what's known as the 'Yayy Without Boo' framework.

Some examples:

Watch This If You Want To Build A Website Without Hiring An Expensive Programmer

(use something like this if you are taking someone to a webpage with a video on it)

Read This For 3 Simple Tips To Save At Least £1,000 On Your Next Tax Bill

(use something like this if you are taking someone to an article)

Click This To Make Your Bed Nice and Warm In Less Than 5 Minutes.

(use something like this if you are selling a physical item in an ecommerce store)

3 Now create one adset per broad interest (all using the same ad), targeting your chosen country (or countries), ages (keep as broad as you can) and make the daily budget just $5, as this makes Meta's algorithm work harder for you.

4 Create as many adsets as your budget can handle but before you submit them to Meta for approval, make sure all your adsets apart from one are set to draft. That way, if your ad is disapproved, you only get one 'strike' and not multiple 'strikes'.

5 If your ad is approved, then you should be OK to switch all your other adsets on (since they're all using the same ad) and you should be good to go.

6 Let your campaign run for 3–5 days – do not touch anything if there are no problems, and only then look at your results and see if you're getting any sales or leads.

7 Turn off the adsets that aren't working and slowly increase the daily budgets by 20 per cent a day of the ones that are.

I only have a little space to cover this topic – quite frankly I'd need an entire other book to do this strategy justice with all of the nuances required, so I recommend you spend time on YouTube researching (especially OfficialFrankKern's videos) so you're familiar with the creative side of the process and not just the technical 'setting stuff up' side of things.

Summary

In this chapter you learned that the main uses for PPC are for sales growth (especially big-ticket items and subscriptions) and for testing book titles and book ideas. Make sure you do your keyword research properly and don't just point PPC ads to your home page – you'll end up with high costs per click. When using Facebook PPC, you can get cheaper clicks by pointing to a Facebook page rather than going to an outside website.

Google and Facebook have the power to approve you or disapprove you and your AdWords advertising account. If you are somehow found to be cheating them or their customers, you can be banned for life just as readily as your website. So don't do it.

Make your aim always to find customers/clients who are already interested in what you have to offer in the first place and you are well on your way to a successful PPC campaign.

Fact-check (answers at the back)

1. What does PPC stand for?
   a) Perfectly Politically Correct ❏
   b) Payment Perfectly Considered ❏
   c) Pay Per Click ❏
   d) Panning People Consolidated ❏

2. Who are the main players in PPC?
   a) Facebook ❏
   b) Google ❏
   c) Bing ❏
   d) Everybody else ❏

3. On what should you base a daily limit?
   a) How much you expect to make ❏
   b) Whatever you have in the bank ❏
   c) The size of the market ❏
   d) How much money you can afford to lose ❏

4. What are subscription services?
   a) A good service to use PPC to get clients ❏
   b) A way of driving as much PPC traffic to your site as possible ❏
   c) A high-risk strategy that may or may not work ❏
   d) A complete waste of money ❏

5. In terms of PPC, what's the purpose of your home page?
   a) A good page to use PPC to get clients ❏
   b) A bad idea to drive PPC traffic to ❏
   c) To be the main page for all traffic ❏
   d) To look attractive and draw people in ❏

6. When you do PPC, what should your focus for those clicks be?
   a) Four different options ❏
   b) Three different options ❏
   c) Two different options ❏
   d) One measurable thing that you want them to do ❏

7. Before you start a PPC campaign, what should you know?
   a) Your lifetime client value ❏
   b) How much you are willing to spend ❏
   c) What you want the click to do ❏
   d) All of the above ❏

8. What should you always try to do in your PPC campaign?
   a) Make sales for your efforts ❏
   b) Learn everything about your clients for your efforts ❏
   c) Get at least an email address for your efforts ❏
   d) Have a plan for what to do with the information you glean ❏

9. What are landing pages?
   a) Where the potential client 'lands' after clicking on your ad ❏
   b) One-page sites your clients want to visit ❏
   c) Special pages only for certain users ❏
   d) Website pages run by airlines ❏

10. What should landing pages be?
a) A one-page site with an
   email address ❏
b) Part of a larger site ❏
c) Interactive, but not too much ❏
d) Pages that immediately take
   you to another page ❏

CHAPTER 14

Monitoring and managing your progress

So far in this Part, we've talked all about SEO and SEM essentials and some of the small details that you need to make sure you have covered. You've learned about some of the social media giants you need in your traffic-getting strategies, and we've also discussed the possibility and proper use of PPC as part of your online marketing mix.

You may now have begun to feel a little empowered and started dropping jargon and terms left, right and centre into your conversations. You should now be beginning to plan how you will get traffic to your website over the coming weeks and months. You've come a long way, but there are a few more points to discuss.

In this chapter you'll find out how to:

- use monitoring software to check your progress up the rankings
- make the job a little easier with some automated tools
- outsource the job completely if you wish, or if you don't have any available staff on hand.

Some of these were mentioned in the previous chapters, but they're important enough to discuss again in more detail.

Monitoring software

Now that you have your website up and running and the link 'juice' flowing, the users should be starting to trickle in. How do you know how well you are doing and whether you are progressing or regressing? Now you will learn about the different types of monitoring software out there, free and paid for.

Freeware

Free monitoring software from Google is great to get started with and should be what you go for first, whether or not you want to pay for this assistance later on. You install these tools on your site and they get you aligned with Google.

While they really shouldn't be used by Google to track your site usage or help with ranking, you should assume that they probably are. This is because it's obviously easier for them to track you by just aggregating the data from the free tools already installed on your site without having to send out their spiders and bots all the time.

What to install
Just to be safe, install this first:

● Google Analytics: http://google.com/analytics

This is the online tracking software that shows you how many visitors you have, where they come from (their country of origin), how long they stayed on your site and where they go throughout your site. Go to the page and follow the instructions to install the GA tracking code on every page of your site and you are done. (Hire a geek from oDesk or Elance to do this for you if you're not keen!)

Many of the CMS out there have apps and plug-ins that make this step easy. WordPress has a few plug-ins for adding analytics to your site, including:

● Google Analytics for WordPress:
  https://wordpress.org/plugins/google-analytics-for-wordpress/
● Google Search Console Tools:
  https://search.google.com/search-console

This is where Google provides you with reports and data about your website's ranking and the number of pages you have indexed in Google's search engine results. All you have to do is sign up for an account (using an existing or new Google account), add your website URL, verify that you are the real owner of the site and then Google will start crawling and logging data about your site, such as the number of pages it has indexed and which keywords you are showing up for in search results.

To speed things along, you can upload your sitemap.xml file, mentioned earlier. Google Web Toolkit (GWT) will also show what links Google has found that point to your site and whether you have any serious errors on your web page – such as bad code or missing/broken URLs.

 You can even tie your GWT, Google Analytics and Google AdWords accounts together to get optimum data sharing across the various services.

Be sure to check GWT often, especially in the beginning, to make sure that your SEO efforts are on track. If pages start showing for different keywords from what you were expecting or you start having serious website problems, you'll be able to fix things very quickly.

URL shorteners

URL shorteners are another useful set of tools. These tools include Bitly (bit.ly), TinyURL (http://tinyurl.com), A.GD (http://a.gd) and even Google's own (http://goo.gl).

They will take a really long URL, for example: http://www.superlongdomainname.org/white/space/florida/ songsareawful/end3.html and turn it into a nice, tidy, short URL, such as: http://bit.ly/fds8f9

This is especially good for emails, where the long URL would go over multiple lines and possibly 'break' in some email software, or when you are restricted to the number of characters you can use, as on Twitter – although the latter will automatically shorten links with its own *t.co* URL. Some URL-shortening services will also count the number of clicks each link gets if you sign up for an account with them.

There are two things you need to bear in mind with URL shorteners:

1 Emails containing shortened links are being increasingly blocked by ISP. This is due to fears that they are spam (unsolicited commercial emails), as a result of high abuse from spammers. For more on this, see this blog post: http://blog.wordtothewise.com/2011/06/bitly-gets-you-blocked/

2 Use only URL shorteners that use 301 redirects. A 301 redirect is one that tells Google that a page has permanently moved to a new location. So, for instance, if for some reason you are setting up a new domain and have to change the URL http://yourdomain.com/yourawesomepage.html to this one: http://yournewdomain.com/yourawesomepage.html you wouldn't want to lose the SEO benefits from all the links pointing to your old page URL, so you set up a 301 redirect on your old server that tells Google and the other search engines that here is the new URL to use. Once Google and the other search engines know about this permanent redirect, they will pass any SEO benefits from linking to the old page to this new URL.

The same is true for using shortened URLs. If you spend time creating linking campaigns pointing to shortened URLs, you need to make sure that any search engine benefits are passed from your shortened URL to the destination URL on your server, not Bitly's or TinyURL's. Since you don't own Bitly or TinyURL, don't spend time and money getting those domains ranked and not getting yours ranked.

If you don't use an URL shortener that is a 301 redirect, set up your own shortening URL system on a server you control. For WordPress users, there are plug-ins you can use easily to create shortened links on your own domain that will act as 301 redirects. Do a search on the WordPress plug-in repository here: http://wordpress.org/extend/plugins/

Paid-for tools

While the Google Search Console tools are particularly good, even they – while showing recent changes – don't tell you how you were doing with those keywords months ago.

Here is a list of the better tools that track your rankings over time:

- **Majestic SEO** ← http://majesticseo.com
  Majestic SEO is another excellent tool that is much easier on the pocket. Majestic works in the same way as Yahoo Link Explorer did (see the boxed text above) in that it's a backlink checker that tells you everything you will ever need to know about who is linking to you, and from where. This will show you more about the URLs linking to you than pretty much any other tool. Once you register, you can compare yourself to other sites in your niche, which gives you a clear picture of what you need to do, with many other useful reports and charts.

  There is a free account option but, if you can stretch to a paid account, it's worth it.
- **SEMRush** ← http://semrush.com
  This is a suite of tools that covers keyword research, analysis of your competitors and organic search positions for various keywords. It also tries to find any PPC ads by your competitors, with an estimation of what they're spending and the approximate CTR of each ad. It displays SEO data for your site in nice, easy-to-read graphs you can print out.
- **Moz** ← https://moz.com
  SEOMoz is another similar suite of tools that gives you excellent data, not only on your own social and SEO efforts but also on those of your competition. Open Site Explorer will display all links from SEOMoz pointing to the various URLs on your website (just like Majestic SEO), and you can run competitive analyses, get recommendations on how to improve your on-page and off-page SEO and run reports charting your progress.

The role of outsourcing

For you, the business owner, the role of outsourcing is probably one of the most important things you will ever learn – not just in SEO and SEM but also for your business in general. As soon as you can outsource a task, do it, especially if you are the only person in your business. If you try to do absolutely everything, you will slowly burn yourself out and your business – that you've spent blood, sweat and tears building – will suffer.

This masterclass aims to give you the knowledge and understanding you need, so that:

- you know what needs doing and can assign someone else to do it without blindly saying, 'I don't know what I need; just make my website #1.'
- you decrease the chances of being swindled by unscrupulous SEO engineers because you can ask intelligent questions and discover whether they really know what they're talking about.

As you've probably already figured out, the correct setting up of a website is perhaps only 15–20 per cent of the actual work. The constant content creation and the work on SEO are what are going to take time, probably a lot more of your time than you may have previously imagined. This is where outsourcing really comes into its own. You may already be prepared for the need to outsource tech things to do with your website from time to time but, in the long term, if you don't have the time or inclination for doing SEO and SEM yourself, you're going to need someone else to handle it on a permanent basis, and it needs to be done well.

How to scale

Learning how to 'scale' your efforts is learning the art of telling other people how to do things effectively. It's finding that balance between, at one extreme, spending hours going into too much detail and micromanaging every little thing and, at the other, just handing the task to someone and saying 'Get on with it,' while you go off on holiday.

What is missing in both of the above scenarios is:

- having a plan
- projecting the plan.

Follow these steps when delegating, to make sure you get as much out of it as possible:

1 Create a work breakdown structure

This is where you sit down and decide exactly what you want to outsource. Do you want to outsource the content creation, the product selection, the SEO, the SEM, the ad writing, the website techie stuff, or something else? After that, you break down what you want done into a list of smaller tasks.

For SEO, this would include:

- Track progress
- Perform competitive analysis
- Do a weekly backlink check on all web pages on your site, using Majestic SEO or Open Site Explorer
- Find quality links
- Find guest blogging opportunities

 TIP *You can find free work breakdown structure templates if you search for them on Google, Yahoo or Bing.*

2 Find freelancers and suppliers

Online, great places to find freelancers (people who work for themselves) and suppliers (people who find other people to work for you) are odesk.com, elance.com and freelancer.com. Freelancer recently purchased another large freelancer-type marketplace called Scriptlance, so it's even bigger now. These websites work like a cross between wanted ads and auction sites. Some of the freelancers on these sites are effectively just suppliers but, either way, they get the job done. You post up the job you want done and freelancers will bid against each other to win the work.

The key to using these sites is to:

- know exactly what you want
  Give as much detail as possible. Don't just say you want someone to build links for you. Look at similar jobs posted up and see how they've been worded. Take what you like from them and craft your own.
- know how much you are willing or able to pay
  On these sites, you can get someone for a pound or two an hour or 100 times as much. If you are not sure how much something you are asking for costs, say so and ask for bids. Remember that you often get what you pay for, so people working for a low hourly rate are not likely to be as good as those asking for more.
- be prepared to pay more for creative tasks
  Graphics and content creation will cost more than technical tasks like building websites or fixing HTML. In my experience there are plenty of great geeks out there, but great writers and graphics people are rare.

Other excellent sources of freelancers include local colleges and universities. Students are always looking for ways to earn some extra money. Placing a request in the student magazine or a postcard on a campus bulletin board or asking for a recommendation from a faculty head might get you a great person you can outsource to. Stay-at-home parents are also another potential source of great freelance staff.

Interview your potential freelancers thoroughly, to make sure that they are the perfect fit and know exactly what you require.

 You now have a good idea of what you need to do, but don't necessarily tell a freelancer what you require in exacting detail. Ask them what they think you need; if they give you the right answer, you know they have potential.

3 Manage your freelancers

After hiring your freelancer, have them send reports to you frequently so you can be sure of the quality of their work (especially in areas like SEO), because if they start using tactics Google frowns on, it can hurt your reputation more then it helps!

Whenever I hire a freelancer, I always state in the job specification that I expect daily reports from the beginning. If they don't deliver them, I will cancel the job and let them go. It sounds harsh, but bitter experience has taught me that the maxim of 'Hire slow and fire fast' is true. Your job is not to train them; they are supposed to be the experts before they ask to work for you. That is the definition of a freelancer.

If, after a while, you know that your outsourcer is delivering quality work, you can scale back your checks to once every few days, just to make sure things are going as planned. Then do a thorough review every month to make sure all goals are being met and that your efforts are starting to bear fruit.

Should you hire a project manager?

A project manager is the ultimate compromise between hands-off outsourcing and total task management. A project manager runs everything, including the freelancers, and only tells you about progress, how well things are going and how much money you have made.

Your decision about whether to hire is really a matter of money and time and so, if you have the time to do it, I would recommend doing the job yourself. No one cares about your business as much as you do and it is always difficult to find someone who has the same vision and goals as you do. However, if you really don't have the time or you know that being a manager is just not your thing, this is an option.

Hiring your project manager is your most important hire, though, and you must:

- check and recheck to make sure he or she is invested in the outcome of the project and has a great track record
- make sure all the finances stay under your control: you can never be too careful when it comes to that
- make sure the project manager knows they have to ask before they make any purchases or hires.

Summary

In this chapter you learned about some of the tools that can make the whole SEO process a lot easier. Try them all out if you have time (SEOMoz especially, as they have a 30-day free trial). They can shorten your learning curve considerably and make your experience better. Read my blog for the latest news that could affect you and your business.

You also discovered how to have the work done for you, without spending all your profits in the process, by outsourcing on Upwork.com. Use these places wisely to get the best return for your money. Do not hire a project manager unless you really don't have the time and you can easily afford it.

In this chapter you have discovered that SEO is the foundation of marketing on the Internet today. To see real success, you'll need to have a passion for what you are doing, or at least enjoy doing it. Ultimately, it is about making your content good for your user, so keep this always in your mind. Tricks may work for a bit, but true quality – always in short supply – is far more valuable.

Fact-check (answers at the back)

1. Which two free tools should you put on every website you own?
   a) Market Samurai and SEMRush ❑
   b) Keyword Blaze and Majestic SEO ❑
   c) SEOMoz and SEMRush ❑
   d) Google Analytics and Google Search Console ❑

2. What does Market Samurai help with?
   a) Everything ❑
   b) Mainly keyword research ❑
   c) Finding links to you ❑
   d) Automating keyword research ❑

3. What does Keyword Blaze help with?
   a) Everything ❑
   b) Mainly keyword research ❑
   c) Finding links to you ❑
   d) Automating keyword research ❑

4. What does Majestic SEO help with?
   a) Everything ❑
   b) Mainly keyword research ❑
   c) Finding links to you ❑
   d) Automating keyword research ❑

5. What does SEMRush help with?
   a) Everything ❑
   b) Mainly keyword research ❑
   c) Finding links to you ❑
   d) Automating keyword research ❑

6. What percentage of the work is creating your page and finding your keywords?
   a) 50 per cent ❑
   b) 70 per cent ❑
   c) 90 per cent ❑
   d) 10–20 per cent ❑

7. What is a great site for getting contractors for your project?
   a) odesk.com ❑
   b) freelancer.com ❑
   c) scriptlance.com ❑
   d) elance.com ❑

8. When paying low on oDesk, what do you usually get?
   a) The best work ever ❑
   b) Work that's all right ❑
   c) What you paid for ❑
   d) You never know ❑

9. When hiring a freelancer, what should you expect at the beginning?
   a) Daily reports ❑
   b) Weekly reports ❑
   c) Monthly reports ❑
   d) No reports, just frequent questions ❑

10. What does a project manager need?
    a) Complete control ❑
    b) To be micromanaged ❑
    c) Control, but not over finances ❑
    d) The same vision and goals as you ❑

7 × 7

1 Seven dos of SEO and search marketing

- Do constantly ask friends and colleagues to take an objective look at your website and look to see how easy it is to use. Note down any sticking points and think how they can be rectified. A bad website user experience equals a drop in rankings.
- Do make sure that all content added to your site is unique. Do not copy and paste an article in full from elsewhere (even if it's yours) and put it on your site. Any articles you post should go on your website first and then added to any social network pages/accounts so Google knows you wrote it.
- Do use other media types (podcasting, videos, images) summarizing your new content and link back to you. Don't just rely on text. Videos and images make up the vast majority of online traffic, generally reach more people and are more engaging.
- Do have a specific purpose and destination when doing PPC search marketing. Don't just send visitors to your homepage to 'get the word out'.
- When doing PPC, focus on mastering one ad network (Google AdWords, Facebook PPC, Bing, whatever it is) before moving on to the next. Don't try to do them all at the same time.
- Do constantly be testing, changing and growing. Don't ever just settle for the status quo.
- If you're serious about SEO and PPC search marketing (and why wouldn't you be?), try to keep up to date with the changes and trends as best as possible so you aren't taken by surprise.

2 Seven don'ts of SEO and search marketing

- Don't try to find search engine and traffic 'secrets' or 'hacks'. Almost all of them fail because they are short-term loopholes and eventually may get your website slapped by Google.
- Don't waste your time writing bad or boring content and expect amazing links from 'authorities' to boost your rankings. Spend the time and write quality content that is aimed to inform, educate and, hopefully, move the reader a little closer to buying products and services from you.
- Don't use any technique that Google could class as 'unnatural' such as link spamming, on-page keyword stuffing and so on. It will punish you for it, in some cases permanently penalizing your domain so it will no longer rank for anything, ever again.
- If you outsource your SEO, don't penny-pinch and use services in countries like India (as an example) no matter how low the rate. I guarantee 99.9 per cent of them won't know how to do it properly and you'll risk your site with Google.
- Don't set up your PPC campaigns and forget about them.
- Don't ignore your competition. Make sure you're continually spying on your competition and try to reverse engineer any rises and drops in their rankings using Majestic. Model the good, avoid the bad.
- Don't forget to determine the average lifetime value of each customer. Once you have this, you will know exactly how much you can spend to acquire a customer and still make a profit.

3 Seven best tools and resources

- Adwords Keyword Planner (https://adwords.google.com/o/KeywordTool/)
- Majestic SEO (http://majestic.com)
- http://www.seomoz.org/blog/17-types-of-link-spam-to-avoid (Never do these!)

- Website Analytics Software http://google.com/analytics
- Outsourcing: http://upwork.com
- Get reports on how your site is doing in the rankings here: http://semrush.com
- Find out what Google thinks about your website: http://google.com/webmasters/tools/

4 Seven things to do now (if you haven't yet done them)

- Generate a list of relevant keywords for your website to rank for in Google. Use its Keyword Planner and enter your website URL to start. Pay special attention to keywords with Medium–High ad competition. Keywords with the most Google ads on them will most likely have the highest commercial intent (i.e. buyers). Plug all keywords into a tool like Keyword Blaze or Ultimate Niche Finder to find the easier keywords with the most search volume to rank for initially.
- Make a list of your direct competitors' websites. Note down what they do well and what they don't. Put their URL into Google Keyword Planner and see what other search terms you can find.
- Go through your website and make sure all your On-Page Optimization is correct. Every page should have a unique Meta Title and Description and content should be relevant to the page's topic.
- Make a list of all your website pages and delete/add more content to any that Google might consider as 'thin' or 'low-quality' to help protect against a Google Panda Penalty.
- Use Majestic to examine your backlink profile, making sure you are only getting links with applicable anchor text from authoritative, relevant websites (excluding social media) to help protect against a Google Penguin Penalty. Ask Google to delete any irrelevant links using the Disavow Tool in your Google Search Console Tools account.
- Look in forums, Yahoo Answers, Quora and other 'Q&A' websites to find common questions that people might

enter into Google for answers so you can leverage Google's Hummingbird Update. UberSuggest.com or HQSuggest.com may also help find these.

● Try to get previous customers or clients to post reviews of your products or services to related review sites like Yelp. com and TripAdvisor.com. Google gathers reviews from sites like these (known as 'citations') to help determine relevance for the search term and are extremely powerful, especially for companies that service a specific geographic area.

5 Seven things to do each business day

● Log into your Google Search Console Tools account and look for any new crawling and sitemap errors as well as new irrelevant links that have appeared that can be dealt with quickly.

● Log into Google Analytics and take a look at the sources of yesterday's traffic. Are there any new 'authorities' linking to you or positive reviews of your products or services? Follow up accordingly.

● Set up a Google Alert for your business name and any products or services you offer and have it send new alerts to your email. Since you'll be accessing your Inbox daily anyway, you won't have to 'do' anything extra to see the data.

● Check your PPC campaigns and see if there are any that need optimizing or pausing.

● During your daily surfing, keep an eye out for websites that might be interested in publishing an article of yours (guest blogging) in exchange for a link back to your website.

● Set goals for your website in Google Analytics (depending on the main action that you want them to take that leads to money for you) and check if the goals are being reached – if not, something is wrong.

● Take screenshots of any text or image ads you see that grab your attention and save them to possibly model for your company. Also, save the destination URL to see if that's also something worth adapting.

6 Seven things to do monthly or occasionally

● Check your rankings in Google Search Console tools. You would think this would be daily but it is best not to give much credence to short-term gains or losses but rather look at the big picture.
● Do a full audit of your PPC campaigns and make sure any individual campaigns producing no or not enough profit are axed.
● Do a 'site:yourwebsite.com' search in Google. Hackers and spammers are rampant these days and, if they hack you, you might not even know it. They could just post web pages on your site invisible to you. This way you will see them fast.
● Do a full audit of where visitors are landing on your site and where they are going. They might be landing in unexpected places for unexpected reasons.
● Change your goal values in Google Analytics to more accurately reflect how much money each action earns you.
● Check your website's loading speed to make sure it's nice and fast. This also has a direct effect on your rankings. Make sure that all your website's images are compressed as much as possible without losing quality and there is no unnecessary HTML or Javascript code on the page.
● Put your URL into Google Keyword Planner and see if Google shows new search terms that it thinks you are relevant for. Can they spark new approaches for your SEO efforts?

7 Seven future SEO and search marketing trends to look out for

● Look for Google to clamp down more and more on spam. Aim for your links to just keep getting more and more 'natural looking' (even if they aren't strictly 100-per-cent natural unasked-for links).
● The line is beginning to blur between SEO and social media, with Google looking at 'social signals' (likes, shares, tweets,

etc.) as a way to verify that you are an 'authority' to your audience. I think it's pretty reasonable to say 'social signals' will gain more and more power as Google knows they are much tougher to fake than generating spammy backlinks. This is another reason to produce awesome content that gets organically shared on social media in the hope that it will have a direct positive effect on your rankings, via Authorship.

- The number of people using Google on a mobile is increasing every year. Its 'Mobilegeddon' update to reward websites that are mobile-friendly shows that it is serious about providing an excellent experience for those users. So make sure you do the same and check your website works and looks as best as it can do on a smartphone. This trend is only going to increase for all search engines (not just Google), so investigate how best to take advantage of it for your audience and your market.

- Following on directly from mobile is Voice Searching. With smartphones now coming with built-in voice assistants like Siri, Cortana and Google Now, more people are using that type of communication to get the answers to their questions. Again, this is only going to increase so begin to think about how you can show up in front of a user's eyeballs when they ask questions like 'How can I ...?', 'Where can I find a ...?', 'What is the best ...?'

- Customer/client reviews will gain more power not only for search engine rankings but also for social networks to determine your 'authority' and trustworthiness. Realize that what you do outside of social media may have a direct impact on your social media presence, not just your reputation.

- Interactivity will also be more important. Google is getting better and better at measuring how your visitors interact with your website and using that data to determine whether or not your website is providing a good or bad user experience. If Google thinks it's 'bad', then you can expect to slowly drop down the rankings. So make sure that your website's content is engaging and useful and goes some way to answering your visitors' questions.

● They say that 'Nothing is certain in life except death and taxes'. When it comes to SEO, you can add 'Google Updates' to that. Google is constantly updating its methodology for ranking websites, ensuring the best possible user experience for its visitors: Penguin, Panda and Hummingbird were all designed to do that. So don't panic if you suddenly hear of a new update that's been applied. The sky isn't falling in. It will happen, and when it does see it as an opportunity to leverage your way ahead of your competitors while they all flail around crying that the online world is ending.

PART 3
Your Content Marketing Masterclass

Introduction

Content marketing is one of today's growing marketing trends following fast on the heels of social media. Depending on what you read, it's either heralded as the latest and only way to market anything or it's a big fuss about nothing – because it's actually been around for years and it's just what most marketers do anyway, at least to some extent.

Using content in marketing is of course not new. It could be said that the first direct response advertising which used long copy to set out the benefits of a product or service represents an early form of content marketing. But in those days there was little choice when it came to getting your message out there. There was print advertising and PR and then along came radio and television.

The marketing landscape only changed significantly when the internet arrived and enabled us to do all sorts of exciting things – including publish our own content, easily and cost effectively. How much new content is published online every day is open to debate, but suffice to say it's a truly staggering amount. And that's changed the way we all look for, find and buy things – whether for personal use or in business.

Enter the opportunity for content marketing – marketing through creating and sharing content that potential customers find relevant, useful and valuable in order to attract, engage, convert and retain them. As such it's much more than simply producing a brochure and a set of product sheets to be used primarily by your sales team, or publishing the occasional newsletter or blog post.

It's a strategy that requires careful thought, clear objectives and goals, and a deep understanding of your audience. It requires you to reach out to them with well-planned and well-produced content – in all forms and formats, offline as well as online.

Although some companies may be able to adopt a predominantly content marketing approach, most integrate it with other marketing strategies that work well together and use content to enhance a range of other marketing activities.

In this Part we take a joined-up look at content marketing, the key principles that underpin it, and what it takes to put it into practice in a consistent and fully formed way. And we provide a practical framework for planning it and executing it successfully – whatever the size of your business or your marketing team.

What we know as content marketing today may become the marketing norm for future generations. It takes time to deliver real results and you need to be willing to play the long game and build a relationship and trust with your audience over the long term. Adopting a content marketing approach is certainly not a short term, quick win tactic.

But the chances are it could make a big difference to the effectiveness of your marketing. Let's find out.

CHAPTER 15

Adopt a content marketing mindset

In this chapter we address some of the most commonly asked content marketing questions.

We look at what content marketing is and find out if it really is something new – or something we've been doing by default without realizing it.

Many businesses are focusing on delivering various forms of content to demonstrate their value and differentiate themselves from their competitors, enabled in recent years by developments in technology, the internet and social media.

But not everyone is doing it well. So, what are the key principles and characteristics of content marketing? What do we need to understand in order to be able to plan, manage and put it into practice successfully?

What is content marketing?

Content marketing is the process of marketing through creating and sharing content that potential customers find relevant, useful and valuable in order to attract, engage, convert and retain them.

You provide content that people actually want to receive – that informs, educates or entertains. Rather than marketing or sales interventions that are unwelcome ¬ unwanted, irrelevant or intrusive.

It prepares the ground for a sale, helping you develop a trusted relationship with your prospect and moving them through your marketing and sales process.

At various points in that process you will employ well-crafted, call-to-action and conversion copy, but it will be appropriate and timely. Content marketing is not just advertising by another name – or an excuse to deploy gimmicky sales techniques to grab attention before delivering a hard-hitting 'buy me and buy me now' sales message.

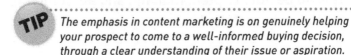

TIP *The emphasis in content marketing is on genuinely helping your prospect to come to a well-informed buying decision, through a clear understanding of their issue or aspiration.*

In many ways you are doing what the best-in-class, consultative sales person is doing during a face-to-face meeting, except that you are doing it with 'content'.

What do we mean by content?

The word 'content' is a bit of a catch-all term. The *New Oxford Dictionary of English* defines 'content' as 'the substance or material dealt with in a speech, literary work, etc. as distinct from its form or style'.

It is essentially *what* you are communicating. But you can present that 'what' – your core content – in different formats, in different places, using different methods of distribution and promotion.

Here's a simple example:

- Your 'what' might be an explanation of how your target audience could resolve a certain problem. For example, remove a red wine stain from a carpet.
- You could write this as a piece of 'how-to' text and publish it as a post on your company's blog.
- Or you could film a short video showing someone actually removing a red wine stain from a carpet and then publish the video on your company's blog and upload it to a video hosting platform such as YouTube or Vimeo.
- You could then draw your customers' attention to it by featuring it in your email newsletter or by sending out a specific email notification.

Content covers whatever you produce in text, image, audio, or video format wherever you publish or present it – on the web, in print, or in person.

Is content marketing new?

This example probably sounds familiar. So, is content marketing really new? Or is it something you've been doing for a long time already, but just not calling it 'content marketing'?

You may already be blogging, creating videos, producing newsletters, using social media and email marketing – plus doing a whole host of other content related activities.

So, is that content marketing?

The most likely answer is that although you may indeed be already using some form of content in your marketing, you may not be embracing content marketing in its fullest form.

If you are simply bolting some ad hoc content activities onto a 'traditional' marketing plan, you'll probably have some significant gaps.

The most likely ones are:

- Lack of a specific content marketing strategy that ties your content tactics together and integrates them with your overall marketing strategy.

- Lack of organization (a plan and tools) to create and publish content regularly to a consistent standard.
- Lack of measurement of content performance and return on investment.

This in itself requires a mindset shift for many marketers.

Although the *theory* of marketing strategy, planning and joined-up thinking is well known, in practice many businesses and marketing departments fall short under pressure to get on and just 'do' marketing – a way of working supported by the fact that, as marketers, we are often measured solely in terms of outputs.

Let's take the example of producing a customer newsletter.

We may be used to producing it four times a year. If we've been doing it for a while, chances are we've lost the connection with why we started the newsletter in the first place. It gets carried forward in the budget each year and we're primarily measured on simply getting it out on time each quarter. We may have some form of loose editorial planning in place but at some stage we get to the point of just wanting to get the thing finished. Once we've got the core article written, we're looking for fillers and scrambling to hit our deadline. We've become almost exclusively focused on the output, so we can tick that box and get on with our next task. And there's little desire or time to assess how well any one newsletter has performed – a difficult task made harder by the fact that we don't really know what we wanted it to achieve in the first place.

This is an example of using content (a collection of articles published in a newsletter) but it is not well executed content marketing.

 TIP *To be successful, content marketing has to be seen and treated as an end-to-end, joined-up process – driven by customer needs and a clear purpose.*

Why an ad hoc approach to content is a bad idea

If you come to content marketing with a predominately 'doing' mindset, with just a glance at strategy and no real plan, you're in danger of becoming very busy writing and producing content and using up a lot of time and resources doing it with no clear idea of what you're getting in return.

In such a scenario getting ongoing support for your content marketing will be at best difficult – whether from your line manager, the management team, your fellow team members or others within your organization who you rely on as subject matter experts.

The seven key principles of content marketing

What then are the key principles and characteristics of content marketing that you have to understand and master in order to become the consummate practitioner?

1. Clearly understand the value you need to create for your audience

Your content is the means by which you will deliver value to your audience. Therefore you need to understand your prospects and customers in a deep and detailed way – to a far greater degree than you may currently be used to. You need to know all about your audience and what will make a real difference to their lives in relation to the products or services you are offering – in order to provide content that they will truly want and value.

2. Provide that value consistently, over the long term

Buying decisions are not usually made in an instant. Even a fairly low-cost product can have a wrapper of decision making around it. When you are in the washing powder aisle of the supermarket, your choice of brand and product is influenced by several factors – all unique to you, your values and beliefs as well economic factors and aesthetic preferences. And our choices are governed by habit. If you are providing a new eco-friendly laundry alternative you may be appealing to an innate desire to be 'green' (knocking on an open door) or have to work harder to educate and persuade someone to buy or switch, keep on buying and recommend your brand. This may take time and the building of rapport and trust – hence why we talk about the need to build relationships over the long term.

This is very different to most marketing campaigns. They tend to take place over months rather than years and have short-term sales goals. Content marketing, by its very nature, is all about playing the long game.

3. Measure results and ROI over the long term

In turn, this means that you can have no expectation of short-term financial pay back. This often presents difficulties in getting your business case for a content marketing approach or initiative adopted – unless your stakeholders and decision makers are all on board. The better news is that a lot of your content marketing efforts will be measurable – especially the part that takes place online as there is a wealth of web and social measurement tools available. The challenge however is to make sure you are setting up your content marketing so that a) you are able to measure it and b) you are selecting relevant, useful metrics to track. You want feedback that will allow you to test and improve performance of the specific content and channels you are deploying.

4. Be crystal clear on strategy and apply joined-up thinking

Content marketing is not the ad hoc execution of random content-based activities. It requires a strategy and plan that integrates with your overall marketing strategy and plan, and specific implementation plans for content creation, production, publishing, distribution, promotion and evaluation. Even when you have a simple strategy, these implementation plans are likely to be complex in the sheer number of schedules and activities to be integrated and mapped. So clear strategic thinking is crucial in order to provide direction and keep focused and on track – while being flexible and adaptable to marketplace changes.

5. Produce content regularly and consistently

Robert Rose, Chief Strategy Officer at the Content Marketing Institute, has referred to content as 'a show that never closes'. It requires commitment and resources to keep it going and maintain standards. It also means that you have to think more like a publisher or broadcaster than a seller of goods and services – and organize your team and workflow accordingly.

This inevitably shifts content from being a collection of marketing collateral to being more of a brand asset. You could be building up a store of valuable intellectual property. It's therefore important to consider where you host, publish and distribute your content and how you protect it. Make sure you own and are in control of the place where you keep and primarily display this asset (e.g. your own web domain) rather than relying on third party hosts (e.g. social media platforms) that can disappear or withdraw services – along with your content and followers – at any time.

6. Understand that distributing and promoting your content is as important as producing it

You can only do so much to get your content found by organic search. Even when you've mastered principles 1 to 5, you still need to build your audience through appropriate and timely distribution and promotion. Just writing and producing great content is not enough, you have to get it out there and, yes, shared and ideally talked about, used and acted on. This means bringing various marketing channels, tools and activities to bear and weaving them seamlessly into your content marketing strategy and plan. Things like email marketing, social media, partnering and even paid advertising.

7. Never neglect your internal communications

In order to get and keep support for your content marketing you are going to have to run and manage your own internal communications and PR campaign. This may involve helping to educate and win over the Board, the management team, your boss, your marketing team and other creatives, your agencies, and those people who you are going to be relying on as subject matter specialists.

When it comes to your marketing people, it's likely you're going to have to ask them to work differently, acquire new skills and take on new responsibilities. You may find yourself having to bring in new people with different skill sets. The old order may get shaken up a little or a lot. Be aware of the challenges and, as your content marketing evolves, ensure you are communicating effectively and involving and managing others appropriately.

Is content marketing a good strategy for every business?

As the concept of content marketing has gained momentum, more companies are producing more content – although not always as part of a well-rounded strategy.

Whenever something new or different comes along we, as marketing leaders or practitioners, ask ourselves, 'Is this something I should be considering?', 'Could this give us better results than our current approach?'

Ultimately, whether a content marketing approach will work for you depends on:

- the nature of your customer base and your customer decision-making processes
- how committed you are to properly planning and executing such an approach
- how willing and able you are to make changes.

In my experience, no broad generalizations hold true – such as that content marketing only works for B2B or B2C, or for those providing services, or producing products. You can use it effectively – to some degree – whatever your market, sector or offering.

That's not to say it's always easy to see how well it could work (or not) when you first start to consider it. In many cases, that's because we're all so used to looking at our business and our marketing in a certain way that's it hard to adjust our thinking. You need to start with a clean slate and no preconceived ideas – especially when it comes to tackling what your customers really want from you.

This may mean that you need to:

- work harder and devote more resources to understanding your customers
- be more creative and inventive in planning and designing content
- be more generous with the information, advice and value you provide as part of the process.

If you are involved in marketing a small business, then your content marketing landscape is going to be less complex than if you are a large, multinational enterprise.

Most companies who approach content marketing in a well thought-out way integrate it into their existing marketing plan alongside other marketing strategies.

Not everyone has the potential to become a fully-fledged brand publisher.

However, most businesses can benefit by thinking about and executing their content activities in a more professional way – looking at the content they are creating from their customers' perspective in order to provide something of genuine value rather than something that still looks like an advert or a sales pitch.

Summary

In this chapter we've looked at what content marketing is and the core principles that underpin an effective content marketing approach. It's much more than simply adding a few content activities (like sending out a newsletter or writing the occasional blog post) into your existing set of marketing activities.

Content marketing is all about giving your customers real value – content that informs, educates or entertains. Content that they actually want and can use, that gives advice and answers questions. In this way it prepares the ground for a sale, attracting interest and keeping people engaged until such time as they are ready to buy. It's therefore a strategy that requires commitment over the long term.

Think for a moment about your own business. What content do you already produce as part of your marketing activities? Do you have scope to improve? Do you need to understand your prospects and customers better?

Briefly assess where you are at the moment and how you might develop, tailor and improve your content marketing approach.

In the next chapter, we look at the different types of content formats and techniques at your disposal.

Fact-check (answers at the back)

1. What is content marketing?
   a) A version of social media marketing ❏
   b) Marketing by providing and sharing content that people find useful and valuable ❏
   c) Another name for advertising ❏
   d) A form of email marketing ❏

2. What is content marketing especially good for?
   a) Annoying customers with unwanted direct mail ❏
   b) Delivering in-your-face 'buy me now' sales messages ❏
   c) Preparing the ground for a sale by developing a trusted relationship with your prospect ❏
   d) Distracting people from all the other things they have to do ❏

3. Is content marketing new?
   a) Absolutely – no one has ever thought of using content in marketing before ❏
   b) Definitely not – after all you've had a newsletter for years ❏
   c) No – it's exactly the same as email marketing ❏
   d) Using content in marketing is not new, but content marketing as a fully formed strategy has only come into its own in recent years ❏

4. When could you be said to have adopted a content marketing approach?
   a) When you throw a couple of blogs and few Tweets and Facebook posts together and call it content marketing ❏
   b) When you develop it as a well thought-out strategy within your marketing plan ❏,
   c) When you bolt a few ad hoc content initiatives on to your existing marketing plan ❏
   d) When you just produce a couple of product sheets each year for your sales team ❏

5. How well do you need to know your audience?
   a) In a deep way so you know how your content can deliver value to them ❏
   b) Not that well, you'll just continue to guess what they want ❏
   c) Just enough to be able to make a sales pitch ❏
   d) It doesn't matter how well you know them, it won't make a difference to what you do ❏

6. Will content marketing always bring you a rapid return on investment?
   a) Yes, it's a short-term, quick-win sales tactic ❏
   b) It might, as long as you spend a lot of money on it in the first place ❏
   c) No, because there's just no way to measure it ❏
   d) No, you should expect to reap the rewards over the long term ❏

7. Why do you need a clear content marketing strategy?
   a) You don't, having a strategy is completely unimportant ❏
   b) It's essential in order to provide direction and keep your content marketing on track ❏
   c) So you can then put it in your drawer and forget about it ❏
   d) So you can feel smug in review meetings ❏

8. Why does thinking like a publisher help?
   a) Because working for a newspaper or magazine seems more exciting than what you do ❏
   b) It doesn't help at all because you're just here to sell stuff ❏
   c) Because you need to take your commitment to content seriously and adopt a professional approach to publishing ❏
   d) Because it will look good on your CV ❏

9. Is it enough just to create good content?
   a) Yes, if you do that people will find it somehow ❏
   b) Yes, as long as it's on your website Google will send you plenty of visitors ❏
   c) No, you have to actively distribute and promote it across all your marketing channels ❏
   d) All you have to do is mention it on social media when you first create it ❏

10. Should you tell anyone in-house about your content marketing?
   a) No, no one within your organization will care what you're up to ❏
   b) Yes, it's crucial you communicate in order to win support from your team, your managers and the Board ❏
   c) Only if someone asks you ❏
   d) No, you haven't got time to do that ❏

CHAPTER 16

Understand the different types of content

In this chapter we take a closer look at what we mean by 'content' and getting clear about the different content formats and options available to us.

We find content throughout our organizations – offline as well as online. I could fill this entire chapter with one long mega-list of different types of content, from white papers to blog posts, conference speeches to video clips.

But I'm not. Instead I'm going to walk you through the basic building blocks of text, image, audio and video, and the different techniques we can use to present our content in an attractive, audience-friendly way.

What I want you to learn is how to think about content in relation to your audience and decide what will work best for them and for you – rather than simply latching on to the latest trend.

Content scope

Over the past ten years, companies have been increasingly taking their marketing online, taking advantage of the opportunities opened up by the internet and developments such as social media.

As the term 'content marketing' has become more prevalent, you could be forgiven for thinking that's it just another form of internet marketing. But content marketing does not just take place online. Your customer's content journey spans the whole of your marketing process – both online and offline.

TIP *What you are aiming for is to develop a seamless content experience for your audience that is consistent and congruent – wherever that audience finds you or interacts with your brand.*

The content items that you use to create this experience can be diverse and numerous or tightly focused and few in number – there is no right or wrong scenario.

Your content will include all your fundamental items, such as product and service descriptions and company information (because at some point in their journey that's likely to be what at least a proportion of your audience will be looking for).

But you'll also be creating new content that will take you beyond this descriptive, passive experience (even if it is already highly customer and benefits focused). You will be developing content that your audience can readily engage with and become involved in.

You'll be looking across your organization, thinking about content in a new way, assessing the role and value of the content items you already have, adding to or replacing some of those items and organizing and managing them in different ways.

At first sight, there can seem to be an overwhelming amount of content already in place and a mesmerizing array of new options.

Deciding what format to use

The one thing I never want you to do is to make a content decision that looks like this.

We must ... Add a blog to our website ... Create a knowledgebase ... Develop an elearning course ... Start a radio show or podcast series ... Develop a suite of videos ... Or any other content initiative you can think of ...

Because ... I've heard it's the 'latest' thing to do ... it seems to work well for [insert name of some well-known brand or competitor] ... we read about it in a book or just got back from a half-day course about a new content creation tool ... or any other similar, poorly thought out or knee jerk reason.

Even if (in fact, *especially* if) your boss, someone in sales, or your CEO suggests it – with no additional strategic rationale.

What ultimately determines the format and type of content you create are these two things:

● Whatever is going to best deliver the experience you want your audience to receive.
● Whatever is going to present your content to best effect and communicate with your audience most efficiently and effectively.

Not the latest trend nor shiny new tool nor a pitch from a product, service or training provider who's made no attempt to understand your business or your audience.

Becoming and remaining clear about the essential ways to categorize and think about content is therefore crucial in being able to successfully plan, organize and manage it. Especially when there seems to be a new flavour of the month ... well, every month.

Just because you hear that podcasting is the new blogging or that every website must have video, it doesn't mean it's right for you. The one thing I can guarantee is that by the time you read this there will be some new (or reinvented) technique that will be the latest 'in' thing. You'll see and hear lots of different people basically promoting and endorsing lots of different approaches and tools.

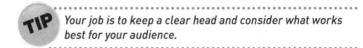

TIP *Your job is to keep a clear head and consider what works best for your audience.*

Keep in mind these simple, fundamental ways of thinking about content and avoid getting confused or distracted.

The basic building blocks – content formats

There are in fact only four basic content formats:

1 Text – words that you read
2 Images – still pictures that you see
3 Audio – words and sounds that you listen to
4 Video – moving pictures that you watch, with or without audio

Before we delve deeper into these, let's consider what each of them has to offer.

Each format gives your audience a different experience. That may sound a bit simplistic but it's easy to overlook this fundamental point when choosing the format for any one piece of content.

In many cases, you will also want to give a choice of formats. We each prefer to consume information in different ways. And our preferred choice can also change according to our circumstances.

● I may be drawn to listening to a half-hour podcast on a topic that interests me, but if I only have five minutes to get the key points, I will want to quickly scan the transcript instead.
● Audio may be great if I'm at home or in the car but impossible if I'm in the office or on the train without a headset or earphones.
● If I'm in research mode, I may want to print off pages.
● If I'm in learning mode, then I may have a preferred way of learning.
● And of course my choice of media and format can be influenced by the device I am using.

Text

Since man first put pen to paper, we've been reading the written word. Just because we've now got alternative media, it doesn't mean text based content is unwanted, boring or ineffective.

Nor should we be seduced or confused by research telling us that only short copy works these days because, thanks to the internet, our attention span is contracting and the competition for it is fierce. We're not talking about online copywriting here (although that will have a part to play in your overall content plan). We're talking about content that people actually want, that solves a problem: well-focused content that people want to engage with and learn from.

Therefore – when you are talking with the right people at the right time – well-written text-based content, whether short form (like blog posts) or long form (like white papers, in-depth case studies, or books) can a) still be the best primary choice and b) often an essential backup resource.

Images

Whether or not you think a picture is worth a thousand words, images can do an excellent job of supporting your text and convey impact and meaning – at a glance.

The main thing to bear in mind here is that images have to be well chosen. If we compare an image to a headline for a moment, they can both grab attention and entice you to 'read on', whether you're using single, full frame shots or creating your own graphics.

Images also send powerful messages, so make sure they support your brand – in both substance and style. Quirky cartoons may be eye catching and fun in certain circumstances, but may not be in alignment with your brand positioning or brand personality.

If you want something professional that goes beyond PowerPoint but stops short of video, then storyboarded static images or stills can be informative and compelling – produced as a Slideshare or video. And an infographic can indeed be used to replace a thousand words – as long as it's well designed.

Audio

As I write this, 'podcasting' is becoming the latest most talked about media option. And audio does indeed have lots of advantages. It immediately gives your audience a richer and more intimate experience. Listening to real voices and real conversations. Hearing your CEO discuss his views on key issues. Hearing one of your customers describe what it's like working with you. In addition, just as images can enhance text, so music can add mood and evoke feeling.

You haven't got the visual element that video gives you, but it is far easier to achieve a professional outcome – not least because you are only working with the dimension of the voice. As soon as you add visual recording, your checklist and performance requirements expand ten-fold. Imagine preparing and rehearsing your CEO for a ten-minute recorded conversation and then what the difference would be if you had to get him comfortable and confident to deliver a professional performance in front of the camera (with apologies to media trained CEOs everywhere).

Video

Video has the power to take the audience experience delivered by audio and deepen it. Done well, this is the closest we can get to experiencing someone or something live, in person. Video can encompass a wide range of different treatments from a short film with cinematic qualities to an animated whiteboard or explainer video – as well as the talking head or in-conversation interview.

It isn't something to adopt lightly – not just because of production quality (which we'll discuss in Chapter 19), but because you're unlikely to want to make just one great video. If you're serious about content marketing, the formats you choose will be part of your strategic decision making and mean a commitment to an approach and technique over the longer term.

The second dimension – content techniques

With those four basic content formats percolating in your brain, let's drill down a little further into this aspect of 'content experience'.

We can think of the job we want our content to do as being the same as we would want a well-trained, consultative, empathetic sales person to do. Yes, that's right, I did say sales person.

Here, I am visualizing someone who, once they have a clear understanding of their prospect's problem or aspiration, explains options, answers questions and makes sure that, as far as possible, that person is making the right decision for them at that time. That might be to buy there and then. Or it might be to defer their decision, keep looking or buy elsewhere. This sales person behaves in a thoroughly professional manner and because of that and their general helpfulness, they will be remembered and the prospect may well return one day or refer them, even if they never actually become a customer themselves.

This is a one-on-one interaction, guided by the sales person. There may well be more than one contact. Rapport is established, a relationship develops.

Picture that scenario. Then imagine that you are putting 'content' in place of the 'sales person'.

Beyond telling

To be successful at content marketing we have to move beyond 'telling'. We have to do more than just produce content that reads, sounds, and looks like an advertisement.

So let's explore a few content techniques that can give your audience a more engaging experience than just being sold to. By and large you can use each of these techniques to produce content in any (or a least more than one) of the four formats described above. And you can blend and mix these techniques up. When deciding how to present your content, it's time to get out of that 'we always do it this way' rut and have some fun with it.

Take a look outside your industry and see what's going on. What media, information and marketing do you find yourself responding to – how could you adapt that for your own use?

Conversation

In our everyday lives we are surrounded by conversations. It's a very natural way for us to communicate. Presenting conversations is therefore a friendly, non-intrusive technique that our audience can easily tune into.

Examples include structured one-on-one interviews, informal 'on the sofa' conversations, panel debates, Q & As, and hosted 'chat show' style discussions.

These can be used to get across a wide range of messaging and facts, and cover areas of opinion and commentary.

Even if you still have to produce an official statement about something, your conversational content can help spread the word by going deeper and exploring key points or issues.

And it's a good way to enhance engagement with technical content, research findings, and white papers.

Explanation

One really easy way to get out of telling mode is to switch to explaining mode. If you mentally precede your piece of content creation with the words 'Let me explain this to you ...' you immediately change your mindset and what follows will naturally be more engaging.

'How-to' content has long been a mainstay of marketing collateral, but see what happens when you apply this process of explanation to content relating to ideas and thought leadership. It helps your spokesperson or brand come across as authoritative while minimizing the risk of sounding arrogant or preachy.

Demonstration

This takes 'explanation' to a different level and brings in a visual dimension. Essentially you are showing someone how to do something.

No longer is this the preserve of live events and product demos – we can be helpful in so many more ways. Consider a DIY flooring supplier who actually shows you how to measure your floor space, including all those tricky corners and alcoves, and calculate the number of flooring packs you'll need. As a customer, you don't have to just figure it out from the written guide, you can watch Jake the DIY man actually doing it – in a room pretty much like yours.

Education

This DIY flooring example is also a form of education because as well as being able to buy the right number of packs with confidence, the customer has also learnt a new skill – how to measure up the floor space accurately. Education can be a little piece of learning like this or it can be a much bigger initiative.

Identifying and matching a specific thirst for learning with something that we can teach is a powerful content technique – always remembering that part of our definition of content marketing is that it prepares the ground for a sale.

Précis and collation

Just as a proportion of our audience may at times want deep and detailed content, others may be seeking just the opposite. This provides us with a huge opportunity to be helpful, by summarizing and writing or producing 'short' versions of things that can be consumed quickly and easily. This masterclass is one example. You don't want to read the latest content marketing 'bible', you want to grasp the basics quickly.

'Short' can also mean very short. For instance a series of 500-word blog posts or two-minute audios that highlight the key learning points from 'must read' but heavyweight business books.

Rounding up and collating also speaks to the time poor – the top five developments to know about in your niche this year, ten of the most useful tools and resources, the three most innovative ideas published on a specific topic this week.

Content segments

Segments are traditionally used on TV and radio – packaged portions of content, easily identified by the audience and often much anticipated. It could be a 20-second news update in between longer features. Or a regular five-minute slot within a programme that tackles a topic in a specific way. There is usually an element of branding and visual identity associated with segments.

This technique helps to make both you and your content appealing and memorable. You can apply it to sections within a newsletter, recurring features within a campaign, or as a regular slot within your podcast.

If you're used to producing collateral such as a customer magazine, you may already be used to applying segment thinking. 'A day in the life' series is a good way of explaining what goes on behind the scenes, featuring a different job role each time to show the care and attention that goes into creating your product or service from different perspectives.

'Two minutes with ...' or 'Lunch with ...' can badge an interview series within your blog, 'The Friday Rant' a segment within your podcast, or 'Five seasonal tips' a regular feature within your newsletter.

Origination vs curation

Finally, a reminder that you don't have to originate all your own content. You can source, select and share other people's quality content that aligns with your own content strategy and meets the needs and expectations of your audience. The key aspect of content curation though is that you must add value.

So, don't just provide a list in your round up of the ten best pest control blogs so far this year – say why you like them and what the key takeaway points are in each case.

Thinking of sharing a financial market commentary from the BBC or a *New York Times* science report? Explain why you are doing it. Do you have a different perspective or interpretation to offer – or alternative food for thought?

Add your own commentary and points of view. This is *your* content – so we want to hear from you, we want your perspective. Curation enables you to share legally, so make sure you stay legal and quote correctly and avoid plagiarism and copyright infringement.

Bringing it all together

There are many different ways to deliver your content objective. As you progress through this masterclass, keep in mind the diversity of content formats and techniques available to you.

Avoid getting stuck in a rut or default thinking. For example, that a 'newsletter' has to be in a certain format or that, in order to create great 'content', you have to be producing lots of written material.

But equally avoid getting carried away by a whizzy, all bells and whistles approach – just because you can or because someone says you should.

When choosing how to deliver your content, keep 'audience' and 'purpose' firmly in the forefront of your mind. What combination of formats and techniques:

● are best suited to your audience?
● will best enable or trigger your desired call-to-action?
● will best deliver on your content objective – are you setting out to entertain, inform or educate?

Then secondly, think about your content itself and if it naturally lends itself to a particular format or technique.

Summary

In this chapter we've delved a little deeper into the world of content. We've learnt that content can be found everywhere within an organization and that our aim with content marketing is to develop a seamless content experience for our audience – wherever they find us.

We looked at:

- How to decide what content format to use
- The four basic building blocks – text, image, audio and video
- A variety of content techniques we can use to move us beyond telling and selling

We need to keep our content fresh but avoid becoming distracted or misled by the latest, most-talked-about approach. We need to assess if it actually has the potential to work for us.

When it comes to any specific piece of content, choose a format and technique that is well suited to helping you achieve your content objective – what you want your audience to experience, feel or do as a result of engaging with it.

It's also easy to overlook the obvious fact that different people like to consume content in different ways at different times, so where appropriate, it's good to offer your audience a choice.

If you now think about the content you already work with, how might you change or develop it to make it more appealing to your audience?

In the next chapter, we move on and look at how to develop your content marketing strategy.

Fact-check (answers at the back)

1. How do you decide on the best content format to use?
   a) Just produce whatever the CEO says he wants to see ❏
   b) Adopt whatever is currently being talked about on the internet ❏
   c) Consider what is going to give your audience the best content experience ❏
   d) See what your main competitor is doing and copy them ❏

2. Why is it a good idea to give your audience a choice of formats?
   a) Because we all like to consume content in different ways at different times ❏
   b) It's not, because you just don't have time to do that ❏
   c) Because you can – technology makes it easy ❏
   d) It's not, people can just use whatever you decide to give them ❏

3. Do people still like to read in-depth text based content?
   a) No, people just want to look at pictures and listen to sound bites ❏
   b) No, there's no use publishing anything longer than 200 words ❏
   c) Yes, when they've found something they want and find useful ❏
   d) Only if they have nothing better to do ❏

4. What are images really good for?
   a) Distracting people from your copy ❏
   b) Conveying impact and meaning at a glance ❏
   c) Competing with your headline ❏
   d) Making fun of your brand ❏

5. What should be your overall aim when presenting content?
   a) To make it look and sound like an advert ❏
   b) To make it difficult for people to find the answers to their questions ❏
   c) To focus only on what you want to tell people ❏
   d) To mirror what a well-trained sales person with a consultative, empathetic approach would do ❏

6. The technique of explanation is good because
   a) It quickly and easily gets you out of 'telling' mode ❏
   b) It allows you ramble on until you've got nothing left to say ❏
   c) You don't have to think very much ❏
   d) You can easily make stuff up to fill the page ❏

7. Why is education a powerful content technique?
a) It allows you to create an e-course – even if no one ever subscribes to it ❏
b) It's not, no one is interested in essentially having to go back to school ❏
c) It gives your content matter experts something to do ❏
d) It allows you to tap into people's thirst for learning ❏

8. How can you be helpful to those with little time to spare?
a) Leave them alone, they've got enough to do ❏
b) Provide a forceful argument on why they should read your latest white paper ❏
c) Provide round-ups and summaries of key topics of interest to them ❏
d) Send them emails every day in the hope that they'll read at least one of them ❏

9. What is a content segment?
a) Easily identified, packaged portions of content traditionally used on TV and radio ❏
b) Something only found in soap operas ❏
c) The bit down the edge of a web page that contains adverts ❏
d) A new form of product packaging ❏

10. Do you have to produce all original content?
a) No, you can just copy and paste stuff from the internet ❏
b) Yes, it's the only way to be credible ❏
c) No, you can curate content and add value by adding your own comments and perspective ❏
d) Yes, otherwise you could be accused of copyright infringement ❏

CHAPTER 17

Develop your content marketing strategy

In this chapter we look at what you need to do and have in place at the strategic level in order to plan, manage and make things happen successfully at the implementation level.

We look at what it takes to fully home in on and understand your audience, find out what makes them tick, how they make their decision to buy from you – and how that helps you with your various content decisions.

We also go a little deeper into buyer behaviour to further develop your thinking before turning our attention to your content marketing goals and how you decide where to deploy your content within your marketing process.

We finish with a summary of what to include when you document your content marketing strategy.

Putting the customer first

In many ways your content has to do the same job as your product or service – it has to deliver value to the person using it.

It is very easy to approach content the wrong way round. To reach first for the content you already have or concentrate only on what you want to say – without fully considering what your audience really wants to hear about.

We all have a tendency to focus on ourselves – *our* company, *our* people, *our* products, *our* services, what *we* are doing. And as marketers we often get pushed in that direction by various parts of our organization, from the Board to the sales department.

Yes, marketing has to support and drive the achievement of business objectives and sales goals. But we must ensure our messaging and content actually speaks to our audience.

 If we don't consider our audience, we'll be talking, but no one will be listening.

So, to develop a content marketing dimension to your overall marketing strategy and shape a top line, strategic plan, you need to think carefully about your audience groups and decide how to use content to influence each groups' buyer behaviour.

The work we do in this chapter will give overall direction to your content marketing and a framework within which to manage and implement it.

Home in on your audience

As marketers we know our prospects and customers come first. Without them we'd have no business. We have to understand their needs, their problems, their pain points and their aspirations in order to provide products and services that they will want to buy.

You probably already have some sort of target market or market segment analysis in place. But it's more than likely you'll now have to carry out more detailed and in-depth work in order to create useful, distinct 'personas' in order for your content marketing to be successful.

A persona is a detailed portrait or description of a specific group of prospects or customers – a distinct audience that you can reach and influence through content marketing.

Each persona is defined by:

- their unique set of characteristics and interests
- how they decide whether or not to buy or use your product or service
- the stages they go through when making their decision
- and what influences them at each stage.

In order to create truly useful personas we need to go beyond demographics to understand what makes each persona tick. And in a business-to-business market we need to go beyond job titles, to see and get to know the people and the reality of their everyday environment, challenges and priorities.

How do you get this level of detail and understanding?

1 Focus on real people actually within your target market.
2 Avoid falling into the trap of assuming you know what people want or believing that they want what you want.
3 Go and actually meet and spend time with real customers and potential customers.
4 Interview people within your customer facing teams – others who engage directly with buyers and users in a sales, customer service or delivery situation.
5 Use your opt-in subscriber lists to ask questions and carry out appropriate and well thought out surveys.
6 Use social media as a research and 'listening' tool.

How do you create or describe a persona?

What you are aiming for is to describe each persona in enough detail for you to be able to make useful content decisions about them.

It's not an exercise you just do once and then consign your notes to a filing cabinet. Rather you will use it as a planning tool, regularly checking and updating your personas through ongoing contact with your market and customer facing teams and keeping them aligned as your organization's overall business and marketing plan evolves.

How many personas you have depends on the number of market segments you have and the complexity of the decision making process within each.

- Your personas should be separate and distinct from one another – each with a set of common characteristics and behaviours.
- Each persona will have a different decision-making process, governed by different considerations.
- Ultimately, your content strategy will be different for each one – because each one will require different content in terms of what, why, how, when, and where.

If you find you get confused or have problems, questions or gaps when it comes to deciding on and planning your content, revisit your personas because it's likely you've drawn them too superficially and lack understanding in some key areas.

If you end up with a lot of personas, first check that they are indeed separate and discrete groups. If they are, you may then want to assess and select those best suited to a content marketing strategy vs another marketing strategy. Or implement a staged content marketing roll-out in order to effectively manage your resources – an approach which has the added advantage of allowing you to 'learn by doing' over the longer term.

Factors to consider when developing a B2C persona

- Shopping behaviour and preferences
- Media behaviour and preferences
- Social profile – how they relate to family, friends and work colleagues

- Who and what influences them
- How sophisticated they are when it comes to technology
- Meaningful demographic and socio-economic information
- Buying patterns and behaviours
- The different reasons they might buy from you
- Why they would use your product or service in preference to a competitor
- What might stop them buying from you
- Values and beliefs – what's important to them generally
- What motivates them
- What's important to them in relation to your product or service
- What problems they have that you can help them solve
- What aspirations they have that you can help them achieve
- What unique value you can offer them.

Questions to consider when developing a B2B persona

- In their job role, what are they responsible for?
- What are they tasked with achieving?
- What are their challenges, frustrations or problems?
- How do they go about tackling these challenges or resolving these problems?
- What's the environment like that they are working in?
- What are their preferred methods of research?
- What type of media and information do they read or engage with?
- Are they the final decision maker or do they only influence the decision-making process?
- Do they make the decision alone or with others?
- How do they interact with others in the decision-making process?
- Outside of others in the decision-making chain, what are their other sources of information or recommendation?
- If they are an influencer, who do they influence, what type of influence do they have and how strong is it?
- In relation to the type of products and services that you offer, what questions do they ask?

- What language, words and phrases do they use when talking about them?
- Are there any seasonal or other patterns to their purchase behaviour?
- What unique value can you offer this persona?
- Why would this persona want to do business with you as opposed to all the other options open to them?

How does a persona help you when it comes to content?

When defining your content strategy and at the tactical level, there are lots of content decisions to make. Well-crafted personas help with:

- what content topics are likely to be of interest
- the type of stories likely to be most appealing
- the depth of content likely to be of interest
- how best to present this content – formats and techniques
- the best ways to get the content in front of your target persona – either directly or via others
- trigger words or phrases likely to get attention
- keeping your messaging consistent, focused and on track over time
- developing content themes and storylines over time to help refresh and recycle content.

The bottom line is that defining and using personas makes you approach content from the perspective of your customer or prospect and actually gives you the best chance of providing content that they want and that will be of value to them.

TIP *Without personas it's all too easy to slip into thinking about content predominately from your own perspective and get stuck on the 'it's all about us' treadmill.*

Delve deeper into buyer behaviour

I've mentioned the need to understand each persona's buyer or user decision-making process. Using a simple yet powerful communications model like AIDCA helps to add depth and richness to your content strategy.

Awareness (or Attention)
Interest
Desire
Conviction
Action

The original AIDA model was developed by Edward Strong and included in his 1925 book *The Psychology of Selling and Advertising*.

When we are in the process of buying something, we first become aware of it, then we develop an interest in it, then we get a desire for it. It is likely that we are moving away from the purely logical to the more emotional. Then sometimes reality kicks back in at the 'conviction' stage. Is this really the best option, is it the right time, can we afford it?

Ticking the 'conviction' box triggers our intention and converts it into 'action' – i.e. we buy.

If we accept that our customers will be experiencing this sequence (or something similar) when making up their minds about buying from us, there are two key factors at work that will influence their behaviour at each stage – the two Cs of 'confidence' and 'comfort'.

You need to be giving your prospect both the confidence (head or logic centred) and the comfort (heart or emotion centred) they need at each stage in order for them to take the next step and keep on moving forward through the engagement process.

To develop your content marketing strategy, take each of your personas in turn and walk with them through the AIDCA model.

● What does each one need to know, experience and feel at each stage?

- What type of content is most likely to help you achieve this? Think about your core 'what' (information, message or story) and also how best to present it (format and technique).

If you are already using this or a similar model to help develop your overall marketing strategy, you can now add in this content dimension.

One key thing to highlight here is that content marketing is often the ideal means of moving people through the AIDCA stages – especially the latter ones.

Often marketers think their marketing process isn't working because they're not getting enough results at the 'action' end. In reality they could be doing a great job of, for example, raising 'awareness' and converting that to 'interest' only to have people stuck at the 'desire' or 'conviction' stage.

If they get stuck it's because there's something missing – information, a piece of the story, understanding, emotional or practical engagement. Whatever it is, their 'desire' or 'conviction' box has not been ticked – either consciously or subconsciously. And it's holding them up.

This is quite different to having people drop out of your process because they've actively rejected you. Often all you have to do to get them moving again is to supply the missing piece of the puzzle – and using some form of content can be one of the best ways to do this.

Decide what you what to achieve

So far in this chapter we've been focusing on your prospects and customers – your audience, the people who will be receiving and consuming your content, even actively seeking it out.

The other side of the equation is to clearly understand and articulate what you want to achieve with your content marketing.

Set content marketing goals

You need to set some content marketing goals and be sure that they are specific and realistic. Typical content marketing goals can relate to:

- building brand awareness and supporting your brand positioning
- generating sales leads
- converting leads (via a call-to-action)
- starting and/or growing an opt-in subscriber list
- nurturing leads
- converting subscribers to customers – whether as an online process or in support of your direct, in-person sales process
- delivering after sales customer service
- retaining customers and fostering customer loyalty over the long term
- up-selling and cross-selling
- supporting referral and recommendation strategies.

Look familiar? Yes, you can obviously use other marketing strategies to achieve these same goals and you are likely to already have a selection of them somewhere in your overall marketing plan.

So, ask yourself:

- What is the unique or incremental value that content marketing (vs other types of marketing) can contribute to each goal?
- What is the specific opportunity in relation to each goal that content marketing (vs other types of marketing) has the potential to deliver?
- Can we achieve more in relation to each goal by enhancing or replacing current strategies with content marketing?

Map your customer journeys

Unless you are a new start-up, you're going to be introducing content marketing into your existing marketing process. Even if to date you haven't consciously designed this process, you will have one. Every company does. Because you have sales people out there working a sales process and you have customers out there buying from you. And those customers will be finding you and finding out about you somehow.

The final piece in this chapter's strategy puzzle is their journey. The path they take to your door. The touch points – the points of contact or interaction with your brand – that they encounter along the way.

In most organizations, the customer journey has two distinct phases – before and after the sales process kicks in.

Before, the prospective customer is interacting with your wider marketing and today is more in charge of how they find, choose and buy products and services than ever before.

As marketers we've always had to decide where and when to place our marketing collateral, activities and events.

So now you need to take each persona and map their customer journey and touch points to:

- help you decide where and when to publish, distribute and promote your content
- tailor your content for the specific platforms and channels you choose to use
- ensure that you achieve a cohesive, joined up process to offset the risk of prospects falling into gaps or becoming stuck in dead ends.

Once their journey takes them into your sales process, then you need to assess how to present and produce your content to enhance this process and support your sales people.

Your seven-point strategy framework

I've taken you through this chapter in a particular way in order to develop your thinking. Just as with any marketing strategy or plan, there's no definitive way to document it.

If you're starting from scratch, document it in a way that makes most sense and is most useful to you. If you already have a robust marketing planning process and plan format in place, then ensure you are updating it appropriately to reflect your new-found content marketing thinking.

Here's a summary of what to include:

1 The case for content marketing. Why you have chosen to adopt this approach and the unique value it will bring to

your brand. How it will integrate with your other marketing strategies and activities.

2 A set of specific content marketing goals with an explanation of how you will measure progress towards and achievement of them.

3 An overview of each persona, backed up with the detailed description and an explanation of each persona's typical buyer behaviour pattern and decision making process.

4 A top-line summary of the type of content you propose to deploy to move each persona through the AIDCA engagement process.

5 An indication of the platforms and channels you will use to reach each persona and why you have selected them.

6 How you intend to measure the performance of your content, platforms and channels.

7 Your content marketing budget.

Remember, this is your strategic snapshot – a top-level summary. If you're running a traditional marketing planning process, this is what you will be addressing each year as part of your three-year (or longer) term view.

As we progress through the rest of this Part we will cover various content topics in more detail. This will probably mean that you will continue to develop your understanding and clarify your strategic thinking around content, platforms, channels and evaluation.

So, at the end of this masterclass, come back to this strategy framework, review it and add in any points that you feel would be useful and valuable to hold at this strategic planning level.

The 2015 annual 'Content Marketing: Benchmarks, Budgets and Trends' research by the Content Marketing Institute showed that the two main differentiators between the not-so-good and the great content marketers were that they were a) writing their strategy down and b) following it closely on a consistent basis (www.contentmarketinginstitute.com/research).

Summary

In this chapter we've covered the thinking and work you need to do in order to develop a sound content marketing strategy.

We looked at:

- How to fully focus on your audience so that you can make useful decisions about what content to create
  - The concept of personas and how you actually develop them
  - How to use the AIDCA model to further understand buyer behaviour
  - Setting specific content marketing goals
  - Mapping your customer journeys to help you decide where and when to deploy your content.
  - What to document – your seven-point strategy framework.

Your content marketing strategy gives you direction, keeps you on course and helps with tactical decisions as new content ideas and options pop up.

If you are introducing a content marketing strategy or extending your current level of content activity, then you will need to integrate your 'content' thinking into your existing marketing plan. This may mean you have to dig deeper into your customers' behaviour, preferences and desires than you have done to date – and get closer to them in order to do so.

In the next chapter, we look at content planning – how to manage the creation, production, publication, distribution and promotion of your content.

Fact-check (answers at the back)

1. Developing a content marketing strategy gives you
   a) An excuse to spend lots of time out of the office ❏
   b) Something to talk about in marketing meetings ❏
   c) A framework within which to manage and implement your content marketing ❏
   d) A lot of hard work ❏

2. How important is it to fully understand your prospects and customers?
   a) It doesn't matter that much because it wouldn't make any difference to what you already do ❏
   b) It's vitally important to help you create an effective content marketing strategy ❏
   c) Not that important because you've not bothered much about it so far ❏
   d) It might help you, but only if there's a risk you'll miss your sales targets this year ❏

3. What is a persona?
   a) A list of your customers' job titles ❏
   b) A detailed portrait or description of a well-defined, specific group of prospects or customers ❏
   c) Something to do with opera ❏
   d) The demographic breakdown of your market segments ❏

4. How many personas should you have?
   a) One is enough ❏
   b) The more the better – it makes you look busy ❏
   c) It depends on how many distinct audience groups and decision-making processes you identify ❏
   d) It depends on how many customers you have ❏

5. How do personas help you with content marketing?
   a) They help you decide what content topics, formats and techniques will be most appealing ❏
   b) They don't help at all, you can just guess what content to produce ❏
   c) They only help if you get stuck for something to say ❏
   d) They only help if you have to manage some sort of PR crisis ❏

6. What is AIDCA?
   a) An out-of-date advertising model that's of no use today ❏
   b) A communications model that helps you understand your audience's buying psychology ❏
   c) Something that looks impressive in presentations ❏
   d) A form of social media marketing ❏

7. Why is AIDCA useful in developing your content marketing strategy?

a) It helps you focus on what people need to know, experience and feel at each stage of the buying process ❏

b) It's not much use at all because all you have to do is focus on creating awareness ❏

c) It makes you sound knowledgeable when talking with your boss ❏

d) It's a good way to put pressure on your web developers and ad agency ❏

8. What marketing goals can content marketing help you achieve?

a) It can only impact awareness of your brand and your products and services ❏

b) It doesn't really help you achieve any of your goals ❏

c) It's only good for helping you cross-sell once someone has already bought from you ❏

d) All of them, but you have to be clear about the unique value that content marketing can contribute in each case ❏

9. Why is mapping your customer journeys important?

a) It allows you to spend lots of time with the sales team ❏

b) It's not, it's a step you can easily skip ❏

c) It helps you decide where and when to publish, distribute and promote your content ❏

d) It allows you to use your new process mapping software ❏

10. How should you document your content marketing strategy?

a) Write it up as quickly as possible so you can file it away and get on with other stuff ❏

b) Create a strategic snapshot covering all the key areas in enough detail to be useful and valuable ❏

c) Create the biggest document possible to impress the management team ❏

d) Don't bother documenting it, it's easy to remember ❏

CHAPTER 18

Get started with content planning

By now you have a good grasp of how to think about and design your content marketing at the strategic level. In Chapter 16 we thought about content itself and the various formats and techniques to use when presenting it.

In this chapter, we start to work with the detail – coming up with a number of specific pieces of content for each of your personas and then planning when, where and how to deploy them.

We look at three specific planning tools to ensure:

- each content item you create and publish is aligned with your strategy – your master planning matrix
- you are able to publish to professional standards on a consistent and regular basis – your workflow
- you successfully manage and track your content through all the stages of the publishing process – your editorial calendar.

Your master planning matrix

Your master planning matrix acts as your master control and helps ensure that each item of content you plan to produce has a clear and specific purpose, linked to a specific persona and a specific marketing goal. In other words, it aligns with your content marketing strategy. For each persona map out each item of content to publish, noting:

1 The 'what' – the core topic, message or story this item will deliver (aligned with what each persona needs to know, experience and feel)
2 What content format you are going to use – what version of text, image, audio, video or combination
3 What content technique you are going to use – how best to get your 'what' across
4 Where you will publish it – your primary platform or channel and any other ones
5 What the purpose of this piece is in terms of call-to-action – what you want your persona to do as a result of engaging with it
6 When you will publish it
7 What specific keyword phrases you are going to optimize this piece for (if any)
8 How and where you will distribute it and promote it
9 How you will evaluate it
10 What content marketing goal this piece is designed to impact.

What you are aiming to do is sketch out your content plan in overview with enough detail to make it meaningful. As well as ending up with a list of core content items, you will be able to start to identify things like your most common formats and channels, and how complex your evaluation plan might be. We'll be adding another layer of detail later. For example, here you would plot roughly when you might publish it, say which quarter, month, or season. Later you will assign a specific date.

In terms of time frame, start with the next 12 months and, on a rolling basis, tackle the next 3 or 6 months in more detail than the rest of the year.

A simple example

Let's take a look at a very simple example for a company making eco-cleaning products.

Persona summarized as 'green' consumers motivated to reduce their use of 'toxic', chemical laden cleaning products in the home while maintaining a high standard of hygiene and cleanliness.

Core 'what' – show that our products contain a very small number of non-toxic ingredients and explain the science behind how those ingredients work together as well as the major mainstream brands.

Format – text explanation, image of an 'our' and 'their' pack comparing ingredient listing, audio explanation of science part

Technique – audio interview with one of our product developers

Primary platform/channel – consumer blog on company website

Purpose/CTA – encourage trial/request a product sample

When publish – Spring/April

Optimization/keyword phrase – 'effective eco-cleaning'

Distribution/promotion – Facebook, Twitter, e-newsletter

Other platforms/channels – eco-bloggers, PR

Evaluation – website: referral sources, time spent on page, audio listens, other website pages visited, number of sample requests

Goal impacted – lead conversion, subscriber list growth

A tactical planning process

OK, you may have spotted that this is starting to look a lot like a planning process. The good news is you'll be able to integrate this content element into an existing process fairly easily. However, some companies prefer to keep their content planning separate and even call it something like 'editorial planning', especially if they have got more into the publishing mindset. Whatever you do, you're going to find it more challenging if you haven't already got a robust marketing planning process in place covering your other marketing tactics.

If that sounds like you and you've decided you're going to give this content marketing thing a go, you're going to have to get smarter and at least get a planning process in place for your content. Otherwise you're likely to end up with a hit-and-miss publishing schedule and patchy results.

Be realistic

I've given just one example above and you can see that it won't take many content items before you're planning and managing a fairly complex matrix. How complex depends on the size and complexity of your market, products and services.

The key is to avoid trying to do too much too soon. It's better to build your content marketing muscle slowly and focus on doing a small number of things well – rather than being over ambitious. Otherwise you risk:

- making fundamental mistakes in execution
- producing poor quality content – and there's enough of that out there already
- failing to hit your publishing schedule
- failing to engage your audience
- losing the support of people within your organization.

So taking a pragmatic approach, you could, for example, get started by taking one persona and crafting a very specific 12-month awareness or education programme using one primary platform or channel.

In this way you can also essentially pilot content marketing and use the results to assess how well the approach might work for your company and then plan future strategy and develop your people and skills – based on a more evidence-based business case.

Even if you are keeping it simple, you still need to be realistic about exactly what it takes – time and resources – to create and produce good quality content (as you will see as we work through the rest of this chapter).

Once you've mapped out your master planning matrix, it's time to think about just how your content is going to get produced and published. What are the key steps and tasks involved and what people with what skills do you need to make them happen? This process is known as your workflow.

Designing your workflow

A typical content plan contains multiple types of content, activities, platforms and channels. A workflow is the ordered sequence of steps or tasks required to create, produce, publish, distribute and evaluate your content.

Having a clear, documented workflow enables you to produce content to time, regularly and to a consistently high standard.

Even when they have set up a specific content platform or channel, many companies fail to publish to schedule. You'd wonder what was going on if your favourite newspaper or magazine didn't appear one day or if it was littered with blank spaces.

Consciously planning your content as we are in this chapter and thinking through your workflow will help you understand exactly what has to happen to get your content out there and who you need in your team to make it happen.

How to identify your workflow

A documented workflow includes:

- the step or task itself
- the role responsible for making it happen
- when it needs to be done – a deadline or a timescale or a lead time.

You may be able to design one workflow that is flexible enough to cover all your content, or it may make sense to have separate workflows if you are managing several activities made up of significantly different steps or tasks. For example, text-based vs broadcast production, online vs printed media.

Map out the steps involved from start to finish. A good way to do this is to use sticky notes and a wall, whiteboard, large piece of paper or table top. Make each step or task as specific as possible – one single step or task on each sticky note. Then arrange them in a logical order. Typical steps include:

1 Identifying your source or input materials
2 Identifying a subject matter expert
3 Assigning roles
4 The different elements of content creation – researching, writing, scripting, designing, or recording
5 Content optimization
6 Reviewing for alignment with guidelines
7 Editing
8 Producing – getting the content looking or sounding good and fit for publication
9 Proofing
10 Legal authorization
11 Signing off
12 Publishing – making the content live
13 Specific channel management
14 Specific channel or platform promotion
15 Evaluation and measurement

Your workflow will include a number of different roles, each responsible for a different set of tasks or part of the process. And these roles may be carried out by different people depending on the type of content and channels you are working with. Someone also has to be responsible for managing the process as a whole.

One of the mistakes that many new content marketers make is to underestimate the steps involved and resources required to actually produce quality content to professional standards. They focus almost exclusively on creating it and then skip happily on to publishing and promotion.

Assess timescales

Once you've mapped out your workflow it's easier to assess how much time is required to complete the whole process properly to schedule. If you work backwards from your publication date, you get a sense of when the preceding steps in your workflow have to happen.

In the beginning, this might involve a fair bit of guesswork but the more you run the process, the more you will be able to fine-tune it – refining timings and also spotting any gaps or missed tasks.

Make it repeatable

The whole point of mapping and documenting this workflow is so that you can repeat it consistently each time to the same standard. Many brand content initiatives fail simply because individuals and teams start from scratch each time. This takes up more time and energy, and usually ends up using more resources.

What you still need to do is think like a professional publisher to make sure you are aware of all the necessary steps and tasks. Consider setting up a visit to your regional newspaper or other media company for half a day and get to know their end-to-end publishing process first hand – and also exactly what the various roles actually entail.

Building your content team

Once you've got this far, the next task is to decide exactly who will be performing the various roles within your workflow.

Chances are you have identified some roles and skills not currently found in your marketing team. If you are managing this team or a particular area of work, you'll have to decide how to manage your resources in order to fill the gaps.

- Who in your team or elsewhere in the company has the skills you now need?
- How might you re-engineer the team to take account of new or enhanced roles?
- Does it make sense to combine roles and re-train or upskill certain people?
- Does it make sense to outsource specific roles or skills to a freelancer?
- Is the role already covered by an existing agency relationship – and, if not, could it be?

If you are an individual within the marketing team or someone who works closely with them, the key question is how you can best use or improve your skills and realize your potential within this new content marketing landscape.

Creating your editorial calendar

The editorial calendar adds a final, practical and detailed layer to your planning. Think of your workflow as your template for how to get your content published on time, time after time. Your editorial calendar then addresses a specific timescale, and adds the detail of who will do what, on specific dates – and tracks progress.

If you're working with a small number of activities or channels, you may only need one editorial calendar. If you've got more going on, then it may be more effective to have a number of editorial calendars for specific activities or channels.

The concept is similar to the tracker you might use to plan and manage other marketing activities such as events, exhibitions, speaker programmes, email marketing, and PR.

What you want to aim for is something that is genuinely useful and avoid creating a complicated monster. If you are already using some sort of scheduling tool, by all means see if you can adapt it for this purpose. Otherwise, I advise starting off with a spreadsheet and the most simple design possible so you get used to using it and learn what works for you – you can always enhance it as you go.

If we take a simple example of an editorial calendar for your blog, your calendar might contain:

- the scheduled publication date
- the author/writer
- the subject matter expert or source (if different from the author/writer)
- the editor and/or the person responsible for sign off
- the post topic
- the title of the published post
- the persona/audience for the post
- the current status (the stage it's reached within your workflow)
- any key dates – for example, the date the draft must be ready for editing or approval.

You may also want to add some of the other items from your planning matrix above. For example, if you want your editorial calendar to act as a useful aide-memoire for your writers, you may want to add:

- the specific call-to-action for the post
- any specific keyword phrases you want to include in the post.

 TIP *Bear in mind what you want to achieve with your editorial calendar and who will be using it as an everyday tool.*

You can use a similar approach to manage and track the distribution and promotion of your content across your various channels and platforms.

Clear thinking required

Take care to remain clear about the purpose of each of these planning tools as you adapt them for your own circumstances.

1 Your master planning matrix helps you create a content plan in overview and ensures that each item of content you create is aligned to a specific audience and has a clear purpose.
2 Your workflow, like a checklist, maps the steps, tasks and roles required to get each type of content published successfully, enabling you to keep to a regular schedule and consistent standards.
3 Your editorial calendar acts as a tracker and gives the practical detail necessary to plan and manage a specific content activity or channel – listing each item of content (e.g. every blog post for the next six months), the person assigned to each role, specific delivery dates and deadlines.

The danger of jumping straight to creating an editorial calendar and ignoring the first two steps is that:

- Without the thought that goes into your master planning matrix, you risk your first focus being an 'internal' one and, continuing the blog example, your posts soon become all about you.

- Without consciously thinking about and designing your workflow, you may miss out important steps and tasks and fail to fully grasp the complete end-to-end process and how long it takes.

Irrespective of how many people are involved, content is a team effort. So, share your plans, workflows and calendars with everyone involved. This has several benefits:

- It helps people understand their role and how they fit in with everyone else – and the consequences of missed deadlines.
- It helps people step in or step up in times of unplanned absences or when circumstances or priorities change.
- It gives visibility to your stakeholders and budget holders, so they know what you are setting out to achieve and how well you are progressing.

If you are recruited into a content team ask to see these plans, workflows and calendars if they are not immediately. Make sure you are not being asked to work in the dark or as part of a disorganized team. ... Unless of course you want to make a bid for getting things set up and properly organized yourself!

Summary

In this chapter we looked at how to get organized and plan at the detailed task level to ensure we create, produce, publish, distribute, promote and evaluate our content successfully.

● Our master planning matrix integrates with our overall marketing planning process and helps us remain focused on our audience and content marketing goals as we plan what pieces of content to publish.

● Designing our workflow ensures we understand all the steps required to get our content out on time and to a professional standard.

● Creating our editorial calendar allows us to assign specific people and deadlines to specific tasks and manage the whole content process.

The more items of content you publish, the more complex your planning will be. But it is essential if you are going to publish consistently and in line with your content marketing strategy.

This is the point where you are designing and setting up the process that will allow you to execute your strategy successfully. Once up and running, like a well-oiled machine, it will allow you to run, manage, evaluate and refine your content marketing in order to continuously develop it and keep it going over the long term.

In the next chapter, we look at content creation in more detail and how to make your content as compelling as possible.

Fact-check (answers at the back)

1. What does a master planning matrix help with?
   a) Deciding what date to publish a specific blog post ❏
   b) Ensuring each piece of content has a clear purpose and links to a specific persona and goal ❏
   c) Finding a last-minute filler for your customer magazine ❏
   d) Assessing if you should still be using email marketing in five years' time ❏

2. What would help you when setting up and using a master planning matrix?
   a) Delegating it to your social media team ❏
   b) Having to write an annual report for your board ❏
   c) Already having a robust planning process in place for your other marketing activities ❏
   d) Only thinking about what you have to do next week ❏

3. What is a workflow?
   a) A process made up of tasks, steps, roles and lead times required to publish successfully ❏
   b) A type of electronic time sheet ❏
   c) Something they use in the IT department ❏
   d) A wall planner to record people's annual holidays ❏

4. What typical steps might you find in a publishing workflow?
   a) Taking coffee breaks and lunch breaks ❏
   b) Meetings when you have to explain to your boss why you missed a deadline ❏
   c) Ordering new cartridges for the office printer ❏
   d) Writing, editing and proof reading ❏

5. What does a workflow help you to do?
   a) Take more time off for holidays ❏
   b) Publish consistently to time and to a professional standard ❏
   c) Work out why no one is reading your newsletter ❏
   d) Improve your writing skills ❏

6. How might you effectively resource any new skills required?
   a) Outsource specific roles to a freelancer ❏
   b) Hope for the best and just muddle through ❏
   c) Let an existing team member get on with it without retraining ❏
   d) Not bother – if you don't have the skills, it just won't get done ❏

7. What is an editorial calendar?
a) Something to help you feel like you work in the media ❑
b) Something only used by PR people ❑
c) A detailed publishing schedule for a specific channel like your blog ❑
d) A giveaway from your office supplies company ❑

8. What is always included in an editorial calendar?
a) The dates when you are due to take your agency team to lunch ❑
b) A keyword phrase ❑
c) How much you're paying any freelancers ❑
d) The publication date and the name of the content creator ❑

9. Why is it a good idea to share your plans, workflows and calendars?
a) It's not, you don't want people to know what you're up to ❑
b) It helps everyone involved see how they fit in to the process and the consequences of missing a deadline ❑
c) It keeps you busy ❑
d) It means you don't then actually have to talk to anyone ❑

10. If you're brought into a content team, should you:
a) Expect to have to do everything at the last minute? ❑
b) Just respond to whatever you're asked to do, however ad hoc it seems? ❑
c) Work out how soon you can go to lunch? ❑
d) Ask to see the workflow and editorial calendar? ❑

CHAPTER 19

Create compelling content

As we saw yesterday, taking a piece of content from an idea to publication is a team effort.

It's beyond the scope of this chapter to teach you specific writing or graphic design skills – there are other books for that. What I want to share are some of the key principles that underpin the creation of compelling content and how you can put those into practice.

By compelling I mean content that attracts the attention and holds the interest of your audience – content that keeps your audience coming back for more.

What can you do to ensure the content you are creating and producing has appeal, presents your brand in the best light and has the best chance of being shared?

Leverage the power of the story

Much is written about the art of storytelling and how effective it is as a technique or framework for creating compelling content.

The human psyche loves a story. Who can forget the sense of anticipation when, as a child, we heard the words 'Once upon a time in a land far, far away ...'?

TIP *Stories have the power to captivate and engage us. Perhaps it's because our subconscious is still on the lookout for the handsome prince or the pot of gold?*

All good stories have a structure – a framework within which you organize your characters, events and detail and tell your story. Whether it's your brand story or a very specific story that addresses one of your persona's problems or aspirations, your story must be believable and have the power to draw in your audience.

A well-known structure is that of the Hero's Journey where the story takes the reader through the stages of:

- Orientation – *This is a story about a King who has a beautiful daughter ...*
- Crisis – *One day the kingdom is threatened by a savage dragon who captures the princess*
- The call – *Our hero, a Prince from another land, arrives to save the day*
- Problems – *Our hero struggles to defeat the dragon, beset by a hoard of the dragon's supporters*
- Resolution – *Our hero defeats the dragon and saves the princess*
- Moral or Conclusion – *Good triumphs over evil and they all live happily ever after*

An online search will give you various versions of the Hero's Journey and you can also use the persuasive AIDCA sequence we met in Chapter 17. The key thing is that you understand the structure you are using and how it can impact the power of whatever story you are telling. You can adapt the Hero's Journey for your particular company or content type and express it in language more readily understood by your contributors or writers – for example, to create a case study or article template, or to storyboard a video.

Go where the stories are

In any company, the real stories are rarely found in your office. They are out there on the front line – where your customers are, where those you are helping carry on their everyday lives, where your people interact with them. Good PR people are used to getting out and about, but marketing people less so.

You need to get a clear picture of who your primary content sources are and where they are. Within your own organization, those people are often your content matter experts. The product developers and designers, the engineers, the service deliverers, the front line workers.

Then you need to establish a means of tapping into them and even involving them in the creation process. Blanket initiatives, such as insisting everyone writes a blog post once a month, often fail because of lack of buy-in. Understandably so. Most people have enough to do already and they may be unused to writing or presenting for the type of audience you are addressing. So you will need a well thought-out and planned approach to reach out to and engage your internal content sources.

- Consider the individuals involved. Is there anyone who might actually enjoy sharing their knowledge or aspects of their work in a little more depth or with new audiences?
- Are there groups who perhaps already do this as part of their current role? For example, give tours or talks to visitors or business or school groups. Perhaps they go to industry events and produce some sort of content for internal dissemination? Look for where and how they are already sharing – even though it is in a different context.
- Then consider how you can tap into this – through interviewing them or recording them in action.

- You may find people who are already creating content for their own use. Those who are passionate about their subject. They may be writing a personal blog or journal, or taking photographs of or filming their work. You may find they have valuable content to share and are only too willing to be recruited into your content team.

Sales and customer service people know the most common questions that prospects and customers ask and the advice they seek. They'll usually be happy to talk with you, let you work alongside them for a day and take you out on customer visits. The key thing once again is to make it easy for them to help you get to the heart of those stories.

 Whether you are looking for an idea, to develop a storyline, for facts, opinions, or real life experiences, one moment of insight on or from the front line is worth hours of guess-work at your desk.

Adopt the mindset and skills of a journalist

Journalists are well known for asking lots of questions and are unafraid of asking tricky or difficult ones. They dig away beneath the surface of a story and come up with new angles – the real 'hook' that's going to appeal to their audience. They have a nose for a story and they are endlessly curious.

When planning your story, when interviewing and when reviewing your own or someone else's work, imagine you are coming to the subject for the first time. Be curious about it. Your reader may see the subject in very different light to you. Ask yourself:

- What's the burning question our audience is asking about this subject right now?
- How does it impact their lives?
- How can we best answer that question for them?
- How does our message or opinion relate to them?

- What's the key takeaway for them?
- What's the real story here?

Once they've got the story, a journalist then knows how to write or present it in order to hold the attention of their audience. They work out the main point of the piece and they get to it quickly, then the rest of the story unfolds.

Create and maintain a consistent voice

We've discussed how content marketing is all about building relationships and trust over the long term. Just as we want to hold our audience's attention during the sharing of one story, so we want to hold it for the duration of our time together. That means maintaining the same voice – the same distinctive tone and style – across all our content marketing efforts. We need the same brand personality to turn up time after time. This means you need to be clear about what that personality is in the first place and then ensure your content always reflects it.

To do this you need to have a process and materials in place in order to brief your content creators and implementers effectively – not just to keep a consistent voice but also to ensure they conform to standards and deliver to your expectations.

If you already have brand guidelines, that's good but make sure they are fit for purpose when it comes to, what could now be quite a different set of content items – and crucially more people with more diverse roles creating it. If you haven't issued a specific brief, you can't really complain if your guest contributor provides a 1500 word blog post with language that's too technical for your audience when you were expecting 500 words of chatty repartee.

- Ensure everyone knows what you mean by basic terms such as article, case study, blog post or video script.
- State any specific criteria. Equally make it clear what can be included or done at the author's discretion.
- Provide guidance on word count or length.
- Make it clear what persona or audience the piece is aimed at.

- Explain the desired tone and style – whatever the media format, whether text or image based.
- Give deadlines.
- Say if and how their work may be edited.

Always aim for a professional standard

A bit like ensuring a consistent voice, this means first defining your production standards and then ensuring that you adhere to them. You also need to understand what it takes to achieve those standards. However funny, quirky or eye catching a piece of content, you'll fail to hold your audience's attention if the quality of the piece falls below a certain standard – because it won't be fit for purpose. Not only will it not do its job of communicating effectively, your audience is likely to make a value judgement, consciously or unconsciously, about your brand if your content is slipshod and comes across as unprofessional – whether that's a rambling story, a poorly composed image, or text with typos.

Be clear about production values

There are some types of content that you are more likely to outsource than others. Video production, for example. If you're outsourcing anything to an agency or a specialist, then you are benefiting from their expertise. However, learn enough about the subject in order to make informed decisions and be able to manage the process properly. Taking video as an example, know what standard or production value you need for your publication or distribution platform. Understand how your video may need to be adapted for different devices. You want your audience to have the same quality of user experience, wherever and however they are consuming your content.

Ensure your content is well written

This means ensuring that each piece has a clear purpose, with a clear audience, is well structured, uses language appropriate for your audience in simple, uncomplicated sentence structures. Well written content is easy to read and understand. Very few marketing communications professionals actually have much, if any, writing training or coaching. As well as improving technique, good training can also help you write better faster, and show you how to improve key aspects like planning and structuring your pieces and ensuring clarity and understanding from the reader's perspective.

Ensure your visual content is well designed

There are lots of free and low-cost tools around that allow you to manipulate images and create graphics easily and quickly. But DIY tools can equal DIY results if used by someone with few design or layout skills. Well-composed and well-designed images can make a huge difference to content performance – helping to attract attention and encourage sharing. Just make sure yours are of an appropriate standard. You can always get templates designed by a professional graphic designer for use by a less skilled person to ensure consistency and quality, especially for high volume usage like social media or blog posts.

Pay attention to the gap between origination and publishing

Whatever your content format, whether written material, audio or visual, the job's a long way from done when the first draft appears. Professional publishers put content through a rigorous 'polishing' process so that the end result is as good as it can be whilst still hitting the deadline. This means editing and proofing, checking facts, grammar, keyword phrases, alignment with style guidelines, and ensuring legal compliance.

Rehearse, rehearse, rehearse

There are very few people who can actually perform well 'off the cuff' and it's a mistake to believe that rapid content creation means just turning on a microphone or pointing a camera and playing it by ear. You wouldn't walk on stage in front of a thousand people without preparing your material and rehearsing, so your audio and video performances should be no different if you want to achieve a professional outcome. Whether you are filming a short 'talking head' or 'in conversation' video or recording a podcast, here are some tips for preparing well whilst keeping some flexibility and achieving a natural outcome.

- Create a logical framework for your piece in the same way you'd structure a written article or write bullet points to manage a talk or presentation. This might be a brief outline of the story you are going to tell or a short list of questions you are going to ask and have answered.
- For a 'talking head', work with your spokesperson to ensure they understand the audience for and the purpose of the piece, and create a loose script to help them stay on message and keep on track with the story.
- For an 'in conversation', let the interviewer lead and be the one who manages the direction and flow of the conversation, adapting questions to get the value you want out of it.
- For video, make sure your performers rehearse (with or without you) to get used to the material before performing the piece on camera for the first time. Unless they are used to being filmed, allow time for them to do some practice runs to get used to the camera environment, especially if you are using a studio.
- Take the advice of the camera operator or person acting as director when it comes to where people should sit or stand and how they should interact with the camera – they know how to make even the nervous come across to best advantage.
- For audio, consider supporting people with voice coaching. Just a short time practising with a voice coach can help correct the wide range of little issues we all experience when talking into a microphone.

Tailor your content to suit your publishing platform

Think for a moment as a consumer of content rather than as a creator. What are the media, platforms and networks you use and visit on a regular basis? They're probably quite diverse and you're used to reading, hearing and seeing things in certain ways depending on where you are.

In the early days of the web, many companies created their first website by simply taking their existing corporate brochure and turning it into static website pages. We wouldn't dream of doing that today and yet we still sometimes fall into the trap of creating something once and then publishing it in several different places without adapting it and without much thought about what it will look like there.

Avoid simply replicating a piece of content or auto-posting it across different platforms, rather craft it specifically for each place. It might need no more than a little tweaking, but the effort will be worth it. It will look like it belongs and will have the best chance of being noticed, picked up and shared.

Furthermore, your audience may be in a very different state of mind in different places – Facebook vs Twitter vs LinkedIn, for example. This may mean you have to present your story slightly differently in different places. For instance a short, well-chosen clip from your video on Facebook or LinkedIn vs the full video on your website or YouTube channel, or a different tone of voice on Twitter vs LinkedIn.

Create content that people will want to share

Sharing is something that we all, generally speaking, like to do. So as well as creating content that your target audience finds useful, valuable and entertaining themselves, think about what they might also want to share.

A study by The New York Times Customer Insight Group revealed five motivations for sharing:

1 To bring valuable and entertaining content to others: 49 per cent say sharing allows them to inform others of products they care about and potentially change opinions or encourage action and 94 per cent carefully consider how the information they share will be useful to the recipient.
2 To define ourselves to others: 68 per cent share to give people a better sense of who they are and what they care about.
3 To grow and nourish our relationships: 78 per cent share information online because it lets them stay connected to people they may not otherwise stay in touch with, while 73 per cent share information because it helps them connect with others who share their interests.
4 Self-fulfillment: 69 per cent share information because it allows them to feel more involved in the world.
5 To get the word out about causes or brands: 84 per cent share because it is a way to support causes or issues they care about.

Source: The New York Times Customer Insight Group, The Psychology of Sharing: Why Do People Share Online?

So, when you're coming up with content ideas, crafting your stories, and looking for interesting angles, think about this list and how you can appeal to one of those motivations.

Summary

None of us want to produce bland, dull, ordinary content so in this chapter we looked at some of the key principles that underpin the creation and production of compelling content. That's content that attracts the attention and holds the interest of your audience. Content that they find irresistible.

In this chapter we have looked at the following:

- How to leverage the power of storytelling
- How to uncover and tap into the real stories hidden within your organization
- How thinking like a journalist will help you craft your story
- How to maintain a consistent voice to hold your audience's attention
- How to achieve professional content standards
- How to tailor your content to engage people across different platforms
- How to create content that people want to share

We're no longer at the stage where content is scarce and it's exciting just to be able to sign up for a free newsletter or download a PDF. Your content is competing for your audience's attention. You need to achieve a healthy balance of substance and presentation in order to have the impact you desire. And each content item must be of a defined, consistent, and appropriate standard – well-written and well-produced.

Once you've created your content it's time to get it out there. In the next chapter we consider the key aspects of distributing and promoting your content.

Fact-check (answers at the back)

1. What is the Hero's Journey?
   a) A TV show on Netflix ❑
   b) A framework for telling a compelling story ❑
   c) A children's storybook ❑
   d) The title of the next Bond film ❑

2. What's a good way of getting story detail from one of your subject matter experts?
   a) Keep emailing them until they give in ❑
   b) Tell them they have to write it up themselves or you'll tell their boss ❑
   c) Arrange a convenient time to go and interview them ❑
   d) Waylay them at the coffee machine ❑

3. What are all good journalists good at?
   a) Being annoying ❑
   b) Spending a lot of time travelling the world ❑
   c) Giving PR people a hard time ❑
   d) Being curious and asking lots of questions to uncover the real story ❑

4. Why is it a good idea to fully brief your content creators?
   a) To ensure they know exactly what you want them to deliver ❑
   b) It's not, it takes too long and you can't spare the time ❑
   c) It's a good excuse for another meeting ❑
   d) So they can adopt whatever tone and style suits them ❑

5. Does achieving a professional standard every time matter?
   a) No, on the web no one cares about quality ❑
   b) Yes, because sloppy content reflects badly on your brand ❑
   c) No, it only matters if it's so bad it's unusable ❑
   d) No, because no one will remember what they've seen previously ❑

6. What is a feature of 'well written' content?
   a) It's designed to make you laugh ❑
   b) It uses language a 12-year old would understand ❑
   c) It is well structured to make it easy to read and understand ❑
   d) It's very short ❑

7. Is it OK to create something and then publish without further checks?
   a) Yes, hitting the deadline is the most important thing, irrespective of quality ❑
   b) Only if there's no one available to check it ❑
   c) Yes, no one will notice if there's a few mistakes or it could be improved ❑
   d) No, editing and proofing are important steps in the publishing process ❑

8. How important is it to rehearse before filming a video?
a) It's vitally important in order to achieve a natural, professional outcome ❏
b) It's not important at all, it's better if you don't prepare ❏
c) It's only important if you're talking about a sensitive topic ❏
d) It's unimportant because it's the camera operator's job to make you look good ❏

9. What's the challenge when publishing on different platforms?
a) Sourcing enough quirky images ❏
b) There isn't one, you just replicate the same piece of content everywhere ❏
c) Adapting your content to look good and be effective on each platform ❏
d) Finding enough entertaining content to post on social media ❏

10. A key motivation for people to share content online is
a) They need to do something while waiting for the train or plane ❏
b) They want to appear busy ❏
c) They want to get the word out about causes or brands ❏
d) They want to impress the people they work with ❏

CHAPTER 20

Get ready to share

Having addressed strategy and planning in earlier chapters, we now look more closely at the distribution and promotion of your content.

It's a myth that if you simply focus on publishing good quality content, then your audience will beat a path to your door.

You've put a lot of time, effort and resources into creating and producing your content, so don't neglect it now and allow it to languish unnoticed on your website. You need more than just a few tweets to get it out there, picked up, consumed and shared.

In this chapter we consider some of the techniques commonly used to distribute and promote content and the key things you need to think about in each case.

Get your content noticed

A key mistake many companies make is failing to do enough to get their content out there and in front of their audience. Even though you might well be publishing quite a lot of your content, if not all of it, online, you still have to draw people's attention to it.

Otherwise it's like producing a well-designed, well-written, beautifully printed brochure and keeping the supply under your desk waiting for someone to ask for it. Or simply putting a few copies in reception (if you have offices) for visitors to pick up should they happen to stop by for any reason.

Although you can reasonably expect people to find your online content through search or by visiting your website, you also need to get it noticed by having a specific plan for distributing it and promoting it. Depending on the type of content asset you've produced, you can also make it (or a version of it) available as part of your other marketing strategies or activities.

Equally something that you've produced for, say, an exhibition or a conference like a show reel, giveaway, speech or presentation can be turned into useful online content.

Here are some of the key aspects to consider when managing the distribution and promotion part of your content marketing process.

Owned, paid and earned media

One way to think about and plan content distribution and promotion is to use the three-point 'owned, paid and earned' model. If you're using a lot of platforms and channels, it's a useful way of grouping them up.

Owned refers to media that you wholly own and manage – your website, your blog, your social media accounts, your video channel, your newsletter and magazines, and so on. OK, you don't actually own platforms like Twitter and Facebook in the same way that you own your website, but you do have control over your accounts and, within the differing rules of each platform, control over what you publish and share there.

Paid means anything that you pay for in order to get your content noticed – advertising, sponsored or promoted content, and paid search. 'Native' advertising is any paid item that matches the design and style of the media it appears in and therefore appears more like editorial than actual advertising. It tends to blend in with the content that surrounds it and hence it can be more persuasive than an obvious advert.

Earned is essentially any means by which your content gets distributed and promoted because it's earned it, i.e. it's worth sharing. This covers quite a range from traditional PR and being picked up by bloggers and influencers to being shared by individuals on social media.

Earned is often referred to as the area where you need to work the hardest because it means creating good content that people actually want to share and that is easy to share. But frankly you shouldn't be producing any other sort of content anyway. What is true is that 'earned' distribution and promotion is the one that is best for building credibility and trust in your brand and your products and services – in much the same way as true editorial exposure has always held the edge over advertising and advertorial.

Look at the big picture

Even when companies wake up to having to put effort into distributing and promoting their content as well as creating it, it's still easy to think too narrowly about just how to do this. Remember your content marketing strategy is part of your overall marketing strategy. It may over time become your *leading* strategy, but it will still be integrated with and supported by your other marketing activities – offline and online. Therefore when planning how to get your content out there, consider all ways and means of doing so.

For example, a white paper can be turned into both an online download and a printed document for your sales people to use as a leave behind. Extracts can be used for a series of blog posts, promoted through social media channels and also used in trade exhibitions, email marketing and/or direct mail campaigns. If valuable or niche enough it could also be used as a subscriber incentive, with sign-ups converted via optimized landing pages and a degree of paid advertising. And you can seek influencer endorsement for and comment on your white paper and reach out to partners and stakeholders to ask them to share it as well as using traditional PR.

Build your own audience

Essentially your content is pretty useless if it doesn't have an audience. And there's nothing like having a close, loyal audience of your very own – an audience that has already taken some sort of action to show you that they are interested in what you have to offer. In other words your own, opt-in subscriber list – one of your most valuable assets. Unlike social media followers and connections, you know who each of these people really are, you have their details securely held in your own system, and you can communicate with them directly in various ways. No third party can take this audience away from you. Plus they are already 'engaged' to some degree and in many cases already fans.

Therefore it makes sense to focus resources on growing this list, ensuring you remain targeted on your specific personas and prioritize quality over quantity.

 Your own opt-in list is likely to be your most responsive and fertile content marketing channel through which to distribute and promote your content and get shares and feedback.

Use social media effectively

You can use many social media platforms both as a place to publish content and as a means to distribute and promote it. This means it's versatile but also that you can end up in a bit of a muddle if you're not careful. Let's look at LinkedIn as an example.

1 You can publish a post – an article published directly on LinkedIn itself.

2 You can also share an update in order to promote and link to an article on your own website.
3 In addition, other people can share both your post and your update with their connections and in the case of your post, they can also share it on other social media platforms.

So, when you're considering how to use social media, aim for clarity. Simply having a note in your editorial calendar or distribution plan that says 'LinkedIn' is not good enough – you need to be much more explicit. Especially if someone is going to pick up your workflow at the point of publication. Without clear instructions, what exactly might they do with the article in this example if their only clue is 'LinkedIn'?

Once you're clear about how you are using any one social media platform, make sure you know all the tips and tricks to posting on it – from how to write text and tailor visuals to achieve maximum impact, to when and how often to post.

 You can find lots of useful statistics on social media posting, but remember what really matters is what works for you.

It's important to use any advice as a guideline and experiment to find out what's most effective for you in practice. Ideally assign a specialist to manage and evaluate your key social media channels and stay on top of trends.

Use specific landing pages

A landing page is a specific web page that has just one purpose – to convert. The design, layout and copy work together without distraction to present a clear yes/no decision – subscribe or leave. It plays a crucial role in persuading people to take that final step to get their hands on your content offer – usually for a valuable content asset such as a white paper, book, or course, in electronic format or print, free or paid-for.

A landing page is concise, well crafted and persuasive. You can create different versions for each persona or niche audience or channel by focusing on different benefits, customizing the headline, and using very targeted language, graphics and images.

The promise and content that sent your visitor to your landing page should be matched by the offer and content on the landing page. For example, if your promotional e-shot promises a 'free ten-part e-course to help introverts become confident networkers' ensure your landing page uses the same headline or strapline, features the same image and reinforces your e-shot messaging.

Consider paid advertising

The idea of promoting your content using paid advertising can be very seductive – especially if you have a marketing background in which brand and product advertising features heavily. And it can work well if it's planned and managed well – but don't think it's the easy option.

- Use it in support of your most valuable content goals and select your best and most appropriate content. For example, a goal that is a specific and measurable step towards a sale or some other significant conversion.
- Maximize your ad spend by ensuring that all the elements and steps in your advertising and conversion process are as good as they can be – landing pages, copy, graphic design, ad monitoring and performance.
- Just because technology and online platforms make it easy for you to 'do it yourself', it doesn't mean producing an effective advert is easy. The devil is in the detail, especially online where one word or a specific colour or call-to-action can make the difference between an advert that works and one that fails. Get to know the relevant best practice and ensure you are using people with appropriate skills.

Encourage sharing

So, you've got a compelling piece of content ready to share. When it comes to distributing and promoting it, make sure you are doing all you can actually encourage and persuade people to do just that, share it.

- When you post on social media sites, customize those posts and links using the format of the specific platform to best advantage. For example, if you are promoting your latest blog post, how and what you post on Facebook should be different to how and what you post on Twitter. Avoid auto-posting across platforms. Optimal text length and image dimensions are different. Take special care with visuals and crop or size them to display to full effect on each platform.
- Make those posts compelling in themselves – not only does it give the reader a reason to click to read, they're more likely to be happy to share something enticing than something bland.
- Likewise ensure content like blog posts have appealing meta descriptions – that's the bit that many social sites pull in when displaying linked content.
- On social media, reference specific influencers, contributors, or sources mentioned in your original piece of content to encourage them to share it.
- Make it easy for your website visitors to share – ensure your web page social share buttons are easy to spot.
- Don't rely on default share messages. Customize yours to be effective. If the share is to Twitter, for example, ensure the share message includes your @handle. I'm very happy when I hit a Twitter share button and I'm presented with a well-designed Tweet and a little disgruntled if I have to tailor it myself for it to be effective. I may just not bother.
- Promote more than once. Keep promoting specific content items across your various platforms. Not everyone is going to see it the first time and you can present and introduce it differently as you reuse and recycle it, mixing it up with your newer and more time sensitive posts.

- In your monitoring, keep track of individuals who regularly share your content and reward them with a friendly comment or thank you every now and again – a little interaction goes a long way and will make you stand out from the crowd.

Use pre-scheduling wisely

Opinion is somewhat divided on whether or not it's a good idea to automate or pre-schedule the distribution of your content. As with many aspects of marketing it rather depends on how well it's done. Whatever the scale of your content operation, a degree of sensible automation can help make efficient use of your time.

- Avoid obvious repetition – schedule different versions of the same post when re-posting. Especially when you've just released something new like a blog post and you are promoting it frequently during the first week or so of publication.
- Don't schedule too far in advance – pay conscious attention to setting up your schedule at regular intervals. This helps ensure you don't post out of date content without noticing or inadvertently post something inappropriate in relation to a sensitive breaking news story.
- Don't auto-post across social media channels; as we've seen one size does not fit all. Set up separate schedules using a tool like Buffer that allows you to easily customize posts for different platforms.
- Don't automate everything. Ensure there's a degree of real time content posting going on, especially in response to real time conversations and questions on social media.
- Monitor what's going on constantly – automating part of your process doesn't mean setting it up once and then allowing it to happen on unattended auto pilot. No technology is foolproof and if human error has crept in, you want to be on hand to put it right.

Understand content optimization

Throughout this Part we've been talking about compelling content that your audience finds useful, valuable or entertaining and that ideally they want to share. If your content is being picked up, read, watched, listened to, engaged with, linked to and shared, then you are already optimizing it for your audience. Today it is 'natural' engagement factors like these that are increasingly influential with search engine algorithms.

Keyword phrases are still important but primarily because these are the phrases that represent the topics, specific information and answers that your audience is seeking – in the language that they are using when searching. People who find your content through search engines are also important because, usually, they arrive with much more intent and willingness to engage – after all they've just found what they have been looking for.

So the main thing is to continue to understand and write for your particular audience – doing your research at the start of your content planning and creation process.

 Make sure you have a stage in your workflow when you sanity check your draft content and publishing protocols for current search best practice – and keep up with emerging trends.

Promote internally

So far we've been talking about reaching outside of your organization. Remember also to distribute and promote your content internally and with stakeholders and associates so that everyone is aware of it and has the opportunity to share it with their networks in a timely fashion.

● Encourage sharing by making sure people know the rules. Revisit your social media policy or communication guidelines to check that you've got this aspect covered and consider raising awareness of what you would like them to do from time to time in order to encourage them.

- Be even more specific with your sales team and brief them regularly on upcoming content. Plan updates about content in the same way you would communicate an upcoming marketing campaign for a new product launch or event.

Summary

In this chapter we've looked at the key aspects to consider when managing the distribution and promotion of your content – an important part of your content marketing process and one that's often neglected by many companies.

We covered:

- What 'owned, paid, and earned' media means
- How content can be made available by various means throughout your organization
- Why building your own opt-in mailing list is important
- How to use social media effectively to promote your content
- Why you should use landing pages
- Key considerations when using paid advertising
- How to encourage sharing
- How to use pre-scheduling wisely
- The key things to understand about optimization
- How to encourage your colleagues to share your content.

This is another area where joined-up thinking is key. Avoid narrow or short term planning. Distribution and promotion can and should extend across the whole range of your marketing and sales activities. Some content assets have the potential for a long shelf life, working hard online and as part of offline or in person events – as long as they are reviewed and updated regularly.

Next, we move on to the final piece of our content marketing puzzle and look at the area of measurement and evaluation.

Fact-check (answers at the back)

1. What type of channel best builds credibility and trust?
   a) Owned media – it's yours so surely people believe you ❑
   b) Paid media – a lot of the time you don't even know it's an advert ❑
   c) Earned media – because it shows your content is worth sharing ❑
   d) None of them are that good ❑

2. What's one of the best ways of building an audience for your content?
   a) Post every day on Twitter ❑
   b) Build your own opt-in subscriber list ❑
   c) Ask your salespeople to hand out your newsletter ❑
   d) Get your CEO on local radio ❑

3. When it comes to content, social media is
   a) A versatile place to both post and promote your content ❑
   b) A waste of time ❑
   c) The only way to distribute your content ❑
   d) Only good for sharing photos ❑

4. Why would you use a landing page?
   a) To make a long, complicated sales pitch ❑
   b) To display a photo of your customer service team ❑
   c) To return a 'thank you' message ❑
   d) For conversion – to encourage someone to take a specific action ❑

5. When would you use paid advertising to promote your content?
   a) Whenever you need quick sales ❑
   b) To promote your best content and support high value goals ❑
   c) When it's a video of your CEO announcing your annual results ❑
   d) Just before the start of the weekend ❑

6. What can you do to encourage people to share your content?
   a) Nothing – people either will or they won't ❑
   b) Keep on tweeting 'Read our latest blog post' ❑
   c) Customize social media posts for each platform and make them enticing ❑
   d) Auto-post to as many social media platforms as possible ❑

7. Is it a good idea to pre-schedule the distribution of content?
   a) Only as long as you consciously set up your schedules and monitor them frequently ❑
   b) Yes, schedule as far ahead as possible and then leave on auto pilot ❑
   c) Yes, because then you can just repeat the same social media post over and over again ❑
   d) Yes, because then you avoid having to turn up in real time on social media ❑

8. Content optimization means
   a) Writing specifically for search engines ❏
   b) Needing to go on a course to understand the Google algorithm ❏
   c) Producing content that your audience easily finds, engages with, links to and shares ❏
   d) Having to write in a very unnatural style ❏

9. Is it worth promoting your content internally?
   a) No, no one internally is interested in what you produce ❏
   b) Yes, it gives your people the opportunity to share it with their networks in a timely fashion ❏
   c) Only when you're desperate ❏
   d) Only when your boss tells you to ❏

10. Do you have to promote content that you publish on your website?
    a) No, people will just find it when they visit your home page ❏
    b) It depends how big your website is ❏
    c) Yes, relatively few people will notice it unless you actively promote it across other relevant channels ❏
    d) No, you just need to rely on Google to index your web pages ❏

CHAPTER 21

Learn how to measure success

In this chapter we tackle measurement and evaluation. This is traditionally a challenging area for many marketers. We want to know how well our marketing is performing but it's not always easy to measure. Meanwhile, sales, finance and the management team are chasing us to find out what marketing is contributing to the bottom line.

At least with content marketing the measurement part is easier because much online activity is trackable and therefore measurable. In fact there's almost too much choice, so working out what to measure and why is key.

In this chapter we look at the main principles of successful content marketing measurement and evaluation, the methods and tools available to help us, and how to report results for our own use and to satisfy others.

Meaningful measurement

Once you've got your content marketing up and running you're going to want to know if it's working. Just how successful it is as a strategy. And also how well each of the different parts of your process are performing.

If you have brought content marketing into your marketing mix, how you approach this will depend on how you are currently monitoring, measuring, and evaluating your other marketing strategies and activities. What you essentially need to do, as with your planning, is to develop a content layer within your existing evaluation process and reporting.

Whether you are building on an existing evaluation process or starting with a clean sheet, let's first go back to basics.

- The most important thing is to think about measurement and evaluation at the planning stage. Get clear about what you want to measure and why – before you start implementing.
- Choose measurements that show you how well you are progressing towards the achievement of your goals.
- The ultimate question for many will be what is content marketing achieving in terms of sales – in the same way that, at the top level, that's most likely the question being asked about marketing generally.

So, as you develop your content marketing strategy, think about evaluation at every stage. You've looked at your persona customer journeys and your marketing and sales process. Then you made a deliberate decision to bring content marketing into that mix. When developing your master planning matrix, you mapped what content you were going to deploy, with what purpose, at what time and through which channels.

When thinking about measurement and evaluation:

- First think about what you want to happen at each of the touch points in your process – the points where audience meets content. What counts as a measure of success? Then work out if and how you can measure that. And make that measurement meaningful. This means measuring some sort of content consumption, engagement or sharing.

- Then think about where each specific touch point sits within this process. How well is your content performing in terms of moving your prospect through the process? This means measuring response to a call-to-action or a conversion.

What do we mean by meaningful?

Essentially this is making sure that the metric you are looking at is a true indicator of what you want to measure.

Let's take engagement as an example. If by this you mean how well a piece of content, say a blog post, 'engages' your audience – how interested they are in the topic and how well it pulls them in to your website, then 'page views' or numbers of page visitors is not that meaningful. The time spent on the page is a better indicator, along with specific actions taken (such as clicking on internal links to related content, or social shares) and where else people go on leaving the page (behaviour flow).

It's very easy to get bogged down in meaningless metrics, so carefully choose a small number of meaningful ones to track.

 TIP *Be guided by measuring effectiveness or impact, not just quantity of transactions or events.*

Eco-cleaning example

Take a moment to return to and re-read the simple example we looked at in Chapter 18 for the company making eco-cleaning products. Our measurement and evaluation thinking would go something like this:

Overall measures of success:

1 How interested people are in our topic (how appealing/popular is our chosen story angle).
2 How successful the post was in triggering the CTA (request a product sample).

Website:

- How many visitors and what percentage of visitors came to the page via which social media channels – Twitter and Facebook?

- How many visitors and what percentage of visitors came to the page via our e-newsletter?
- How many visitors and what percentage of visitors found the page via search?
- How many visitors and what percentage of visitors came to the page via other sources – other blogs, online media?
- Did visitors read the post – how long did visitors spend on the page?
- Did the audio add value, did visitors listen to it – how many and what percentage clicked to listen?
- How many and what percentage clicked to request a product sample?
- How many completed the product sample fulfilment process and therefore converted to a lead and got added to our opt-in subscriber list?
- Were there any differences by referral channel (Twitter/Facebook/e-newsletter)?
- Have we generated any new awareness/interest – what percentage were first time vs returning visitors?
- What was the behaviour flow of visitors to this page (where did they go next on the site or did they exit)?
- Were there any differences by referral channel (Twitter/Facebook/e-newsletter) or first time vs returning visitors?

Social
- Number of shares and likes/favourites.
- Detail of comments when sharing or comments left on Facebook.
- Pick up and coverage by eco-bloggers.

Email
- E-newsletter opens, clicks and forwards.

PR
- Pick up and placement in consumer, specialist and trade media.

Therefore
- How many new subscribers did we add to our opt-in list?

- How many leads did we generate?
- How many of these leads eventually converted to a sale, at what total value?
- What were the most successful website referral sources?

This example looks at just one piece of content. Remember each content item has a role to play in your process and should directly link to or impact at least one content marketing goal.

Measurement methods and tools

Having now got an understanding of what to measure, let's consider what tools we have at our disposal to help us.

 If you do any sort of web search for content marketing measurement tools, you'll uncover quite a long list. Once again, choose a small number and use them wisely. Most web tools are free or have a free version or free trial period so you can experiment before signing up to paid plans. However, before going off in search of new tools, make sure you are putting the ones you already have to best use and are using them to track meaningful, customized information – rather than just glancing at default reports.

- **Website analytics:** If you've got a website, then you've got some form of web analytics – most likely Google Analytics. Take the time to find out exactly what it can do for you. Get yourself on a basic training course where you can take along your own strategy and plan and create a useful set of customized metrics. With Google Analytics you can see where people come from and what they do and where they go when on your site. You can also track specific 'goals' and 'events' to measure how often visitors take certain actions – like sign up to something, download something, click on a specific icon. In other words you can measure specific conversions.
- **Email marketing analytics:** If you're using an email marketing system, use the analytics to measure the performance of

your newsletters and e-shots as a content channel as well as interest in the content they contain. If you are linking to website content, you can track who clicks to read or view.

- **Social analytics:** As well as looking at the analytics within your specific accounts, consider using one or two other social tools like Buzzsumo that shows how your website content is shared across social networks, or Buffer to see what posts are getting you the most shares, likes and comments.

- **Your CRM:** If you have a CRM or some other contact management or sales system, then review what you are currently tracking and see how you might add in or link to your content. For example, if your sales people are using or linking to specific content items in their sales process, networking or social selling activities. Track what content prospects and customers have been exposed to in the same way you would specific marketing campaigns or events.

- **More sophisticated, integrated, end-to-end systems:** Once you've got more experience with content marketing, you may want to consider upgrading to more powerful technology. Once again there are a number of systems on the market, typically described as inbound marketing and sales systems or automated sales and marketing systems. They allow you to set up and manage the whole of the marketing and sales funnel, tracking not just aggregated general trends but the behaviour of individual subscribers. Check out Hubspot, Infusionsoft or Marketo (to name but three) to get a sense of what they can do. Naturally such systems require a significant investment, so it's important that you first hone and fully understand your own marketing process. Then choose what technology you need to support it.

- **Sales insights:** Putting analytics and tools to one side, let's not forget the low-tech means of tapping in to what's going on. Things like feedback from your sales and customer service people. If you've been briefing them and keeping them up to date on the content aspects of your marketing, then they'll be motivated to tell you how well it's working at the coal face. This type of anecdotal feedback can be hugely valuable as you'll get a sense of how useful certain content is in supporting and even improving the sales process, whether that's in initial conversations or helping to close the sale by acting on those 'conviction' and 'action' triggers.

- **Social listening:** Whilst your analytics tools are looking at behaviour, the detail of what people are saying on social platforms is also important and, just like insights from sales, can tell you a lot about what people think about your content, how they are using it, and how useful or entertaining they find it. So keep on top of what comments people are adding when they share on social media and in response to blog posts. This is also your chance to get involved in and encourage those conversations.
- **Direct outreach:** You can also get feedback on your content by simply asking those people consuming it. You may already be running surveys with your customer and opt-in subscriber lists for brand, product or campaign awareness or recall, so think about adapting those to include interaction and engagement with specific content. If your content is a course, book or white paper, then you can also weave a specific survey into your ongoing keep in touch activity to test interest, usefulness, what they liked or disliked most about it, and gather ideas for product or topic development.
- **Take a composite view:** There are many different ways to monitor and measure content performance using a variety of tools and techniques. There's no one solution that will do everything, so you'll be pulling various measures together from different sources.

How to report your results

Using the approach and tools above, you can build aggregated pictures for groups of content items or specific channels and give different people the evaluation view they require. For example, your management team is likely to only be interested in total sales or cost impact this month while your implementers will want a much more granular analysis. Your researchers, writers, designers, producers, channel managers, social media and email experts will want to see how well their specialist area is performing and if there are clues as to how they can improve.

For management reporting, agree relevant key performance indicators (KPIs) and present your evidence. One way to do this is to develop a scorecard or at-a-glance report, tailored for each area if necessary (like CEO, finance or sales), to show how your content marketing strategy is contributing to overall or annual business objectives and goals over time.

You may need to remind people about the long-term nature of a content marketing approach. Although we've just looked at the measurement of a single piece of content, real momentum and therefore a true sense of how successful the approach is proving to be only comes over time – when you've got a long enough track record to refer to. This is quite different to deploying a short term sales tactic or a campaign for something like a product launch.

Over the course of 12 months and beyond, you can start to see the impact of your content marketing on areas such as brand awareness and changes in customer perceptions or attitude to your brand. And be able at least to start to assess the incremental benefit and impact of using content in place of or in addition to whatever you were using before.

Testing and experimenting

One of the great benefits when you have part if not all of your content marketing taking place online is the ability to test different techniques and versions of your content to see what works best.

- Did this headline get more clicks or shares than this one?
- Did video convert more than straight text on this landing page?
- Did the placement of the call-to-action button work better on the right than on the left of the page?
- Did version A of the landing page convert more sign ups than version B?
- Did the page optimized for keyword phrase A deliver more traffic than the one optimized for keyword phrase B?

And so on. This is known as split testing or, not surprisingly, A/B testing. This experimentation is essential to improving your performance over time. While it would be silly to try and test everything, you may have one or two aspects that you want to improve – aspects that have the potential to make a significant difference.

- This could be finding the tone and style that's a perfect match for your audience or for a specific persona. Testing could include different writing styles, language and blog post lengths, different ways of presenting information (how to posts, Q&As, interviews), different media formats, right down to different styles and length of headline.
- Or it could be honing the effectiveness of landing pages as a lead conversion tool – design, layout, writing style, content length, text vs video.

With an ongoing programme of testing and evaluation, you're improving your performance over time and making gradual improvements to your content marketing process and the platforms, techniques and activities that make up that process. It also helps you to manage your budget and phase investment – based on something more substantial than pure guesswork. Which bring us to …

Return on investment

Traditionally a tricky area for most marketers, return on investment (ROI) calculations are at least made easier with content marketing when you're able to measure the results of your efforts in the way we've discussed above. The other dimension you need of course is to understand what each part of your content marketing process costs you. For anyone with budget responsibility this is an important dimension to consider.

Creating content is resource heavy. Whether you have to manage an existing budget or make the case for new funds, you are at some point going to have to make choices. You have to balance how well a particular content activity is performing in terms of meeting audience and business goals with how much it's costing you and therefore the return you're getting on that investment.

To calculate ROI you need to:

1 Track what content is delivering in the sales funnel and put a monetary value to it. This could be actual sales or the value

of a specific set of leads or other conversions. You'll need to work with your sales team to understand what value they assign to leads.

2 Work out what that content cost you.

3 Calculate ROI as (A – B) / B

So, if you conclude that a content-based initiative has generated £2000 and creating, producing and distributing the content has cost you £500, then your ROI is 3 or 300%.

The other side of the coin is how much content marketing is saving you. In deploying content are you making less use of something else? Paid advertising, sponsorship, direct mail, print, and perhaps even direct sales or customer service time?

If you've been used to calculating marketing ROI before adopting a content marketing approach, you can also compare the incremental ROI of content vs whatever you were doing before.

Understanding your costs will also help you to manage your resources more efficiently – especially when deciding to use in-house or external resources. For example, would using a freelance designer or writer be more cost effective than assigning a task to one of your own team or doing it yourself? You have to take into account not just the relative per hour per head cost, but also the cost of any additional training (in-house) or support or supervision (outsource) that may be required. Can you maintain quality or achieve better quality at lower cost by outsourcing and therefore make better use of your budget?

Summary

We've wrapped up this masterclass with a look at content marketing measurement and evaluation. Although it happens at the end of the process, planning what you measure and why must always be done at the start – when you are developing strategy, setting goals, and doing your planning.

It's important to measure things that are meaningful – focusing on effectiveness, impact and outcomes, not just numbers for the sake of numbers.

We looked at:
- What we mean by meaningful measurement, and looked at a simple example
- The measurement methods and tools available to us – online analytics as well as some traditional low-tech options
- How to report results
- Why testing and experimenting is a good idea
- How to develop a return on investment calculation

Whether you are new to marketing or a more seasoned professional picking up content marketing for the first time, don't neglect these aspects of measurement and evaluation because they will enable you to continuously improve your content marketing over time – always remember you are playing the long game.

Fact-check (answers at the back)

1. When should you plan how to measure your content?
   a) Once you've finished creating and distributing it ❏
   b) About a year after you've developed your strategy ❏
   c) Right at the start of your content marketing planning ❏
   d) Whenever you can fit it in ❏

2. What do we mean by a 'meaningful' measurement?
   a) One that gives you the biggest or highest number possible ❏
   b) A metric that is a true indicator of what you want to measure ❏
   c) One that impresses the Board ❏
   d) One that's easy to explain ❏

3. How does an individual item of content relate to your content marketing goals?
   a) They're not related at all ❏
   b) In a very loose way in the sense that your content sometimes helps generate sales leads ❏
   c) They're only connected when you try and match them up at the end of the year ❏
   d) Each item of content should directly link to or impact at least one goal ❏

4. When it comes to measurement, a good starting point is:
   a) To make sure you put the measurement tools you already have to best use ❏
   b) To go out and buy this month's most talked about social media tool ❏
   c) To take a quick look at the web stats your IT department issues once a month ❏
   d) To wait until your boss asks you a question about how your content is performing ❏

5. Can Google Analytics measure specific website conversions?
   a) Yes, you can measure how often people take certain actions on your website ❏
   b) No, it only shows numbers of visitors and which pages are read the most ❏
   c) Only if you have an e-commerce website ❏
   d) Only if someone actually buys something ❏

6. When should you investigate using an automated sales and marketing system?
a) As soon as possible as it'll mean less work for you ❏
b) When the sales director says it's time for you to get one ❏
c) Once you fully understand your marketing process and can choose the right technology to support it ❏
d) When your marketing communications manager resigns ❏

7. Are there additional ways to measure content effectiveness other than web-based systems?
a) No, measurement always takes place online ❏
b) It depends on what products or services you sell ❏
c) Yes, insights from sales people on what customers think about and do with your content can be hugely valuable ❏
d) No, because we only publish our content on our website ❏

8. How can you best report your evaluation results?
a) Write the longest report possible every month as that will impress people ❏
b) Simply distribute a standard Google Analytics report ❏
c) Do nothing – no one will read a report anyway ❏
d) Compile an at-a-glance snapshot for different groups, tailored to show the KPIs they are most interested in ❏

9. What's the benefit of split testing?
a) It gives your team something to do on Fridays ❏
b) It allows you to find out what works best and improve your content performance over time ❏
c) There is no benefit, guessing works just as well ❏
d) It keeps you busy and gives you a good excuse to avoid unnecessary meetings ❏

10. To calculate return on investment you need to know
a) How many website visitors you had this year ❏
b) The monetary value of what your content delivers in the sales funnel and the cost of creating that content ❏
c) How often people shared your content on social media last month ❏
d) Whether your boss is recommending you for a bonus this year ❏

7 × 7

1 Seven useful ways of thinking

Content marketing success is often not so much about what you do as how you go about it, especially the way you think about and approach it.

- Put yourself in your customer's shoes – see and understand the world through their lens.
- Look at a topic from different angles – different perspectives spark different ideas. Get up and move around – both physically and mentally.
- Find a way to the heart of your topic – the main point, the real story, the pot of gold.
- Connect the dots – think in a joined-up way about everything from strategy to execution.
- Adopt an analytical approach – test, observe, and interpret the results to find out what works for you.
- Seek to learn – unleash your curiosity. Keep asking yourself how you can improve and keep on top of emerging trends.
- Learn to think in stories – weave a compelling and honest tale to captivate your audience.

2 Seven in-demand skills

As marketing evolves and more businesses and organizations take more of a content marketing approach, certain skills are much in demand.

- Good writing skills – being able to write well is key not just to creating compelling content but also to brief others in your content team and communicate more widely across your organization.
- Organizational skills – being well organized is essential for keeping the content marketing process running smoothly.

- Understanding what makes content sharable – what it takes to get it picked up and shared across different networks and communities.
- Having an eye for detail – whether that's working with design or words or processes.
- Being able to manage projects and people appropriately, knowing the best techniques to use, when.
- Financial understanding – knowing how to make a business case for content management, setting and making the most of your budget as well as calculating ROI.
- Understanding the psychology of the buyer and learning what the evolving field of neuroscience can contribute to the field of marketing.

3 Seven critical job roles

Content marketing combines traditional marketing roles with those found in publishing, so there are new opportunities to be had inside many of today's evolving marketing departments.

- Researcher – investigating and researching content ideas, conducting interviews and running focus group sessions with audience groups to uncover hot topics.
- Writer – using journalistic skills to turn content ideas into well-crafted, compelling written content.
- Visual content creator – working with images, graphics, and film to create appealing visual content with impact.
- Editor – keeping an eye on consistency of tone, style and quality across all content items and ensuring the desired brand story evolves and is successfully maintained.
- Social media communicator – working with content across social media channels to listen, engage and respond, keeping the conversations going.
- Analyst – using technology and common sense to measure content performance, turn data into actionable information and communicate the results.
- Content team leader – responsible for the process as a whole, keeping the team motivated and on track and

ensuring all the necessary tools and resources are in place and working effectively.

4 Seven key budget considerations

When you consider your content marketing budget, you may first think of salaries and if you will need more people. Here are some of the other key aspects to think about.

- Visual and audio content production – the tools to produce images, graphics, podcasts and video, including studio time and specialist editing.
- Software, systems and tools – to handle monitoring, analysis and management of processes like email marketing right up to a fully formed automated sales and marketing system.
- Website development – to ensure your website is fit for purpose as a publishing and marketing platform and can be easily updated by your content team.
- Paid advertising and sponsorship – for when you need to bring in a little paid help to get your content launched and out there.
- Optimization – specialist support to keep on top of keyword phrase development and spot opportunities, especially if you are a niche player.
- People – recognize the true investment required to hire people with the right skills, whether in-house or through outsourcing.
- Training and networking – no one knows it all and the best content marketers need to hone their skills and keep up to date, whether through formal training, learning from their peers or attending events.

5 Seven common myths

Content marketing is growing but there are still some misconceptions out there – although of course *you* now know better!

- Content marketing doesn't cost you anything. You need resources and a budget just as for any other marketing strategy. In addition content marketing is resource heavy – just look at all that time, commitment and skill required.
- Create content and people will come. Getting your content noticed, picked up and shared does not happen by magic. Distributing and promoting it is as important as creating it.
- Anyone can write. Anyone can write something, but not everyone can write compelling content and all the best writers write a lot and continuously strive to improve their skills.
- It's all about rapid content creation – just turn on the mic or camera and press 'go'. You can get away with this only if you're working with a charismatic, media savvy person. Many of your content sources are not natural performers, so need handling accordingly.
- It's all about quantity. Volume of content is not as important as quality. Whilst you need to understand how much content you need to publish to gain 'traction', quality must always come first.
- It only happens online. Content can be published and consumed anywhere. Some of the most successful initiatives integrate content across online, offline and in-person channels.
- Optimization is just for search engines. Search engines are just tools that people use to find things, so always write for your audience first and foremost.

6 Seven inspiring quotes

Content marketing can be a little challenging at times, so here are a few helpful hints.

- 'Marketing is no longer about the stuff that you make but about the stories you tell.' Seth Godin
- 'Traditional marketing and advertising is telling the world you're a rock star. Content Marketing is showing the world that you are one.' Robert Rose, Chief Strategy Officer, Content Marketing Institute

- 'I don't know the rules of grammar. If you're trying to persuade people to do something, or buy something, it seems to me you should use their language.' David Ogilvy
- 'Here's everything you need to know about creating killer content in three simple words: Clear. Concise. Compelling.' Demian Farnworth, Chief Content Writer at Copyblogger Media
- 'If you sell something, you can make a customer today. If you help someone, you can create a customer for life.' Jay Baer, author of *Youtility* (Penguin, 2013)
- 'The scariest moment is always just before you start.' Stephen King, *On Writing: A Memoir of the Craft* (Simon & Schuster, 2002)
- 'Success is not final, failure is not fatal: it is the courage to continue that counts.' Winston Churchill (*OK, he's not talking about content marketing – but he could be!*)

7 Seven next steps

Now you've read the masterclass, what next?

- Check out the latest Content Marketing: Benchmarks, Budgets and Trends research covering North America, UK, and Australia from the Content Marketing Institute: www.contentmarketinginstitute.com/research.
- Think about your marketing and how you might benefit from adopting a content marketing approach or enhancing existing activities with some form of content.
- Carry out a content audit and see just what types of content you are currently producing, when and how often.
- Carry out an audience audit and see to what degree you are already communicating with specific, well defined audiences.
- Spend a day with some of your sales or other customer facing people to see if you can uncover any new appealing content themes or topics.
- Using a real piece of upcoming content, plan how you could improve it and practise your storytelling technique.
- Decide who else to share your new-found content marketing knowledge with!

PART 4

Your Mobile Marketing Masterclass

Introduction

The other day I was walking through my local shopping centre and I saw a mobile virtual reality headset for sale – the type that you put your mobile phone in and instantly get transported to another world.

I grew up in the generation where things like that were the stuff of the Jetsons or Thunderbirds (now that's aged me). I grew up with *Encyclopedia Britannica*, the *A to Z* and MS-DOS.

I know what it means to have to go to a library for research, and how to properly cite something (but don't ask me to do it now). I know what it is like to have dial-up internet.

Heck I can remember connecting to bulletin board systems via a 1200/75 modem just like in the *War Games* movie! Ask any kid on the street today and they will have no idea what you're talking about.

Now I have all the world's knowledge, whether from Wikipedia, from the online *Encyclopedia Britannica* or some other source, constantly updated every second of every day … in my pocket.

With my phone I can video chat with friends and family anywhere in the world and I can pop it into a headset and have virtual reality within seconds.

I can ask my phone to not only tell me how far away a specific location is, but also give me directions to it.

The phone I have right now blows away the laptop I used five years ago and could probably run 99.9 per cent of my daily business tasks (short of using Photoshop) on it.

Things are moving scarily fast. Like 'blink and miss it' fast. Especially when it comes to mobile. Right now more than two-thirds of all internet traffic in the USA is mobile (http://bit.ly/2NhKL1T).

On Black Friday 2021, 42.4 per cent of the $8.9 billion in US online sales came from smartphones and other mobile devices, a 2.9 per cent increase from 2020 and an increase of 23 per cent over Cyber Monday 2021, reversing a trend from the last few years where Cyber Monday has been generating more sales than Black Friday (source: https://bit.ly/3MbTjXF).

These trends are becoming a wave, and we businesspeople better learn to surf it or we'll be crushed by companies that do. The world isn't going to stop because of my age or experience and it won't stop for yours.

If you're reading this masterclass you are most likely in the same boat most business owners are in: trying to figure out what the heck is going on, and then trying to figure out how to generate revenue with it.

While I am far from a 'guru' or 'master' in this domain (as if anyone can be since these trends started happening practically yesterday), I *can* help you apply solid online marketing principles to this new 'mobile' generation.

The key is not only knowing how things are changing, but more importantly how people's minds are changing with them, because marketing is mostly a psychological game.

When you know that, you'll be in a better position than your competitors.

Blessed are the flexible for they will not be broken.

So prepare to enter a whole new world.

CHAPTER 22

What's the big deal with mobile?

It is inevitable.

Two reasons:

1 Technology: Mobile internet speeds are getting faster and data compression is constantly improving.
2 Cost: It's never been cheaper to get online. You can buy a decent, no-contract Android smartphone for under $100 (at the time of writing).

I could also go into detail about the law of accelerating returns and direct you to an excellent but dryer-than-the-Sahara technical article, but the main reason it will happen is because people *want* it to.

The fact of the matter is, there are BILLIONS of people around the world who are happy to spend countless hours scrolling through their newsfeeds and watching cute kitten videos on their smart-phone every day.

I'm not ashamed to say I love my smartphone. I was with a friend the other day listening to some music streaming in from a radio station *on my phone* and he wondered out loud who had just sung that song. I fired up my web browser *on my phone*, did a quick search for part of a lyric I managed to remember and within a few seconds I had the answer.

The future is mobile

I use my phone to connect with my project manager and staff when I am on the road. I can even work on my laptop at my desk at home while riding in a car using TeamViewer or LogMeIn apps.

If I wanted to I could probably write, edit and format this whole Part on my mobile phone using Google Docs Voice Typing function. It doesn't require any training to recognize my voice, is very accurate (minimal corrections) and is completely free! No matter where I am in the world, I can dictate a chapter into my phone, make any edits I want, and share the document in the cloud with my editor so he can see in real time what I am doing. (Err, not sure I should have mentioned that as it might give him ideas.) Do that and 'BAM!, I have a chapter in maybe an hour or two of talk time, and then I can put my feet up, call it a day and relax.

Here's a list of some other (not all) ways the world is going mobile and will continue to do so over the next few years:

Knowledge is mobile

People may not know where a business or organization is located or what the capital of Venezuela is, but they do know *where* to go to find that information. Instead of having to know everything, they can whip out their mobile phone and hit Google for the most current information.

Do you remember the last time you looked at an encyclopedia? Nope, me neither. They don't even make the physical Britannica encyclopedias anymore. They went the way of the dodo thanks to Wikipedia.

Photographs and images are mobile

Instagram, Facebook, Flickr and more all cater to a market that uploads photos on the go. Almost every smartphone now has a camera in it that can take photos almost as well as a dedicated digital camera. In fact, digital cameras themselves are becoming more of a professional product than a consumer product, as shipments of all digital cameras continue to fall dramatically from a peak of 16.2 million units in 2012 to just 2.16 million units in 2021 (source: https://bit.ly/39eM9TM).

Video is mobile

The sheer size of statistics covering online video is mind-boggling.

- 694,000 hours of videos are streamed on YouTube every minute.
- YouTube Shorts are viewed 15 billion times a day.
- Over 1.7 billion people watch YouTube videos every month.
- Live streaming as whole generated 8.99 billion across all platforms during Q2 2021 (source: https://bit.ly/39WiBL7)

(Sources: https://bit.ly/3wh1ZGN)

Not so very long ago, if you wanted to film something, you used your camcorder. Not anymore. The latest generation of smartphones can shoot in 4K (four times higher definition than Blu-ray discs) and if you need an even more professional result, you can purchase all manner of semi-pro add-ons like high-quality lenses, stabilizers and drones to get those sweet aerial shots.

So-called 'action cameras' like GoPros let you attach your tiny video camera to your bike or your helmet strap and record your activities. And with a click or a tap, you can upload the finished results to Facebook, Instagram, YouTube etc. and share your creations with the world.

If you don't want to mess about with editing your footage, you can always livestream to millions of people from your phone or GoPro and becoming your own TV channel.

If that's not your bag and you just want to stick to watching TV and movies, no problem. Most TV companies have sections on their website or dedicated apps that will let you catch up with your favourite show you missed a couple of nights ago, which you can watch on your phone. There are plenty of dedicated movie apps like Netflix, Amazon Prime Video and Sky Cinema, where you can get your movie fix (not to mention exclusive award-winning and highly-regarded TV shows they produce themselves), all available on the go through your smartphone.

Books are mobile

During 2021 (the most up-to-date figures at the time of writing) one out of every six books purchased were e-books (source: NPD.com) which is down around 8 per cent on 2020 but is still 8 per cent higher than in pre-pandemic 2019.

You may have seen stories in the news talking about the 'death of e-books' and the resurgence of print. This isn't telling the whole story. It's true that e-book sales from major publishers have been generally slowing mainly due to price increases, they still account for $1.1 billion in 2021 (sources: https://bit.ly/3l5PUxC and https://bit.ly/37HNBxG).

Just as stand-alone, digital cameras are dying, so are standalone GPS sat-nav systems like TomTom and Garmin. Thanks to most smartphones today having built-in maps and sat-nav systems and a plethora of third-party apps and services, all designed to help you get around with minimal disruption, global sales of dedicated sat-nav systems have consistently fallen over the years. As an example, for TomTom, one of the biggest sat-nav system makers, consumer sales revenue fell 563.3 million euros in 2016, to just 112.95 million euros in 2021, a drop of 79.95 per cent in revenue over just five years (source: https://bit.ly/3l7b4LC)

As nice as it is to snuggle up with a book, people find it just too much to cart around hardcover books. It is much easier to buy it online and download it on whatever e-book reading device they own.

Navigation is mobile

Just as stand-alone, digital cameras are dying, so are stand-alone GPS sat-nav systems like TomTom and Garmin. Thanks to most smartphones today having built-in maps and sat-nav systems and a plethora of third-party apps and services, all designed to help you get around with minimal disruption, sales of dedicated sat-nav fell from a peak of 48 million units in 2011 to just 3.2 million units in 2015 (the most current figures available; source: http://bit.ly/2xU8mRK).

Notebooks/cabinet files are mobile

Not only are the obvious things going mobile, but even note-taking via Evernote, Dropbox, Microsoft's OneNote and other services are making documents and notes you have made accessible with just a few taps of your finger.

Wonder if that invoice has been paid? Check your Dropbox...

Did you write something down on a piece of paper but are worried about losing it? Break out your smartphone, snap a picture of it and have it instantly uploaded to your Evernote account, which will automatically use writing recognition software so you can search for the note later by typing in a few keywords.

Magazines/newspapers are mobile

Print is dying a slow and painful death as pretty much every publication is going digital, and by extension also going online and mobile. No more inky fingers or having to queue to get your morning paper while you wait for your train.

Why wait till tomorrow morning to find out what is happening in the news today, when you can find out instantly on Twitter from news organizations or the papers who print it?

You can get up-to-the-minute info simply by grabbing your phone, heading over to BBC News, CNN or Reddit.com to find out all the info the papers won't have for another 24 hours.

All via mobile technology.

Thinking like the mobile generation

I have gone to great lengths here to show that everything which can go mobile is going mobile. So what does this mean for your business? It means you *need* to start thinking about going mobile as soon as possible if your market is heading that way. Position yourself early or you will find yourself playing catch up, and I'm talking about much more than just having a mobile-enabled website (which of course you should have).

Studies have shown that our brains literally change shape and pathways depending on the technology we use (source: http://bit.ly/3LbPNN4) and in time this will also change our psychology.

Most people do *not* buy rationally but through their emotions, then justify their purchase with logic, and as such you need to make sure your mobile visitors *feel* right when they visit you.

Let's look at this in more detail:

The mobile customer wants things fast

Everywhere and in every way speed is becoming more of an issue. In many places around the world, truly unlimited 4G mobile data is becoming a reality.

Your customer is now carrying around something that can (to all intents and purposes) tell them anything they want to know, and they are now learning that it can get them anything they want – fast.

Customers want instant gratification and their smartphone allows them to get it! Same-day delivery is already available from some companies on items as large as refrigerators if you order before a certain time, and Amazon is experimenting with same-day delivery using a fleet of drones to carry packages, so they can get purchases to their customers as quickly as possible.

If ecommerce companies are looking into using drones to transport items, you can bet your bottom dollar couriers like FedEx, UPS and DHL and even postal companies like the UK Royal Mail will also be looking into it to stay competitive.

As bonkers as thousands of unmanned drones criss-crossing the sky sounds, these companies are continually looking to the future and you should do the same.

I'm not suggesting you must invest in a fleet of drones but you need to take it *very seriously* that your customer wants things as fast as is physically possible. If you're not able to deliver fast and your competitor is, you're in for a painful time.

The mobile customer wants a simple user experience

When you start attracting mobile traffic to your business, you need to make sure the process for the customer to complete the order or gather more information is as ridiculously easy as possible.

It's better for both parties if the user creates an account for your website so they can repeat order quickly and so you can follow up with additional related offers. But if the customer has to create an account to purchase that teddy bear for little Angelina, and has to type on their smartphone while they're rushing to catch the next train home from work, it is going to be a nightmare for them if they have to manually enter all their information by hand and are suffering from constant FFEs (Fat Finger Errors). As one of the twenty-first century's greatest thinkers once said, 'Ain't nobody got time for that!'

Your customer *will likely* give up and find someone else selling that teddy bear who's a darn sight easier to order from. You need to remove as many reasons for them to type whenever possible.

For instance, instead of forcing users to manually enter their data, give them the option to create an account using their Facebook, Twitter, Google or Instagram accounts. Or if you're using an ecommerce platform like Shopify or Magento you can use plugins and extensions to automatically copy over customer information into a mailing list provider like Mailchimp for you to send follow-up offers.

And don't stop with account creation and the ordering process. Make sure your customer support options are also dead simple. Put your contact phone number front and centre on your website in the mobile browser. Make it so they can call with one touch.

Give them options to email you, text you, Facebook message you, Tweet you etc. Think about the networks and services your customers use every day and make sure you're there and contactable.

Just being quickly reachable is such a ridiculously simple step towards giving amazing customer service that I'm surprised it's still not the norm. It doesn't have to be super technical or convoluted. A simple statement on your website like:

'Any problems? Text, Instagram, FB Message or email us your order number and the problem and we'll get back to you ASAP!'

And lastly, make sure you have a much-simplified version of your website showing when someone visits on a mobile device with everything laid out as clearly as possible.

Make it fast to load and cut out anything that doesn't absolutely need to be there: 53% of visitors to a mobile website abandon it if it takes longer than three seconds to load. For every second delay it takes to load the website, conversions fall by 12% (Google, 2018).

If you don't have a ton of money to invest in a mobile version of your website with all the ordering functionality, just have people call you to place their order.

(IMPORTANT: Speak with your credit card processor first to make sure you're allowed to manually enter your customer's credit card information.)

Ideally this shouldn't be the only purchase option you offer as not everyone will be comfortable giving their credit card information over the phone, but it *is* a quick and simple way for some people to order without you having to spend a ton of money having something coded.

Think of it this way: if someone has never been to your mobile website before, will they be able to figure out where they need to go in as few clicks or taps as possible? Ask friends and family for *honest* feedback on your mobile website. Once you've ironed out all the issues then you may have a winner on your hands, so make it live and see what happens. Ask your customers what they think – offer them a discount for any help they can give.

Any time you offer a discount to someone for their help, if your discount system is computerized, make sure the voucher/discount code can only be used once per customer. That way they can't take advantage of you or share it around the internet. If it's not computerized, just keep a simple Excel spreadsheet of all the people you've given a discount to and how much and check all orders against it. When they've ordered, delete them from the spreadsheet.

The mobile customer wants it the way they want it

Not only do your customers want something fast, they want it fast and ideally *customized* to them. If you sell ties and people want a 24-inch, green and yellow polka-dot, waterproof tie, you better make sure a) the ordering process is super-easy and b) you give them customizing options (HINT: people pay more for custom stuff).

Technology has made it possible for users to customize their day-to-day mobile experience. They can see the posts that they want from friends/pages that they want. A few taps and they can see the latest weather reports for their area, which movies starring their favourite actor are on at their local cinema or on TV tonight and so on.

This means you need to offer flexibility. Where can they change their order? Can they have it in a different colour? Different size? Do they want it gift-wrapped? With a personalized note? What can you offer to make a purchase more special for the customer before their order goes out the door?

This is where it is good to keep up to date with not only what's possible in your industry but also in other industries.

An example

You have a dog grooming business. What could you do to save your customer's time? Could you offer a mobile version of your service?

1 Just the fact of coming to a customer's home means less time spent and inconvenience of having to catch little Fluffy and get them to you and less stress for Fluffy being in an unfamiliar environment.
2 The VIP same-day service: Great Aunt Mabel just phoned and has invited herself round for dinner but Fluffy looks like she's been out chasing rabbits around the woods. How are you going to cook dinner *and* clean Fluffy? No problem – if you select the VIP option and contact us before 12pm, we'll come to you today.

3 Give customers a simple process to sign up for an account, give their phone number and address, set the time when they want you to show up and what style they want Fluffy coiffured into. There are always a million options here but pick the most common options that most of your customers choose (think of the 80/20 rule).

I know the above might be a bit much to do all at once but the key is to focus on one step at a time and you will already be light-years ahead of your competition.

OK let's go start attracting these mobile customers!

Summary

The aim of this chapter has been to point out how the advances in mobile technology are rapidly changing the way we interact with each other, our purchasing behaviour and the effects (positive and negative) it can have on our productivity.

We often take technology for granted and don't notice its effects on our day-to-day lives, but to maximize our business successes, it's vital we try to see where it is ultimately going and, most importantly, profit from it by positioning ourselves and our businesses correctly.

A massive shift is happening and when it is complete it will seem like it happened 'overnight' while you were sleeping.

Don't let this happen.

Using the examples in this chapter, start thinking about the various ways in which you can reach mobile users today. Pose this question to your subconscious as you drift off to dreaming about puppies and rainbows ...

'How can I make my business(es), better positioned for the mobile future, starting tomorrow?'

Keep this question in mind while you go through the rest of the chapters, tweaking and adding to it as you progress.

Fact-check (answers at the back)

1. How many hours of video are watched on YouTube every day?
   a) 10 million ❏
   b) 1 billion ❏
   c) 270,000 ❏
   d) 14.67 ❏
   e) 100 million ❏

2. In 2017, e-books made up what percentage of online book sales?
   a) 46% ❏
   b) 27% ❏
   c) 55% ❏
   d) 9% ❏
   e) 34% ❏

3. Most people do not make rational purchasing decisions. Instead they purchase using:
   a) a credit card and hide the bill when it comes in ❏
   b) logic and then justify with emotion ❏
   c) with cash ❏
   d) emotion and then justify with logic ❏
   e) instinct ❏

4. What was the *Encyclopedia Britannica* killer?
   a) WhatsApp ❏
   b) Facebook ❏
   c) Wikipedia ❏
   d) Twitter ❏
   e) MayoClinic ❏

5. Which options should you give customers to contact you:
   a) Email ❏
   b) Phone ❏
   c) Twitter ❏
   d) SMS/Text ❏
   e) All of the above (and more) ❏

6. Mobile users want their products:
   a) Slowly ❏
   b) Fast ❏
   c) Instantly ❏
   d) b and c (if possible) ❏

7. Mobile users love complicated and hard-to-navigate websites.
   a) True ❏
   b) False ❏

8. Do mobile users like to give things a custom spin?
   a) Yes ❏
   b) No ❏

9. What is one way to get feedback on your website?
   a) Ask family ❏
   b) Look through the site and guess ❏
   c) Ask customers ❏
   d) a and c ❏

10. One question you can ask yourself to appeal to the mobile consumer is:
    a) How can I make things more complicated? ❏
    b) How can I make them more money? ❏
    c) What can I do to save them time? ❏

CHAPTER 23

Simple mobile SEO tactics

It doesn't matter how great your website may look or how fast it loads, if nobody knows about it – it might as well not exist.

One of the most effective tools to bring a continual stream of prospective customers to your business' website is from a specific search that's performed in one of the main search engines like Google, Bing or Yahoo.

However, as search engines have billions of results in their indexes, today's business owner must use a mix of art and science to attempt to reverse-engineer the secretive algorithms and ranking criteria Google and others use to determine which of your webpages is seen by the search engines as the most relevant result for a query.

This reverse-engineering strategy is called search engine optimization, or SEO, and in this chapter I'll cover some of the simple things you can do to increase your chances of generating visitors for little or no monetary cost by using mobile-specific search engine optimization (SEO).

But first here's something you probably don't know ...

Mobile traffic

If you have a website, you're almost certainly getting mobile traffic in some form already.

Don't believe me?

Go into your analytics software (which is probably Google Analytics since it is the most popular) and look at your visitors. Now look at the types of visitor to see whether they're mobile devices or not...

You probably have a good percentage of mobile visitors. When I randomly check the stats for my websites, I can see around 15 per cent of my traffic is mobile.

The truth about the mobile internet is that *it is the internet now*. This shouldn't come as any surprise. Mobile internet usage overtook desktop internet activity back in 2016 (source: http://bit.ly/2Cu98sk) and globally more than 6.64 billion users own a smartphone, which equates to 83.72 per cent of the world's population (source: https://bit.ly/3FU2idP).

Sure, many of those users have both but the reality for a lot of people is it's more convenient to surf the web on their tablet or phone. And now the mobile market has matured, people are more confident with purchasing goods and services using their phone, especially with the development of Wallet apps built-in to iOS and Android, and technologies like Near Field Communication (NFC) enabling people to pay by physically touching their phones to a keypad to send payments.

Now that mobile users are becoming a higher quality visitor, you're not limited to which type of traffic you get: whether it's from Google search results, social media or from paid media (Google AdWords, Facebook Ads, etc.).

Before we look at how to use Google to get your business in front of your audience on their mobiles, it's worth spending a little time defining exactly *who* your audience is.

I'm not talking about people aged between X and Y, or 'Millennials', I'm talking about fleshing out your audience by creating a customer avatar – an individual persona that describes your ideal customer in detail.

Why go to all this trouble? Once you know exactly who your buyers are, their behaviours, where they go online, what their hopes and desires are for using your product or service etc. then it becomes a lot easier for you to market to that 'person' – make sense?

Creating your customer avatar

To create your customer avatar, start by thinking about the primary product or service you're offering. If you have existing customers go through their information and pull out any data you can think of that might be useful. If you can find them on Facebook, look at their occupations, the kind of things they like. Are there any common denominators?

If you don't have any customers yet, guess as best as you can. If you're still drawing a blank, hire someone from a freelancing site like UpWork.com to help you create an avatar.

Now write a short biography about your ideal customer. Use the following example to help.

> ### Hoboken Dog-Grooming: customer avatar
>
> Customer data reveals that, for a dog-grooming business based in Hoboken, New Jersey, most customers are women aged between 35 and 44 who live within a 20-mile radius.

This is just an example: yours will probably be less detailed than this in the beginning but you can build it up as you add to it over time and as you learn more about your audience.

When crafting your avatar, be as detailed as possible with the data you have or can find – try asking questions such as:

- Would Jill and Mike be interested in this?
- Will it save them time or money?
- Will it be entertaining to them enough that they take a minute to watch a quick video?
- Would the headline catch their attention if they happened to see it while browsing YouTube?
- What about the video thumbnail image?

If it doesn't appeal to your customer avatar, then you need to go back to the drawing board. You need content that is laser targeted to your avatar, not boring, generic messages.

Leveraging mobile search

With more and more people surfing and searching from mobile devices, it's important to do everything you can to take advantage of these users. One of the best ways is to optimize the pages on your website to show up in the Top 10 results when people enter a specific search term. This is known as search engine optimization (SEO).

There are certain things you need to make sure you've done in order to optimize your webpages for organic search (i.e. the main results section, not the paid ads at the top or bottom) and there are additional things you need to do to optimize for mobile search.

Title and description meta tags

Title Tag
The Title Tag is the text that displays when you hover over a tab in your browser and is one of the primary methods Google uses to try to figure out what the page is about.

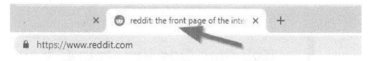

Keep your Title Tag to no longer than 70 characters with important keywords towards the beginning. Every webpage on your site should have a unique Title Tag and should only focus on one main keyword at a time.

Description Tag
This is commonly used by search engines to describe what the page is about within its results.

```
<meta name="author" content="Lucy Alexander">
<meta name="description" content="Find out what digital marketing is today, the tactics involved, the types of
content you can create, and the purpose digital marketing serves to your overall marketing strategy.">
<meta name="generator" content="HubSpot">
<title>What Is Digital Marketing?</title>
```

What Is Digital Marketing? - HubSpot Blog
https://blog.hubspot.com/marketing/what-is-digital-marketing ▾
26 Jun 2018 - Find out what digital marketing is today, the tactics involved, the types
of content you can create, and the purpose digital marketing serves to ...

Digital marketing - Wikipedia
https://en.wikipedia.org/wiki/Digital_marketing ▾
Digital marketing is the marketing of products or services using digital technologies,
mainly on the Internet, but also including mobile phones, display advertising, ...
Digital marketing · Digital marketing system · Digital marketing engineer · Promotion

What is digital marketing? | SAS UK
https://www.sas.com/en_gb/insights/marketing/digital-marketing.html ▾
Learn all about what digital marketing is from our marketing insights – and find out
why it is so different from traditional marketing. Read more!

It's best practice to keep your Description to around
150–155 characters with each webpage having a unique Meta
Description and a call-to-action (CTA) within it.

Also having a CTA like 'Click here ...' is incredibly important
because Google tracks and compares the number of people
that click each link in their results pages. If your link gets
more clickthroughs than your competition, and people stay
on your site, Google will reward that link with a bump in their
search rankings because it's more relevant to the original
search query.

Google does NOT like multiple webpages on the same site
having the same Meta Title and/or Meta Description.

> ## Hoboken Dog Grooming: Title and Meta Description
>
> **TITLE**: Peggy's Pooch Pampering: **Hoboken Dog Grooming** Expert
>
> **DESCRIPTION**: Peggy's is Hoboken's favorite place for coiffured canines since 1989. As used by Jersey Shore's Snooki. **Click here to get the first trim free.**

Image Alt Tags

Make sure the *alt="one-of-the-search-terms-you-are-trying-to-rank-for"* markup is added to each main image on your webpage to help give Google more information on what your webpage is about.

NOTE: Do Not Spam each image with multiple keywords or keep using the same keywords in each image. Related ones in other images are fine.

URL canonicalization

This is just a fancy way of saying 'make sure Google knows which webpage URL is the correct one'. One of the most common errors I see is unnecessary URL duplication. For example:

- http://yourdomain.com
- http://www.yourdomain.com
- http://yourdomain.com/index.html
- http://www.yourdomain.com/index.html

and so on ...

This happens a lot, and over time people or staff enter the wrong URL into local online directories, posting a promotional article on a third-party website. I know and you know they all mean the same thing (i.e. your homepage) but sometimes Google sees them as distinct, individual webpage URLs, so you need to let Google know which URL for each webpage on your website is the correct one.

Fortunately, this is easily done with one line of HTML code in your page:

←link rel="canonical" href="http://yourdomain.com/page-name"/→

Put the correct page URL in the 'href' section and paste that code above the closing ←/head→ line in your page's markup.

You also need to decide on one URL format to use across your entire website, whether it be:

- http://yourdomain.com

  or

- http://www.yourdomain.com

This again confuses Google and makes it think you may have duplicate content on your website, for which they will 'penalize' you.

Speak with your web developer about setting up your webserver to use one format or the other. For Linux-based webservers, this is done with 'htaccess' and for Windows servers it's the 'web.config' file.

Mobile friendly/first design

One effective way to generate more traffic is to make your website display nicely on mobile devices as Google is currently rewarding websites with a slight nudge in rankings if they're designed to be mobile-friendly (source: http://bit.ly/2R7tDlF).

If your website uses a popular Content Management System (CMS) like WordPress, or you have a third-party ecommerce system like Shopify or BigCommerce, you may already be generating a mobile-friendly version of your website or store. If you're not sure, ask your web designer.

If your website is not generating a mobile-friendly version, then a quick fix can be as simple as creating a 'mobilized' version of your website without any unnecessary bells and whistles and adding two small lines of HTML; one to your main webpage and one to your 'mobilized' version.

On your main/desktop version of your webpage add the following line underneath your Description Meta Tag:

←link rel="alternate" media="only screen and (max-width: 640px)"
href="**http://m.yourdomain.com/page-1**"→

Swap the **URL** for the mobile version of your page which in this case is in a subdomain on your website called "m" (your web designer can set this up).

On the mobile version of the webpage put a Canonical tag as mentioned above.

←link rel="canonical" href="http://yourdomain.com/page-1"/→

This will stop Google getting confused with two different pages having the exact same content on your website and tell them that the desktop/main version of the webpage is the page they should index.

And because Google is dang smart, it should display the mobile version of the webpage for people searching Google on their mobile.

> ## Mobile first
>
> If you don't currently have a website but are looking to build one soon, my advice isn't just to make it mobile friendly, but to make it 'mobile first' – in other words, build the site to be optimized for mobile as the priority – not desktop computers – right from the very beginning.
>
> And honestly, I'd seriously consider redesigning an existing website to be 'mobile first' so you can get a massive jump on your competition by giving your ever-increasing mobile visitors a better experience.

Google's Snack Pack and citations

This isn't really talked about a lot but if you offer products or services to a specific geographic area and you aren't actively leveraging the Snack Pack then you're missing out on a lot of potential Google love.

Well, let's remedy that right now, shall we?

Google's Snack Pack/3-Pack

This appears mainly when you're searching for a type of business in a local area, so for example, the screenshot overleaf shows what comes up when I search for 'dog groomer Hoboken NJ' on my Samsung Galaxy S9.

There's an obvious ad at the top, which a lot of people just ignore but then we have a map with three businesses listed on it and directly below that is a box with more information about the businesses, like their opening times, and a convenient 'tap-to-call' button on the right.

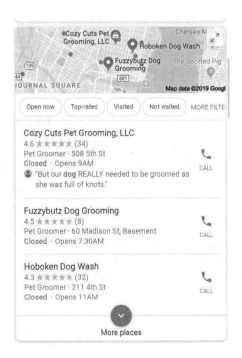

This is the Google 3-Pack (sometimes known as the Snack Pack) and it's important to try to get into the Snack Pack for a couple of reasons, the main one being that on most modern smartphones it will appear 'above the fold' (on the screen without scrolling).

And as you can see, it's designed to be quite eye-catching so wouldn't it be better to also be in the Snack Pack so the user doesn't scroll past it to get to the regular organic search results where you're fighting with nine other results, instead of just two?

So how do you get into it?

First you need to set up an account on Google My Business (google.com/business). Go through the whole process. Fill in all your business information and request the postcard to verify your address – should take about a week to come through.

TIP *Look at your competition's category in the Snack Pack. That's the category you need to use too. If you're not sure, Google released a complete list of all the correct GMB categories to use for each country. See: http://bit.ly/2Rds99H*

Now you need to generate local and business-related citations.

Citations

A citation is just a link from an authority website that is either from your locality, your industry or ideally both. The types of citation link you get differ according to your location and your product. For example, for the best citation sources by US city see: http://bit.ly/2R9W02o.

TIP *These are constantly changing so doing searches for terms like 'best US citation sources' or 'best UK citation sources' will help get you started. For business-related citations, think about professional bodies like associations, trade journals, respected niche directory websites etc.*

As a rule, I aim to get as many highly authoritative citations as I can, with a minimum of at least 50 as the first target. Finding and submitting all the relevant citations will take time, so outsource this to a staff member or alternatively use a third-party freelancing website like UpWork.com or Fiverr.com.

Reviews

From what we know, getting lots of positive reviews doesn't seem to have a massive direct impact on your rankings within the Snack Pack. For example, I searched for 'emergency dentist Liverpool' and the results showed a website with three reviews and a 2.7 out of 5 outranking one with nine reviews averaging a 4 out of 5 (see overleaf).

However, common sense tells us that more good reviews will make our listing stand out, and make our business seem like a better option compared to our competition and hopefully generate more clicks to our website or calls to us.

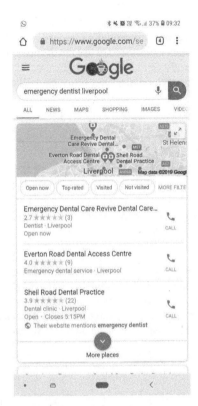

The Rules

Google are just as hot on people trying to 'game' review getting as they are with other spammy SEO practices so first here's what NOT to do:

1. Compulsory: Don't incentivize people with money or anything else to write reviews for your business or write negative reviews to your competitors.

2. Compulsory: Don't hire third-party companies to create fake Google reviews. They might be under Google's radar for now, but should they be found out all companies that used them run the risk of being penalized.

Best case scenario: you lose all the reviews you paid for (wasted money).

> *Worst case scenario:* Google bans you from the Snack Pack and applies a site penalty that affects your regular rankings.
>
> Don't risk it.
>
> **3. Compulsory:** Do not set up a specialized area or kiosk in your place of business for gaining customer reviews. The main reason this isn't a good idea is that it's trivial for Google to detect this since all the reviews would come from the same IP address as your business and would be an immediate 'footprint'.
>
> **4. Advisory:** Try to avoid running periodic 'big push' campaigns to generate reviews. Having a sizable number of reviews suddenly appear on your listing looks suspicious to Google and might be mistaken for trying to 'game' the system.

So what are the best ways to get reviews? Just keep it natural. For every new customer you get, ask them if they would leave an honest review on Google.

This gives you a normal pattern of reviews, spread over time from lots of different residential IP addresses within a local area.

NOTE: If you're a business that services customers or clients over a larger area or nationally, don't worry – Google will know to expect reviews from all over the country and not just one local area.

Printed reviews

If you have customers that come to your place of business or you deal in mail order, you can give them a printed sheet that asks for the review along with instructions on how to do it.

 For an online Review Handout Generator see (free account required): http://bit.ly/2R8y6ED.

Online reviews

Once you are verified in Google My Business, you can generate a 'Leave a Review' link for your website with the following free online tool that will take the visitor directly to the review form for your business: http://bit.ly/2R8mwcy.

To make it easier to remember and to use in print, get your web designer to set up a redirect to the link using a URL like: http://yourdomain.com/review.

Dealing with spam/fake/bad reviews

Not everyone is going to like you or your business and nowadays they can instantly vocalize their displeasure by leaving a negative review in any number of places: Google, Yelp, Facebook etc. If you're actively promoting yourself or your company, as sure as 'eggs is eggs' you are at some point going to run into this issue but don't worry, it really isn't the end of the world.

Before you run screaming to Google, Yelp or whoever to attempt to have it removed think carefully if it's a legitimate complaint. If it is, reply and apologize publicly for it. Do whatever is possible to rectify the situation as best you can. Can you offer them a refund of the item or give them an additional something at no charge? If you're offering a service, can you do something else for them at no extra charge?

No business is perfect but by publicly apologizing and showing that you're trying to make amends helps when other potential customers and clients look at your reviews and see that you care about them.

If the review looks fake (i.e. doesn't talk about a specific order, is vague) then in as unbiased way as possible, check the review against Google's Review Posting Guidelines here: https://bit.ly/3PhlvKv.

If you still feel you have a case, then click the 'Flag as Inappropriate' link next to the review explaining *specifically* why you believe it should be removed. Google will check the review and if they determine it's violated the posting guidelines, they'll remove it but it's not guaranteed.

 Google won't remove bad reviews when companies and customers disagree on specific facts as they have no way to verify them.

Summary

There has been a lot for you to take in at one time here. So let me sum it up as best I can:

First, using your analytics software, check how many people are visiting your website as a mobile user (you probably already have visitors from this whether you know it or not).

Second, create your customer avatar so everything you do from here on out is targeting the right people. You don't want to aim for everyone in the world because only a certain percentage of the population will even think of buying from you. If you are a dog-grooming service, believe it or not, not everyone owns a dog, much less a dog that needs grooming, so make sure you are targeting all your ads and website right.

Next we went through a whole bunch of technical stuff that is all important so don't skip it. Meta Tags, canonicalization and citations, etc. really do matter a lot if you want to get mobile traffic at all.

But don't get lost in it.

We also talked about getting reviews: what not to do and what to do. Always keep in your mind 'Would Google (or whoever) think I am trying to 'game' the system?' You may be asking for an honest review but never give the customers an incentive of any monetary value and never ever use a review service.

Make it your goal to choose one suggestion in this chapter and start on it now. Don't try to get everything done all at once – try working in bite-sized chunks.

Fact-check (answers at the back)

1. What is the most popular analytics software?
   a) Clicky ❏
   b) Piwik ❏
   c) Tableau ❏
   d) Google Analytics ❏

2. To find out who your customer truly is you need a customer:
   a) Avatar ❏
   b) Example ❏
   c) Sample ❏
   d) Survey ❏

3. You need a 'call to action' in your Meta Description because:
   a) It is cool and all the cool people are doing it. ❏
   b) It makes people more likely to click on your listing ❏
   c) Google can read it and know you are better than your competition ❏
   d) It makes your website better. ❏

4. Title and Meta Descriptions should all:
   a) Be the same on every page of your site ❏
   b) Include as many keywords as possible ❏
   c) Be unique and only target one keyword at a time. ❏
   d) Be 200 characters long and full of only your contact info. ❏

5. Images should be 'tagged' with:
   a) One keyword each if possible ❏
   b) Descriptions of the images ❏
   c) Random words ❏
   d) There should be no tags. ❏

6. You should never tell Google which webpage is canonical. You should just let them figure it out themselves.
   a) True ❏
   b) False ❏

7. Websites are all mobile-friendly automatically.
   a) True ❏
   b) False ❏

8. To get Google reviews you should:
   a) Set up your profile on Google My Business. ❏
   b) Avoid spammy ways to get reviews ❏
   c) Get reviews naturally over time by asking everyone to leave a review. ❏
   d) All of the above. ❏

9. To increase the number of reviews you get, you should:
   a) Tell new customers ❏
   b) Tell old customers ❏
   c) Hand out printouts showing people how to do it. ❏
   d) Set up sections of your website and emails to your customers with the info. ❏
   e) All of the above. ❏

10. If you get a bad review:
    a) Panic ❏
    b) Ask for it to get removed immediately ❏
    c) Flag it as spam ❏
    d) Deal with it by trying to set things right first. ❏

CHAPTER 24

Social media marketing

'It takes 20 years to build a reputation, and five minutes to ruin it. If you think about that, you'll do things differently.'

It's seems obvious that this quote from billionaire investing legend Warren Buffet would apply to every aspect of your business (and your personal!) life – what you do and are seen to being doing have consequences and repercussions. But in the online world, these ripples are instantaneous and can reach from one side of the world to the other – in a matter of *seconds* and are archived, copied, retrieved and distributed forever.

But as powerful a tool as social media is for being able to cause huge damage to a company, when used correctly it can really pay off in a massive way and in this chapter I'm going to explain how to achieve this. Not only that but I will show you how to connect with mobile users through social media.

Benefits of social media in the mobile marketing mix

When it comes to using social media, it's important not to expect an immediate return on your investment and effort. It's not as simple as spending money on ads and then checking how many sales you have made. Social media doesn't work that way.

It is going to takes time for you to build your following, for people to get used to seeing your company name in their various feeds. It's not something that happens overnight (unless you're very lucky!).

So what are some of the benefits you can get from utilizing social media?

Building your brand

Social media is a powerful tool for brand building. It allows you to determine how you want to position your company to your target audience. It enables you to tell people about your business and highlight the people in it. Using social media effectively means you can describe and show the benefits of your products or services to your target audience. It only takes a small amount of effort and content to really make an impact.

Exposure

It's said that for a customer or client to buy from you, they had to have been exposed to your marketing messages anywhere between six and twenty times. Social media allows you to generate a *lot* of repeat exposure.

Depending on how long your average sales cycle is, it's possible to get in front of your potential customers, and clients, eyeballs tens if not dozens of times (maybe even more?) educating them on what your company can do for them.

If your products and services appeal to a wide number of different industries and you produce stellar content, who knows – it ends up being shared virally all over social media, doubling if not tripling (more?) your exposure.

Building relationships

Social media is all about building relationships, whether it's with existing customers or prospective ones. People can follow you and you them. You can find out what they like, how they use your products, how your services improved their lives or business. It's incredibly powerful. Here's a simple example:

Let's say you're perusing one of your best clients' Twitter feed on your phone and you notice they're a Chelsea supporter by the number of times they comment about the club's performance. How gobsmacked do you think they'd be if you sent them a Chelsea shirt signed by their favourite player as a birthday gift or just as a random 'Customer Appreciation' thank you? Do you think that would make them more or less inclined to do extra business with you ... or refer your company to their business colleagues?

How many other companies out there do you think are cultivating their business relationships in that way? How often has that happened to you? Yeah, me too.

Happens all the time ... Not ...

Though to be fair I did get a nice paperweight from a realtor once.

With social media you have instant, in-depth access to your followers, customers and clients who then become members of your community. Through social media, you can find out what they like, and what they don't. What they love and what drives them mad. Can you discover a gap in the market no-one is filling just from your followers' frustrated Tweets?

This level of communication and research used to take a lot of time and cost a lot of money with specialist firms but now you can accomplish almost as much with just a few social media accounts and it doesn't cost you a penny.

Establishing authority

Social media works especially well for helping companies in the business-to-business (B2B) space establish their authority on their chosen topics. Whether you're a coach, a consultant, service provider or speaker it's simple to leverage social media to 'prove' to your market that you are an expert on your subject.

All it takes is getting content out there in your area of expertise and soon enough your audience will be trained to think of you as the 'go-to-guy' or 'go-to-girl'. If people have questions, try to answer as many of them as possible – leave no question behind.

The more you can demonstrate your authority and expertise, the more content your audience will be exposed to and the easier it will be to attract new prospects, clients and other potential business partners to get in touch.

Generating website and mobile traffic

Social media when done correctly can increase the traffic to your website. However, although it is great for sharing information, sometimes it doesn't give you enough 'space' to be able to say everything you want to say to educate and inform your market. It's at times like this that you want to try and drive followers from your Facebook Page (for example) to your website.

One way of doing this, if you're a service provider, is to write (or have ghostwritten) a list-based article (for example '10 greatest myths about XYZ'), go into detail on the first three, then if people want to read the rest, have them click a link to a post on your website that goes into more detail about the other seven. You can offer them a video which goes into even more detail, or a checklist, schedule or blueprint they can print out to get a specific result, in exchange for their email address – which you can then use to keep in contact with them to offer more useful articles and just follow up with them.

Reminder: you won't get floods of traffic and new leads overnight but you don't want to either. Do you want 10,000 tyre-kickers or 500 buyers?

Competitive advantage

So many businesses still think social media is a 'fad' and that it won't amount to anything. What they don't know but I (and now you) know, is that over the past few years, social media has graduated from a digital water cooler, where we hung out with our friends to talk about last night's episode of much-watch TV, into a serious influencing factor when it comes to buying decisions.

Social commerce is set to become a major driving force for consumer and business purchases in the years to come, especially with networks like Facebook, Instagram and TikTok integrating in-platform purchasing, so there's no need to leave to get the things you want.

Here are just a few statistics to set the stage:

- 70 per cent of Gen Zs said social media ads influenced their purchasing decisions (Statista, June 2021).
- US social buyers are expected to reach 108 million consumers in 2025.
- 11 per cent of social media users immediately make an online purchase after discovering a product.
- 85 per cent of Pinterest shoppers have more in their basket and spend twice as much as other shoppers.

(Sources: https://blog.hubspot.com/marketing/social-commerce-stats)

And don't think this behaviour is limited to consumers: if you're selling products or services to other businesses, you need to pay close attention. This is especially true with Gen Z – their behaviours today are tomorrow's C-suites:

- Over 36 per cent of B2B decision-makers use Instagram to research new products and services.
- 84 per cent of C-level/vice president executives use social media to support purchase decisions.
- 75 per cent of B2B buyers are influenced by information they found on social media.

So it's important to offer assistance to people asking questions to prove your expertise.

I could go on but you get the point. *Social media isn't going away* and with more and more pressure on executives to do the job right the first time, social media as a research tool for B2B and B2C customers is becoming ever more important and you need to treat it as such.

Spend the time and effort to answer the questions coming in. Keep your pages and accounts updated with new content. Take social media seriously, because if you're doing a great job and your competition aren't, you'll be leaps and bounds ahead of them, giving you a great competitive advantage they'll have trouble fighting against.

Content

We've talked about how effective social media can be for pretty much any type of business, but now we need to address the elephant in the room: content.

There's no getting away from it, you are going to have to create and publish content on a regular basis to have any kind of success on social media. When I say 'you' what I really mean is:

1 You
2 Someone in your company OR
3 A person/people outside your company tasked with the role

No matter who does it, content *must* be created because without it, you're not going to show up in anyone's personal Newsfeed giving you exactly ZERO exposure.

The name of the content game is to make sure you're publishing high-quality, relevant content on a regular basis that will keep viewers interested in your business and what's going on.

How often should you publish? There's no right or wrong answer to this, but for most businesses it's better to post daily or at the very least three times a week to ensure you're not far from your target audience's thoughts.

Regardless of how often you decide to post, make sure you're consistent and do whatever you can to make sure you post on the same days every week. That way you'll be 'training' your followers to come back to your Facebook page every time some new content is due.

And always remember to remind them to come back ... 'That's it for today's post. See you on Friday for this week's Friday FAQ when we'll be answering the question ...'. If you *do* decide to alter the publishing schedule, give your readers plenty of notice to get ready for it.

Publishing quality content really isn't that hard. Here are a few pointers:

- Keep it relevant to your business and to your audience. Don't start posting up random funny or 'cool' videos you've seen. Your readers are coming to you for information and education on your field of expertise. If you start posting things that aren't relevant, you may lose them.
- Write in a normal, conversational manner. Don't be too formal with your language as that puts up a subconscious barrier between you and your prospect but at the same time, don't be too 'chummy' with them either. We're looking to build mutually profitable business relationships here.
- Post photos and where possible videos. People *love* to see video. Image and video content make up a large percentage of total social media content.
- Facebook's 1.57 BILLION daily mobile active users are estimated to generate around 8 BILLION average video views a DAY (source: http://bit.ly/2OFrk8j).
- Snapchat (another mobile social network with a younger consumer demographic) is outpacing Facebook with their users generating 10 BILLION video views a DAY (source: http://bit.ly/2OKdGk9).
- Not bad when you consider Snapchat has just a fraction of Facebook's userbase, with 191 million daily mobile users.
- Instagram (also owned by Facebook) has also exploded since copying and implementing some of Snapchat's functionality and now has more than 500 million daily active users (source: http://bit.ly/2OLJDbT) with video watch time increasing 80% year on year (source: http://bit. ly/2OPQIYM).

Video

Don't think you should set up a broadcast centre or hire professional videographers to post video on social media.

This is a masterclass all about mobile marketing, right? If you have a decent modern smartphone with a camera and video function, you should be good to go. If you don't have a smartphone and you're not sure which one to get, just go to Google and type something like 'best smartphone for under XXX'.

Video content doesn't have to be super-slick high quality. A lot of the time 'amateur-looking' video has better engagement because it feels more authentic (because it is!), less staged and creates a deeper relationship with your audience.

- Publish your content at the most appropriate time during the day. Should you publish before 9am, at lunchtime, after 7pm? Some other time? You won't know in the beginning so just post a variety of different types of content (text, image, video) at various times during the day and then closely examine your social media account's analytics to see if that gives you any feedback on which content, which type of post and which time generates the best engagement with your audience.
- If you have more time than clients and customers then by all means handle everything yourself, but when the time comes, and your business begins to attract more and more clients and customers, don't waste a second and automate as much of the publishing process as possible.
- Yes, you need to curate, create and publish content, but you need to do it in the most time-efficient manner possible without sacrificing the quality of the service you provide to your customers. Outsource whatever content creation you can, when you can:
  - If it's an article you can hire a writer with knowledge in your field. Good writers cost around 7 cents a word, so a 1000-word article will be around $70.

○ If you going to publish inspirational quotes or tips in image form, there are thousands of graphic designers out there who will happily do this type of work for you.

○ If it's video, you can create it yourself with your phone or if it's something you can demonstrate on your computer you can use software like Camtasia Studio or Screenflow (Mac) to record your desktop and save it as a video to upload.

○ If it's a more professional type of video, there are tons of videographers as well as writers and graphic artists in freelance marketplace sites like UpWork.com and Freelancer.com.

● Ideally, plan your content out a month in advance and if it's content to be outsourced have them create everything ahead of time, then use services like Buffer.com, Twitterfeed.com or Hootsuite.com to schedule your content to be posted to your accounts.

Before subscribing to a service, make sure they are able to do what you want them to do. Do you want them to automate posting images or videos? Not all of them can. Do your research.

Content ideas

Stuck on what to post? How about any of these?

● Look for birthdays of famous people who are related to your field of expertise. Are there any interesting facts about them you could publish?

● Is there an 'On this day in history ...' related to your field you could publish?

● Ask followers, subscribers or customers for questions and post an answer on a separate day.

● Post breaking news in your industry (find the best blogs in your industry and subscribe to their content using Feedly.com and make that your browser's homepage).

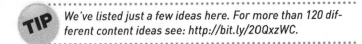

TIP We've listed just a few ideas here. For more than 120 different content ideas see: http://bit.ly/2OQxzWC.

Where to publish

So we've covered what, why, when and how to publish content – now comes the where. Below I'm going to discuss the 'Big Three': Facebook, Twitter and LinkedIn but depending on your audience and the type of business you have, other mobile social networks might be a better fit. For instance:

- If you're an ecommerce operation servicing the teenager/early 20s demographic, you should also seriously consider TikTok and Snapchat.
- If you have anything to do with fashion or health/fitness, start getting experience with Instagram.
- If you sell homewares, then Pinterest could well be your primary mobile social media network, even over Facebook. (Pinterest has a 70 per cent female demographic!)

Facebook

If you don't already have a Facebook Page for your business, you're missing out on possibly one of the best marketing opportunities you can get online. Your Facebook Page can potentially put your business in front of nearly a quarter of all the people on Earth – billions of people. Now maybe your company only serves your local community with a 20-mile radius. Well, because of the sheer numbers of people on Facebook, it's possible for you to market to the majority (if not all) of the targeted people in your service area.

And helpfully, Facebook has given you a tool which will tell you precisely how many people there are in your local area available to target on Facebook. It's called Audience Insights and you'll find it in your Facebook Ad account or you can go directly to it here (FB ad account required).

Audience Insights

- Personal Ad Account: https://www.facebook.com/ads/audience-insights
- Business Ad Account: https://business.facebook.com/ads/audience-insights

A Facebook Page can be created extremely quickly and is completely free to set up.

1 Go to https://www.facebook.com/pages/create/ to begin creating your page.
2 Select a category and Page name for your business.
3 Use your company logo or an image directly associated with your company as your Page's profile picture. The profile image dimensions at the time of writing are 180 × 180 pixels.
4 Write a short sentence or two describing your business (if you're stuck at this stage, open a new tab in your browser and have a look at what other businesses have written).
5 Create a web address for your page that is easy to remember and can be used in your marketing literature. This will help to promote your Facebook Page.
6 The last major thing is your Cover Image – that's the large 851 × 315 (at the time of writing) image at the top of your Facebook Page. This is one of the first things people will see when they view your Facebook Page so it's important to get this right.

 Rather than list out dos and don'ts for creating a Facebook Page, HubSpot.com have a great article on the topic you can go through on their blog here: http://bit.ly/2R7vHdp.

Once the Page is live, you can go in and add more optional information like a phone number, business address, mission statement and so on.

Once your Page is ready for visitors, you can initially reach out to friends, family and customers to 'Like' it and then in due course reach out to targeted prospects via natural organic reach and paid ads.

The type of content that tends to work best with Facebook is:

- Small-to-medium length text (no more than 500 words)
- Images
- Video (particularly FB Live)

If you intend to focus more on mobile marketing, I would concentrate more on image and video on Facebook.

Twitter

Twitter is a popular social media site that works in a similar way to SMS/Text messaging. Messages (called Tweets) are limited to 280 characters but you can also post images and videos up to 30 seconds long.

You decide on what shows up in your Twitter feed by the people and accounts you follow, like Facebook and most other social networks. You can 'Like', 'Favourite', 'Retweet' (share to your own followers) content as well as publicly and privately message (known as Direct Message or DM) other people.

Generally, both parties in a conversation would have to follow each other to be able to DM but you can turn on the ability to allow someone to DM you who hasn't followed you; perfect for companies to allow sales enquiries without the other party having to broadcast their interest to the world.

Twitter is an excellent way to keep up to date with current events and news, particularly when it comes to breaking news and interesting articles being published in real time.

Research has shown that 64 per cent of Twitter users are more likely to buy the products or brands they follow online (source: https://yhoo.it/2R9ZFgM) so whether you're servicing business-to-consumer (B2C) or business-to-business (B2B) you should seriously think about leveraging Twitter in your mobile social media marketing.

Setting up an account is quick, easy and free.

1 Go to http://twitter.com, click the 'Sign Up' button, fill in the email address you want to use and select a password. Then you'll be asked to select a Twitter username.
2 If you're publishing on behalf of your company, try to get your company's name as the username. With 350 million users there's a chance that it may not be available, so you'll need to improvise a little.
3 Once you've got a username you're happy with and that's available, click the 'Create My Account' button and it'll log you in and you're ready to use Twitter. You cannot change the username later so make sure you're 100 per cent happy with it. NOTE: Double check the email address you use because Twitter will send you a verification email with a link inside it that you'll need to click to give you full access to all Twitter's functions.
4 Do the usual things, like adding a short benefit-driven bio and profile pictures (a company logo is fine) and you're good to go.

The type of content that tends to work best with Twitter is more newsy type content, links out to topic content or anything that's easily consumable.

LinkedIn

LinkedIn is a professional social network with over 590 million members. Since it's a professional network made up of entrepreneurs, business owners, executives and the 'C-Suite' (CEO, COO, CMO etc.), if you service businesses in any way, it makes sense for LinkedIn to be a foundation of your mobile social media plan.

If you don't already have a LinkedIn account, here's how to start:

1 Sign up for a personal account (you'll need one of these first before you can create a business one). Just go to http://www.linkedin.com, fill in the form and click the 'Join Now' button. You'll need to verify your email address so check your email and click the confirmation link in the email LinkedIn sends you.

2 After clicking the confirmation link you'll be taken back to LinkedIn where you can choose the type of account you need, based on what you primarily want to use LinkedIn for. There's the basic free account or you can select one of the premium offerings that give you more functionality. Pick the one you want then go to your Profile and begin to edit it putting in all your relevant information.

3 You'll see a field for entering your company's website – use the format http://www.yourwebsite.com. This will create a live link to your company, and any other members of your staff on LinkedIn can also use this hyperlink to link back to your company's website.

Your industry field is searchable so think very carefully what you put in here. I'd advise doing some research into your competitors to see if a) they're on LinkedIn and b) what industry field they've entered. Choosing the right entry makes the difference between being seen or not.

4 Once you've completed your personal profile, create a Company Page (like a Facebook Page) and fill that in with all the appropriate information.

LinkedIn is the same as any social media network. If you want to be seen, you must get involved. Download the app onto your phone and start getting out there. Connect with people you know and start building your network.

The best type of content to post on LinkedIn is informative and educational in nature. The type of content you can post includes:

- Medium to longer text (400+ words)
- Video
- PDFs (case studies, white papers etc.)

A great way to leverage LinkedIn is to look for relevant LinkedIn groups to join – be they related to your field of expertise, your location, a local Chamber of Commerce or something else.

Give help and advice where you can, share insights and just generally contribute. The exposure will help lead you to a bigger audience and eventually to make more contacts which in turn will increase the chance of obtaining new customers and clients.

There are lots of tutorials on how to use LinkedIn on their official YouTube Channel here: https://www.youtube.com/user/LinkedIn.

Summary

Just as the world is going mobile, so it is going social. To get mobile traffic, you need to be active on all the major social networks as much as possible. This helps build both your brand and your relationships with your clients/customers.

Each social network has its own special rules and ways to sign up correctly that I don't possibly have room for in a summary, but they are all mostly common sense (as far as the web is concerned). Just to be safe, be sure to bookmark and/or highlight the sections that deal with the social networks that you will be signing up on.

But there is one thing all social networks want and that is content. To do anything on these sites and drive traffic to you, you need to be producing content that gets the 'click'.

Make sure your content is 'on topic' and relevant to your business. Be down to earth and fun as much as possible – avoid being too formal. Write high-quality content and post cool relevant pictures, but most of all try and produce good videos. Videos tend to get great traction and can lead to serious traffic from YouTube and other social networks if done right.

Depending on your niche and/or business, be sure to have a plan to produce content. Whether it is you, an employee or some other freelancer creating it, make sure it is high quality content and being created consistently.

In this chapter we looked at a general overview of the 'Big Three' social networks and at some of the pluses and minuses with each, but really you should be on all of them. Later we will look at tools you can use to cut down on the time spent managing these networks – so never fear.

Fact-check (answers at the back)

1. Why are we talking about social media in a section on mobile marketing?
   a) Because this masterclass has seven chapters and this fills one of them. ❏
   b) Social media is cool and hip. ❏
   c) Mobile users are all over social media. ❏
   d) I felt like it, what is your problem? ❏

2. Social media benefits:
   a) Your brand ❏
   b) Your visibility ❏
   c) Your relationships with your customers. ❏
   d) All of the above ❏

3. What percentage of people said a company's social media profile influenced their decision to buy once (positively or negatively):
   a) 50% ❏
   b) 25% ❏
   c) 78% ❏
   d) 85% ❏
   e) 56% ❏

4. Businesses don't use social media to make decisions so B2B companies don't need to be on social media.
   a) True ❏
   b) False ❏

5. You need good _____ to succeed on social media.
   a) Cat photos ❏
   b) Witty comments on current events ❏
   c) Random shared items ❏
   d) Content (video or othe ❏
   e) None of the above. ❏

6. The best kind of content currently in most niches is:
   a) Written articles ❏
   b) Video ❏
   c) Photos ❏
   d) Plain comments ❏

7. The demographic of Pinterest is:
   a) 30% female ❏
   b) 55% female ❏
   c) 70% female ❏
   d) 85% female ❏

8. If you are targeting teenagers/20-somethings then you should be on:
   a) Twitter ❏
   b) Instagram ❏
   c) Snapchat ❏
   d) Facebook ❏
   e) Other ❏

9. LinkedIn should be your main social network if:
   a) You do cat videos ❏
   b) You are a B2B company ❏
   c) You are a B2C company ❏
   d) You are a videographer ❏

10. Twitter is best for:
   a) News ❏
   b) Posting content ❏
   c) Engaging with followers ❏
   d) All of the above ❏

CHAPTER 25

Mobile pay-per-click (PPC) marketing

In this chapter we are going to discuss the #1 traffic methodology that every mobile marketer needs to master and that is pay-per-click (PPC) marketing.

SEO and social media are great ways to generate traffic and build brand awareness but if you don't have your sales processes working and optimized, all that traffic will be wasted.

So how do you figure out your sales processes? Using paid traffic to jump start visitors to your website as quickly as possible to test, tweak and improve your sales and conversion processes. Then when you think you've got something working that's profitable, you start ramping up your social media and organic search campaigns.

If there's one thing I want you to take away from reading this Part, it's this: don't choose between paid traffic, or social media marketing or SEO – they all work in synergy **together**.

DISCLAIMER: Just so we're clear I'm not saying that you're guaranteed to make money when you use PPC traffic. No traffic, whether paid, social or organic, is a 'magic money bullet'. What PPC traffic **can** do is generate traffic quickly to your website for you to work with.

I don't know anything about you, your skill set or your offers, so like any other aspect of business, it requires spending time learning how to do it, which may mean (shudder) math and some common sense to be able to make sense of the numbers and apply what you learn from them.

That legal stuff out of the way, let's talk about the state of the mobile PPC market first and then get into how to do it right.

Mobile PPC in a nutshell

Firstly, some context ...

- There are 7.9 billion people on the planet, or which 6.64 billion own a smartphone, but only 4.2 billion own a toothbrush (source: Mobile Marketing Association Asia).
- It takes 26 hours for the average person to report a lost wallet. It takes 68 minutes for them to report a lost phone (source: Unisys).
- Over 52 per cent of all website traffic worldwide is generated by mobile phones (source: Statista).

What does all this mean? People value their mobile phones seemingly more than their teeth or their money. But seriously, now mobile *is* the internet and because there are that many people accessible, mobile paid traffic is a lot cheaper and plentiful than desktop traffic.

You also tend to find with mobile ad networks you have more ways to drill down and optimize your traffic than you do with desktop traffic. For example, some networks will let you filter and optimize your ad campaigns by:

- **Geo:** a specific town, city, state
- **Device:** only showing ads on a certain make or model or type of device
- **Carrier:** want to only show your ad to people on AT&T or Verizon? No problem
- **OS:** you can specify to only show ads to people running iOS, Android etc.
- **Connection:** you can limit your ads to only show to those people on a 3G or 4G/LTE connection but no Wi-Fi.

And some networks have even more ways to filter.

Like desktop traffic, not all sources generate the same quality of visitor.

There are also different types of traffic you can purchase, especially with mobile. Of course, there is Google AdWords, one of the Tier 1 networks where you can place ads to show up on certain searches and you can also advertise within mobile apps that allow ads to be shown within them.

There's YouTube, where you can have ads running before and during a video being played (and on desktop beside the ad on the page).

Then there is Facebook, which is Google's main competitor in the mobile PPC space which can show ads before and during videos, in your newsfeed and within Instagram which it also owns. For me personally, I prefer Facebook's targeting system (which we'll get into later in this chapter) and the amount of targetable data it has about users is amazing.

Then there are the smaller Tier 1 players like Yahoo and Bing PPC, which operate in a similar way to Google with much less advertising inventory, but can generate high quality conversions depending on your offer, of course.

And there are hundreds of other smaller networks, some offering the same type of traffic, others offering completely different types of traffic then the Tier 1s. For example, there are 'pop networks' where traffic is generated from a pop-under or a pop-up. A website owner signs up and places the pop-up/-under code on their website and that website is then added to the network's inventory as a place to run ads.

A business owner can target categories of websites to run ads on with each website showing a pop-up/-under with the business's ad on it. The website owner gets paid a few cents per pop-up and the business owner is charged per pop shown.

Then there are 'redirect networks'. People and companies will buy expired domain names and sell access to those domains to redirect networks who will categorize them and sell access to businesses.

 To get an idea of just how much of this redirect traffic is out there, check out a mobile network called ZeroPark and go to their 'Network Volume' page here: https://zeropark. com/volume. Play around with those settings and prepared to be amazed at how much traffic there is and how little it costs.

So how does mobile PPC marketing work? There are two main types of PPC – keyword related and demographically related.

Google

Keyword related is how Google does it in their Search Network. You bid on which keywords (search terms) your ad will show up above the organic search results and you pay $x.xx or just $.xx every time your advert is clicked.

You can find out the average cost per click (CPC) for each keyword using either the Google Keyword Planner or Google's Traffic Estimator tool (accessible only from within an AdWords account).

The price you pay is a combination of the amount of competition for the keyword and how popular your ad is. The more times your ad is clicked in your PPC campaign, Google rewards you by ever-so-slowly nudging you up the paid ad rankings.

So, if your ad was initially placed fourth and ended up getting more clicks than the third, second and first place ads, it's possible that your ad will jump the queue into first place and you'll still be paying the same amount as you were when you were in fourth place.

Once again, Google rewards relevancy with ranking, and because ads in first place generally get more clicks than lower-positioned ads (assuming it does get the clicks), you'll end up sending more traffic to your website at a lower cost than your competitors!

Google generally has a higher quality of conversion over Facebook because you're able to target those exhibiting an intent to purchase, for example if they're searching for the best type of business near them or a specific product.

Google/AdMob in-app advertising 'network'

In 2006 the AdMob network launched offering advertising within mobile apps and games and was wildly successful. Three years later, they were bought by Google and their network was integrated (assimilated?) into Google's.

You can also use banner images and even advertise using video ads within mobile apps and games as well as showing ads within the regular Google Search results but only from a mobile device.

So for example, if you have a game that you think will appeal to the Candy Crush Saga users on Android, you can bid for your ad to appear at the top of Google search results for people who have downloaded Candy Crush Saga on their Android phone.

Second, you don't bid on keywords shown up from a search; instead you bid to show your ad on pages Google deems relevant to a keyword.

You can pay CPM (Cost Per Mille, the cost per 1,000 impressions. So when Google shows your ad 1,000 times, you pay $x.xx regardless of whether your ads are clicked or not) or even CPA (Cost Per Action) so if you're advertising an app or a game you only pay if it's downloaded.

Facebook mobile ads

Facebook does both PPC and CPM but they are demographic-based which means that instead of targeting what people are searching for, you can target people per *who* they are, for instance the things they like, their occupation, their age, their sex and so on.

Although you can do this type of demographic targeting in Google, it's nowhere as detailed as it is in Facebook, because Google simply doesn't have the data which is likely why Google+ was created originally before it was shut down.

Ad volume is massive (2.19 billion available global Facebook users and growing) and the pricing is extremely good.

The one thing you need to remember about Facebook ads is that they are *interrupting* a person's usage on the platform, just the same as commercials on TV and radio. They aren't explicitly searching for information about a product or service so even with the 100% accurate customer targeting your campaigns aren't going to have as high a conversion rate as keyword-based ones like in Google.

But don't worry, once you have your campaigns dialled in they can be *extremely* profitable regardless.

Bing/Yahoo mobile ads

Bing/Yahoo ads follow similar rules to Google, and even though they have a much lower ad inventory than Google, Yahoo and Facebook in many cases can generate higher quality conversions (especially if your ideal customer is older and less tech-savvy) was OK.

If you're just starting out with mobile PPC, I suggest you focus your efforts on Facebook and Google so you can reach the most people the fastest.

Pros and cons of mobile PPC

Pros

You know that people are at least vaguely interested in what you have – they went and clicked your ad so they must be at least curious to see what is on the other side (if you wrote your ad right that is, more on this later).

You can really focus down to the very nitty-gritty for your visitors.

If you want people from North Dakota who like bubble gum and rock'n'roll, you can find them with Facebook (not quite in such detail as with Google, though you could find people that are searching for terms around rock'n'roll or bubble gum, just not both in the same campaign).

You can say with (almost) certainty that you will get traffic.

When they're on the ball, both Google and Facebook can approve an ad very quickly – I've personally had ads approved and live in less than 10 minutes before but it's normally within an hour or two.

Cons

Costs per click (CPC) are gradually rising and can be unnaturally high unless you do proper research, choose your correct keywords or demographics and point ads to a specific page on your site, not your homepage.

Both Facebook and Google are now public companies, answering to shareholders and having to go out of their way to make sure that they are profitable – and that means extracting as much money as possible from advertisers.

CPCs can range anywhere from 5 cents to $50 a click and sometimes more (it depends on the market and keywords being bid on). So you really have to do your research into every word or interest you are bidding on to make sure that you are getting the best bang for your buck. Even this can get expensive really fast.

Luckily, both Google and Facebook allow you to set daily budgets that you cannot go over, so you shouldn't have to sell a kidney or your firstborn to pay your PPC bill. But that daily limit needs to consider the number of clicks you want; clicks sending people to your website.

Killer tip

When running a PPC campaign, instead of setting a daily budget, set a lifetime budget for the same amount over a set period of days. So for example, instead of setting a daily budget of $20/day, set it for $600 for the month. This gives the ad network's systems time to figure out how best to optimize your campaigns. This trick works especially well with Facebook.

You need to keep in your mind though that you should aim to generate at least 200 visitors a day to your test URLs so you can be reasonably sure which item you're testing is the winner. Here's a great online calculator that will help to tell you whether your testing results are statistically significant: http://bit.ly/2R06PnZ.

Also, make sure that you set your budget high enough so you can get at least 200 daily visitors.

Research and tracking

Some keywords may be expensive but might end up converting less well than other cheaper keywords for you or vice-versa. So you need to do research combined with a lot of tracking. Tracking is where you see where the traffic is coming from and how well it converts (how much people do what you want them to). Compare the keywords to other keywords and narrow down exactly what you need. Both Facebook and Google have free tools that will allow you to track sales, leads or other outcomes and so on.

Mobile PPC advertising strategies

So now you have a focus, how will you set up your campaigns? First you need to watch the relevant tutorial videos provided by Google and Bing to show you the mechanics of creating campaigns and ad groups:

- http://google.com/adwords/onlineclassroom
- https://help.ads.microsoft.com/#apex/ads/en/51193/-1
  (click the Getting Started tab on Bing for even more video tutorials).

Then you can look at structuring your PPC ad campaigns on the Google and Bing search networks. The most common way is to use the 'long-tail keyword' approach by creating multiple ad groups, each revolving around a main root keyword and having similar keywords in the same group.

If we go back to the dog grooming example we used previously, and I type in the keyword 'dog grooming' into Google's Keyword Tool, I get a series of keywords all grouped together by theme like:

KIT:
- dog grooming kit
- dog grooming kits
- grooming kits for dogs
- dog grooming kits for sale
- dog grooming starter kit

TUBS:
- dog grooming tubs
- dog grooming tub
- dog grooming bath tubs
- dog wash tub
- dog grooming tubs for sale
- used dog grooming tubs
- dog bath tub
- dog grooming baths

CLIPPERS:
- dog grooming clippers
- best dog grooming clippers
- dog grooming clippers reviews
- Wahl dog grooming clippers
- clippers for dog grooming
- dog grooming clippers Australia
- best dog clippers
- dog grooming clippers for sale
- clippers dog grooming
- dog grooming clippers UK

Plus a lot more ...

Once you've selected the keywords and ad groups you want to use, you can transfer them into an existing campaign in your Google AdWords account (if you're already logged in) with a couple of mouse clicks by selecting the 'Add To Account' button.

Bing isn't quite as refined a process as Google's so what I generally do is to use the exact same keywords and ad grouping in Bing. If you use the free Google AdWords Editor and Bing Ads Editor software programs, you can easily export your Google campaigns and import them into Bing quickly and easily. Just search in Google for 'Bing Ads Editor' and 'Google AdWords Editor' to get the download links for your country.

Some quick dos and don'ts

Do

- Set a budget you can afford even if it doesn't convert at all.
- Test many different headlines and body texts of your ads and see which work out and which don't.
- Try and focus down on the exact keywords that you want to get clicks on. The more specific, the cheaper and more effective the click becomes.
- Wherever possible, point an ad to a page on your website that is directly related to your ad. Do not just send visitors to your website's homepage.
- If possible, offer something on the webpage you're sending people to in exchange for an email address or phone number. That will let you continue to follow up for free to maximize your chance at making a sale.
- Read Google and Facebook's ad policies carefully before you place a single ad so you know what you can and can't do (and the products you can't advertise) on their networks.

PPC strategies for Facebook

As mentioned before, Facebook is a different beast because there are no keywords as such to bid to show your ad for. Instead, you need to target people interested in related subjects, located in a certain geographic area, by the college or university they went to, their sex or any other combinations of demographic information.

Based upon my own experiences with Facebook PPC, here's how I recommend you structure your campaigns:

Where possible, link your ads to a post on a Facebook Page. Facebook doesn't like it when you take users directly outside of Facebook. In my tests, the costs per click of my campaigns *halved* when I sent people to a Facebook Page instead of an external URL.

If you intend to run a PPC campaign to generate Likes for your company's Facebook Page, also consider creating a Facebook Page for a celebrity or subject that has a broad appeal and is somehow related to your product or service and then running a PPC campaign to generate Likes for that page too.

For example, if you are a weight loss consultant who specializes in helping women lose weight and get fit, you might create a Facebook Page around a female celebrity who has successfully lost weight and now looks great, for instance Jennifer Hudson if you're in the USA or maybe Davina McCall if you're in the UK.

Piggy-backing on a celebrity or broad subject like 'weight loss' should make it easier to generate Likes for that page, targeting people using your criteria (local area, sex, age, etc.) and then you can send occasional 'promoted posts' to your fans with special offers on your company Facebook Page.

Something to ponder

If you have a lot of fans/Likes for your broad subject Facebook page, you might be able to sell 'promoted posts' to other companies not in direct competition with you, generating another revenue stream. Just a thought ...

Oh and BTW, would you be interested in a free resource where you can find around 20,000 examples of Facebook ads categorized by Placements, Industries, Objectives and Type? Here you go: http://bit.ly/2Odgmﬂz.

You're welcome!

Retargeting

Retargeting is a technique that few businesses know how to do, which is a shame because it is phenomenally powerful.

You as the website owner place a special code on all the pages on your website (sometimes called a retargeting pixel or tracking pixel). When someone visits any page on your website, a small text file called a cookie is placed on their computer containing various bits of anonymous information including a unique identifier.

(There's no need to worry about cookies, they're not viruses or anything like that.)

The traffic network is then able to track certain activities on your website like the webpages they view, for how long, if they place an order – things like that.

Over time and using this ever-increasing datastore, you're able to build audiences of people who have performed certain actions on your website and run ads *only to them*.

Here are a couple of examples to get you thinking just how powerful this can be:

1 What if you ran a retargeting ad only to people who visited a specific product on your site *and* abandoned your order page without buying ... and offered them a 10% discount code if they order within 24 hours?
2 What if you ran a retargeting ad only to people who bought your bronze level package within the last 7 days with an offer to get a free 1 hour consulting call worth $xxx if they upgrade to your Silver level package?
3 What if you ran a retargeting ad only to people who bought a specific item (like a formal shirt) and offered a tie and cufflinks set to go with it?

How powerful and effective do you think those types of targeted campaigns would be?

You can also use retargeting to build brand awareness to your audience, seeming like you're everywhere. For instance, if you put a retargeting pixel on your blog you can run a campaign targeting websites in a similar category so when your visitors leave and visit these websites, they'll keep seeing your ads – literally following them around. This can be on everywhere from other Google sites, on Facebook, as well as Yahoo.

As 99 per cent of those people that visit your website through social media/SEO and PPC will not buy right away, this means that those potential customers will now have a chance to come back when they are ready to buy without having to remember your website's name and URL.

Your visitors will suddenly start seeing your ads at their favourite websites and the sites they visit every day like Facebook, causing them to slowly but surely begin to trust you more and more and see you as an authority if only because they saw your ad on the *New York Times* website.

The services I use for this are:

● http://adroll.com
● http://perfectaudience.com
● http://sitescout.com

Most major traffic platforms also offer retargeting within their own platform. Facebook, Instagram and Twitter offer retargeting within themselves and Google offers a service called Remarketing (it's the same thing). All offer simple and elegant solutions and reach a *lot* of users around the world.

YouTube Ads and Facebook

YouTube is the second biggest search engine in the world and it is totally worth your time to create videos to get traffic. Now though, with their pay-per-view program, they have become even more potent.

Say you create a video but you are wondering if it converts real fast? Spend $20 and get a bunch of views to it and see! Out of those views, how many clicked through to your page? How many of those became customers?

At this point you might want to optimize it more and edit it a bit. With YouTube's average view time, you can see where people start to drop off and it might give you an idea of what to change. Or it might make sense to leave the ad up and continue to pay for views. Otherwise, if it still converts and retains your audience but not enough to make sense continuing the ads, just keep it up on YouTube and get natural views.

Either way it is a win–win–win for you by saving time and helping you improve at the same time. Once you get a few good videos converting well on YouTube, consider setting up a campaign on Facebook as well, driving dirt-cheap clicks to these. This way you can get multiple uses out of your successes.

Summary

To sum it all up, there are two major players in PPC (pay-per-click) ads: Facebook and Google (with YouTube a close third). These two are where you should do your tests first – before going anywhere else – and are the easiest to get up and running and get traffic fast. The point at the beginning is risk small, and only lose small. But see what happens and learn big from it.

Don't expect to make any sales at first. Aim to learn. With that in mind, be sure you know what you want the person on the other end to do. Do you want them to give you their email? Or some other info?

There are no hard and fast rules, only guidelines. What works for me and my niche might not work for yours.

Follow my guidelines in this chapter and you should be on the right track from the start. Then once you have started to be profitable in one PPC network (Google or Facebook), you can branch out to YouTube and/or other advertisers like Yahoo. Try to adapt what you learned from before to the new medium and scale from there.

After this consider retargeting. This is a great way to get all those misses to become hits. After all, in a good campaign, literally 95 per cent can leave and not do anything and it could be considered a success. With re-targeting you can cheaply follow up with those people and add a few more percentage points to the board over time.

Fact-check (answers at the back)

1. PPC stands for:
a) Perfectly politically correct ❑
b) Payment potentially considered ❑
c) Pay-per-click ❑
d) Panning people consolidated ❑

2. The main PPC giants are:
a) Facebook ❑
b) Google ❑
c) YouTube ❑
d) Bing ❑
e) Everybody else ❑
f) a, b, and c ❑

3. Be sure and place a daily limit based on:
a) How much you expect to make ❑
b) The size of the market ❑
c) How much you can afford to completely lose ❑

4. CPM stands for:
a) Cost per million impressions ❑
b) Clicks per month ❑
c) Cost per mille (1000) impressions ❑

5. Your home page:
a) Is a good page to use PPC to get clients ❑
b) Is a bad page to drive PPC traffic to ❑
c) May or may not work ❑

6. When you do PPC, it is good to have the focus of those clicks to be:
a) Four different options ❑
b) Three different options ❑
c) Two different options ❑
d) One measurable thing that you want them to do ❑

7. Before you start some PPC campaigns, you should know:
a) Your lifetime client value ❑
b) How much you are willing to spend ❑
c) What you want the click to do ❑
d) What you will do with the information you are going to glean ❑
e) All of the above ❑

8. In your PPC campaign always try to:
a) Make sales for your efforts ❑
b) Learn everything about your clients for your efforts ❑
c) Get at least an email address for your efforts ❑

9. Landing pages are:
a) Where the potential client 'lands' after clicking on your ad ❑
b) One-page sites that you clients want to visit ❑
c) Only for users of private planes ❑

10. Retargeting ads means:
a) Someone visiting your website will now see targeted ads on other pages. ❑
b) You will know where they live to set up your sniper nest. ❑
c) You can now find out everything about this person. ❑
d) b and c ❑

CHAPTER 26

Mobile apps for small business

It's safe to say that one of the reasons (if not the main reason) that smartphones have become so successful in recent years is because of the apps that run on them.

Without the apps, you've got a nice touchscreen phone that can play music and surf the web, which is all great and everything ... but there's nothing particularly special about that.

There were quite a few smartphones before the iPhone but the apps on them were basic, slow and not particularly fun or easy to use. Email was generally only available if your phone was connected to your company's servers and the internet was a 'baby' version.

And then in 2007 the iPhone was released which triggered a seismic shift in the entire mobile phone industry. With the iPhone, you had an operating system based on their desktop OSX, a large (then!) touchscreen that you didn't need a stylus to use, proper email that would work with any normal email system and a web browser that enabled you to surf the full web.

In other words, a true personal computer that fits in your pocket.

At the core, fully-featured, desktop-class software applications that are easier and cheaper to develop, putting them within reach of any size of business.

437

In this chapter, I'm going to go through exactly what an app is, why you might think about having an app developed, how to get one created and how you can make one yourself, whether to give it away or charge for it and how to get your target audience to download it.

What exactly is an 'app'?

An app is just a nickname for a 'program application' that is designed to perform certain functions on your phone, tablet, computer or TV (yes TVs have them now too).

They do all kinds of things. I have one that checks my blood pressure and counts my steps (I am seriously inactive, I need to work out). There's Skype so I can audio/video call and send messages to annoy my staff (they love me really). I have an app that will allow me to connect my phone to the PC in my office and control it like I was sitting in front of it from anywhere in the world with an internet connection.

I can search for houses for sale, get sports results, shop online, buy domain names, check the weather, stream millions of songs into my phone, watch TV and movies, tune my guitar, work out my taxes, learn how to draw, read a magazine, navigate from anywhere to anywhere else in the world. Get from place to place with a map app.

You can play a piano on your phone, track your investments, help you get focused (which is getting harder to do because, you know ... I have dozens of apps on my phone). Not to mention some of the weirdest apps you can imagine serving no purpose, like an app that add cats shooting laser beams out of its eyes to your own photos. I'm not kidding: https://apple.co/2R8nHbY.

And the list goes on and on. It is absolutely nuts. With 3.3 million apps in the Google Play Store (source: Statista) and 1.8 million in Apple's App Store (source Apple) it's safe to say that if you can think of it (and maybe even if you can't think of it) there is probably 'an app for that'.

Why should *I* consider creating an app?

Smartphone users are already preconditioned to download and use apps so this isn't anything they're not already doing and require 'training' for. A custom mobile app specifically designed for your business can give your customer instant access to you, your product and services and any special 'app only' offers you choose to run.

Apps can leverage the incredible marketing power of push notifications, the little message alert boxes that ding up telling you to do something. And you know what? They work like gangbusters, boosting app engagement as much as 88 per cent when used appropriately (e.g. a news site can push more notifications about current events than a retailer without it looking spammy).

 With 600 billion in-phone push notifications sent to 2 billion mobile users worldwide just on the Airship push platform in the first half of 2021 (source: https://bit.ly/3FCOBQh), maybe this is a tactic you could also consider?

WOW! I definitely need an app for my business!

Hold on there, tiger! First you need to make the business case for it.

If you're a retailer or service provider able to take orders and clients from anywhere in the country (or the world) then an app could be a good way to increase your company's visibility and begin to build a great relationship with potential customers and clients.

If you're a business targeting a local geographic area, it's a little trickier because you have much lower number of potential customers and clients so it will all depend on the profit margins you're operating with and the development cost for the app. Let's consider some examples.

Example 1

You're a cosmetic dental surgeon with an average customer value of $10,000 with approx. 40 per cent profit ($4,000).

Let's assume women aged 30+ in California are your potential target audience (at least 9 million people according to Facebook) and your app costs $5,000 to create.

You only need two new clients *ever* to come through the app for it to more than pay for itself.

Example 2

Now let's say you own a stationery store servicing downtown San Diego's 37,000 residents.

Your average order is $75 with a 30 per cent profit margin ($22.50) and your app costs the same $5,000 to build. You are going to need 222 new customers spending at least $75 to recoup your app's investment.

I've plucked figures out of thin air here, so your app may cost a lot more or less to create, depending on how complex or not it is but you see where I'm going with this. I'll share some tools and resources you can use in a while to dramatically reduce development time and costs but my advice is, do your figure work before you commit to having an app developed.

If an app looks like it's practically not feasible to be developed, don't worry – here's another approach that's almost as valuable to your customers and clients and has the advantage of being faster to get up and running. Why not go through Apple's and Google's app stores and see if there are *related* apps on there already you could recommend to make your clients'/customers' lives better? For example if you're an accountant, find the best tax calculator or accounting app. If you're a personal trainer, find an exercise app that's good and offer a meal plan, nutrition tips or advice for perfect form.

You get the drift ...

You could:

- Write a blogpost with screenshots
- Format the blogpost as a PDF report instead and give it away in exchange for their email address
- Record a tutorial video showing how to use it.

Then either write a post about it linking to your website on Facebook and run ads to it or if you have a customer email list you can contact them directly and send them a link to the information.

I've decided to have an app created – what's next?

First you need to figure out what your app is going to do and how much you're going to spend on it (see the examples above), the first having a direct effect on the latter.

Whatever you decide it needs to be genuinely useful *and* act as a direct marketing tool to generate revenue for your business. It should offer an easy way for customers to get in touch with you and shouldn't contain any extra frippery. You don't need to give your app a flashlight or a compass unless you're a survival training consultant. For instance, if you're a dog groomer, how about a simple appointment setting and reminder app that would automatically schedule customers to come by every x weeks or whatever frequency the user would set? Maybe there could be a 'Pooch Panic Button' for when Trixie runs off through a muddy puddle and needs a top-to-tail emergency grooming?

Another use could be for a rewards programme for your business? Every time a customer spends a certain amount, they earn a 'stamp' on their digital card. Once they have collected a certain number of stamps you can offer a free extra 'something' or a percentage off any order over a certain amount. This is a great idea, because it gives the customer a reason to keep the app on their phone (i.e. it saves them money). Which brings me to the second point ...

They need to be customized to the customer.

If you have a business that has a lot of options or is a more 'on demand' type business, then you might consider an app.

For instance, let's say you are a plant hire company (the big machinery type of plant, not the floral kind) and most of your customers are construction firms. What would be genuinely useful to a construction site manager?

In large-scale construction, the harsh reality is that time really is money for a CSM, especially if they're operating on a hard deadline with a hard budget. What about developing an app that interfaces with your stock control system showing the availability and pricing of all your various equipment? A site manager could then hire whatever machinery they need for however long they need it *on their phone* standing in the middle of a building site without having to waste time trying to get someone on the phone to find out what's available.

Or maybe you're a vehicle recovery company and you want a super-simple app your customers could use to alert you that they need your help. Your app could be as simple as hitting a big-red virtual 'Panic Button' that hooks into Google/Apple Maps and texts the person's GPS co-ordinates along with their name, phone number, vehicle make/model and registration (pre-entered by the phone owner in the app's Settings section) to a dedicated phone number.

If this type of app would be great for your company but works out to be a little pricey, why not see if similar companies in other locations around the country who aren't in direct competition with you would be interested in splitting the development cost?

The app would simply contact the nearest recovery company when the button was pressed. Or you could always have the app created and then license it to similar companies in different areas and turn the app into a new revenue stream for your business? Have a think about the ways you could share the costs and the benefits with others.

Other uses for apps

An incident happened the other day that is the perfect example of how apps can be used in business. At an upscale clothing store my wife wanted to try something on, but we couldn't find her size. We showed it to the lady there and she whipped out her mobile phone and scanned the barcode and told us they had her size and to give her a few moments so she could get it.

How awesome is that?

Instead of having to spend thousands for *each* store for barcoding equipment that only has one use, they only had to pay once to come up with an app that does that and the staff just need to download an app to their phone.

Maybe this could also be an option for you and your business? Could you possibly come up with an app that would help your employees do their job faster, easier or better? Maybe they work in a factory and need to be reminded to do certain things on time. Maybe you could get an app made that reminds them exactly what to do and when to do it.

Ask your employees what they have the most problem with during the working day that might be solved with an app? They might have ideas that you never dreamed about.

How much does it cost?

This might be the defining factor for you that determines whether you develop an app or not. You will need to consider the following factors:

- **Obvious:** The more complex the functionality, the longer it will take to create and therefore the more it will cost.
- **Not-so-obvious:** *How* it is coded will affect the cost.

There are three general types of apps: native, hybrid and web.

Native apps

These are apps that have been coded using the specific programming tools for the operating system, will have direct access to all the various functionality and systems that the phone will allow and because of their specific programming (all things being equal) native apps will run faster than other types of apps.

Native apps coded for Apple's iOS will not work on the Android operating system and vice versa.

Hybrid apps

These are apps that have been written in such a way to perform as closely as possible to a native app but that can be run on the major mobile operating systems. This is generally referred to as WORA (Write Once, Run Anywhere).

WORA development systems are getting more and more sophisticated every year and their functionalities are getting larger and larger as other programmers donate modules they've created to perform specific tasks back to the relevant communities – making each generation of hybrid apps easier and quicker (and therefore cheaper!) to develop.

Popular WORA development systems are: React Native, Ionic, PhoneGap, Xamarin and Titanium.

Web apps

Web apps are exactly what they sound like – in essence mobile websites wrapped in a native programming 'shell' to make them appear more like an app on the phone.

However, the difference and distance between web apps and hybrid apps is decreasing thanks to the improvements to HTML webpage markup and Javascript.

The latest HTML standard for webpages, HTML5, is able to do a lot of very clever and powerful things that only a few years ago would be impossible with the HTML available at the time. When HTML5 is paired with Javascript frameworks like Angular. js (used by Google), React.js (used by Facebook and Instagram), Meteor.js and others you end up with incredibly powerful, incredibly fast web-based applications that are quick to create.

If your app idea is a simple one, it's possible that a web-based app could be enough to do the job.

Creating the app

It goes without saying that as a business owner, unless you have a serious geek itch that needs scratching you should absolutely get someone else to create the app.

If you're not into hiring and firing and all that and you just want to talk with someone and they handle all of that, I would check out here for ideas on price: https://www.otreva.com/calculator/.

As you will note it is quite a bit different between the two prices. Don't take this as the final word though. Shop around; you may find someone else willing to do your idea within your budget.

If your app idea is quite simple, there are marketplaces where you can buy pre-built apps that can be quickly and easily customized for your business.

Here's a great article showing nine places where you can buy pre-built app code: http://bit.ly/2R4jQg9.

If you see an app there that doesn't quite do what you want, send a message to the developer to see what they can do.

To reduce the costs even more, you can hire programmers outside of your country. Programmers in the old Eastern Bloc countries, the Philippines, India and Pakistan are a lot cheaper than those in the West and just as capable.

When you write your app's project description, you need to go into as much detail as possible, being as specific as you can be when describing how each part of it should work. The best place to find examples of plain English project specification documents is on the freelancing websites I mentioned earlier.

Once you've printed out a few and looked at them it becomes easy to figure out the sort of information that a developer is going to require.

If you don't know the answer to something like 'What programming language do you want the app coded in?' tell them straight that you don't know, what do they recommend and most importantly WHY!

If they say '… because that's the coding language I work in!' that's not a good enough reason. Regardless of the answers they give, probe them … ask them why this way and not that.

Doing this will save you a lot of time and money from hiring the wrong person for the job and help to eliminate confusion between you and the programmer who ends up building your app.

If your time is valuable, you can of course also hire someone to find and hire the right programmer for the task. You can also find these people on the freelancer websites. If you have the budget, you can also hire a project manager for a fixed amount of time to make sure everything runs smoothly and just to keep you up to date with a daily email or 15-minute chat going over progress. There are plenty of project managers who've dealt with mobile app creation on the freelancer websites.

Getting your app in Apple's App Store and Google's Play Store

Even if you aren't creating an app to give away or sell to the whole world, your best chance of getting it into the hands of your customers and clients is to make it available to download from the official Apple App Store and Google Play Store. This is because:

- Apple and Google review every app that's submitted for any potential behaviour that could be deemed 'unsavoury' and a potential security risk.
- Both Apple and Google require ID and other types of documentation proof just to set up a developer account so there's always a way to track down the creator of a malicious app.
- Just making it available to download from your own website will require you to spend a lot of money upgrading the

security of your servers to minimize the ability of hackers somehow getting in and compromising your app and then getting hold of your customers' and clients' personal information.

Therefore, if you can direct people to search for your app's name on the App Store or Google Play Store, or give them a direct download link to it, it reassures them that your app is legit and will save you a ton of headaches trying to do it yourself.

Rather than write out everything you need to know, here are a couple of videos walking you through the process.

- https://developer.apple.com/programs/enroll/ ⟵= Apple's Developer Program
- https://developer.android.com/distribute/ ⟵= Google's Android Developer Program

Promoting your app

In my opinion, this is the easiest bit, but your approach should be different for existing and new customers:

Existing customers

This can be as simple as setting up a page on your website that links where visitors can download your app from Apple's App Store and/or the Google Play Store. Something like:

http://www.yourdomain.com/downloadapp

And then just remember to include that URL on your marketing material and on your website.

New potential customers

You could simply run ads on Facebook and Twitter to your target audience announcing your app. Just spend a few bucks a day and let the campaign roll for a month or two. Google gives you a couple of great ways to promote your app.

- First, run an AdWords campaign to show up at the top of a relevant mobile Google search (http://bit.ly/2R9WMwk).
- You can use Google's Display Network to drive installs of your app by advertising directly to users of another app (http://bit.ly/2R48lp8).
- Since a lot of people spend a lot of time on YouTube, you could run 'In-Stream' (sometimes known as 'Pre-Roll') ads on YouTube targeting videos that are about similar apps or topics source: http://bit.ly/2RbPY1C.

By being ultra-specific about your targeting (either by location, by topic or both) you can get the exact people you want to download your app without spending a fortune on ads.

Summary

Apps are cool and are all over the place. People download them like crazy and they are a great tool for talking directly with your customers.

But ...

Don't just jump into apps because they are the latest thing. You can do plenty to target mobile users without apps. Do your research before committing time and money to making a full app.

But if it makes sense for you to get one made, don't hesitate too much to get it done. Your competition might already be working on one, or worse have one done already. If they have, download them all and 'pick them apart'. What's good? What isn't? How can they be improved? Note all your ideas down and then implement them into your app.

When you develop it, be sure you take stock of all options and refuse to be overcharged. There are websites that will gladly take $10,000 and give you a 'web app' that cost them a few hundred to make.

Learn the lingo in this chapter for the different programming languages and you will already be a step beyond everyone else. Then if you don't just want to pay a company to do it, you can hire a coder (on any of the sites I mentioned). If you do, spend time reading through previous project submissions to see if there are projects of a similar complexity to get a sense of how much yours could cost.

Once your labour of love is created, promote it to your target audience and, at the very least, to your existing clients and contacts. (This might also be a good time to break out those PPC skills you learned yesterday.)

Fact-check (answers at the back)

1. An app is:
   a) Three-fifths of an apple ❏
   b) An application run
      on a laptop ❏
   c) An application run on a
      smartphone ❏
   d) A technical term for a jump
      shot ❏

2. Why should you consider
   getting an app made?
   a) 90 per cent of time on a
      mobile phone is spent
      within apps ❏
   b) Retailers can generate
      conversions 3x higher
      from an app than a
      mobile website ❏
   c) Both of the above ❏

3. Every company in every
   situation should get an app.
   a) True ❏
   b) False ❏

4. Which of these can an app do?
   a) Take your blood pressure ❏
   b) Count your steps ❏
   c) Do a 3D analysis of
      your home and tell your
      square footage. ❏
   d) Make your phone a
      flashlight ❏
   e) Teach a foreign language ❏
   f) Get someone to wash
      your dog ❏
   g) All of the above and more ❏

5. What should your app do?
   a) One thing well ❏
   b) Five things OK ❏
   c) 27 things terribly ❏

6. There are three kinds of apps:
   a) Native, hybrid, web ❏
   b) Webby, new, old ❏
   c) Web 2.0, domain, social ❏
   d) Darla, Marc, and Rheta ❏

7. The best way to get an app
   made is always to use an app
   developing company.
   a) True ❏
   b) False ❏

8. Some the alternative ways to
   get an app made are:
   a) UpWork.com ❏
   b) eLance.com ❏
   c) EasyOutsource.com ❏
   d) Guru.com ❏
   e) Do it 100% yourself ❏
   f) All of the above ❏

9. You should always get your
   app put into the app stores of
   Google/Apple.
   a) True ❏
   b) False ❏

10. The easiest part of developing
    an app is:
    a) Promoting it ❏
    b) Creating it ❏
    c) Developing it ❏
    d) Designing the look and feel ❏

CHAPTER 27

SMS direct marketing

We as consumers are being bombarded by marketing messages all day, every day. Depending on who you believe, we're exposed to anything between 500 and 5,000 marketing messages and of those 99 per cent have zero impact on us, which makes sense as we just don't have the time or energy to fully process that much information every day.

Our brain ends up 'subconsciously skipping' – it knows we're not really interested and for marketers and business owners, that's wasted time, effort and money trying to get a prospect's or customer's attention.

However for the savvy marketer (which you most certainly are, since you're reading this masterclass) correctly using SMS as part of your online marketing mix could be the Holy Grail for breaking through all the 'noise'. More so than anything else we've discussed previously: more than Facebook, Twitter, Google AdWords, even (in my opinion) email.

So in this chapter, I'm going to cover: what SMS is (in case you've never touched a mobile phone before), why it's imperative you add it as a marketing channel NOW, how to get people to willingly give you their mobile phone number, examples of ideas that work great, the technical bits and bobs you need in place, the legal elements you *must* have in place so you don't fall foul of the authorities and how to automate SMS marketing without spamming.

What is SMS marketing?

SMS (Short Messaging Service) is the proper name for 'text messaging' on a mobile phone and so SMS *marketing* is the practice of collecting your customers' mobile phone numbers to enable you to contact them to inform and educate them on your products, services and offers, just like you would with their email, fax or postal address back in the day.

So how does it work? There are a few ways business owners and marketers do it but the most popular is to set up a shortcode; a special five- or six-digit number to which a lead, prospect or customer can send a text message and receive an automated response back and the business owner can automatically capture the phone number to use in future communications.

You can buy a shortcode exclusively for your business (expensive) or you can buy keywords in an existing shortcode.

Shortcodes

Shortcodes are country-specific so, depending on where you're located and where your customers or clients are, may require some planning on your side of things as to whether you'll need just a single shortcode or a shortcode for each country.

Search for terms like:

- 'SMS shortcode providers [country]'
- 'shared SMS shortcode [country]'
- 'dedicated SMS shortcode [country]'

... to give you an idea of your options.

Once you have a customer's mobile phone number in a database you can repeatedly offer deals and special offers to them, continually driving them back to your business, increasing your sales and profits for very little additional expense.

Adding SMS marketing to the online marketing mix

Since you're reading this masterclass you obviously understand that people are more mobile than ever before and it's getting more and more difficult to reach them via traditional means, let alone getting your message to break through the hundreds (if not thousands) of marketing messages the average person sees every day.

In 2016 62.9% of the world's population owned at least one mobile phone, forecasted to rise to 67% by 2019 and pass 5 billion people globally by 2020 (source: http://bit.ly/2ysZvFT). We're rapidly reaching a point where there will be hardly anyone on the planet who doesn't own a mobile phone and every single one of them can receive SMS messages, completely bypassing the marketing 'noise' around them.

In addition, SMS/text messaging has far better engagement than its older cousin, email.

- Email open rates (avg.): 22%
- SMS open rates (avg.): **98%**

- Email clickthrough rate (avg.): 7%
- SMS clickthrough rate (avg.): **14%**

- Email sales conversion rate (avg.): 2%
- SMS sales conversion rate (avg.): **8%**

- Email time delay to open (avg.): 384 minutes
- SMS time delay to open (avg.): **3 minutes**

> **TIP** *I'm not advocating buying in lists of mobile numbers and spam-dialling them. That is most certainly not SMS marketing. You are going to build lists of people's phone numbers who have specifically requested to receive information from you.*

Later in this chapter we'll be discussing the legal requirements you need to observe so you don't run into the various government regulators who like nothing more than levying fines on unknowing business owners.

And finally, because there is a (albeit small) cost to send a text message, hardcore spammers tend to avoid it as it gets very expensive for them at scale. For instance, I can purchase an account at a bulk mailing service that allows me to send up to 2.5 million emails for $800 a month.

SMS message credits from bulk providers can cost anywhere between 1.5–5 cents per message so for 2.5 million mobile phone numbers it will cost anywhere between $37,500 and $125,000 to spam everyone in the database!

So you can see, it's a lot easier for spammers to generate profits from spending $800 than it is having to spend $125,000 – meaning on the whole, the signal-to-noise ratio for SMS marketing is very good since there isn't a ton of spam being received by users, increasing the chance of your message being seen and engaged with.

SMS list-building strategies

There are plenty of ways to ethically persuade users into giving you their mobile phone number. Here are a few:

Discount coupon

For example, if you were offering a 20 per cent discount coupon code you could say: 'Text GUIDE to 12345 to get 20% off your next order. Just show the unique discount code on your phone to the cashier and your 20% discount will be applied immediately!'

Or for service providers, 'Text AUDIT to 12345 to receive a free social media audit (worth $795) but only for the first 20 businesses so hurry!'

You can post signs promoting the offer around your shop, on your website, in your voicemail holding message; retailers, program your till to add it to every receipt.

Appointment reminders

This can either be a one-off reminder or a short series of texts, depending on how far out the customer is from the date. If they're a couple of weeks out you could have series of reminders as follows:

Immediate

'Hi [NAME], this is to confirm your appointment with [PERSON] is scheduled for [TIME] on [DATE]. Call [PHONE] if you need to cancel or reschedule.'

One week out

'Hi [NAME], just a reminder that in one week today, on [DATE] you have an appointment with [PERSON] at [TIME]. Call [PHONE] if you need to cancel or reschedule.'

Day before

'Hi [NAME], just a reminder that tomorrow, [DATE] your appointment with [PERSON] is at [TIME]. Call [PHONE] if you need to cancel or reschedule.'

The day (OPTIONAL)

'Hi [NAME], just letting you know that your appointment today with [PERSON] at [TIME] is still on. Call us on [PHONE] if you need to change the day or cancel. (No more reminders!)'

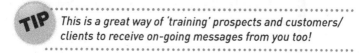

TIP *This is a great way of 'training' prospects and customers/clients to receive on-going messages from you too!*

If you run regular online training/webinar events and your service doesn't support SMS reminders as part of their service, like GotoMeeting or WebinarJam, you could do it yourself. 'Text TRAINING5 to 12345 and I'll send you reminders on the day of the training/webinar so you don't miss it!'

Morning reminder

'Hi, this is Nick. Don't forget the Social Media Success online training starts at 3pm EST this afternoon. See you then!'

Final reminder

'Hi [NAME] The Social Media Success online training starts in 15 mins. Grab a coffee and I'll see you in a bit! P.S. Listen out for the surprise ;-)'

Contests and competitions

Everyone loves the chance to win something so why not organize a 'Text to enter' competition? The prize can be anything but try to make it relevant to your business and have a decent perceived value – something that your audience would genuinely love to win. If you're a retailer, you could offer a prize of $xxx to spend at your store. It will only cost you wholesale for the prizes and you're turning over stock.

Competition tips

TIP 1: Offer all entrants who don't win a one-time percentage discount coupon to drive people back to you and offset your prize costs.

TIP 2: Partner with non-directly-competing businesses and run a super-contest where the winner gets $xxx in store credit from each store? The prize could easily run into $ thousands. Tell each store owner to give a percentage discount coupon away to all non-winners to drive people back to their stores.

TIP 3: For the more entrepreneurial contest organizer, since you now have a list of mobile phone numbers in your system, you could:

● Offer the businesses the ability to market further special offers for a monthly fee + SMS costs. This idea works particularly well with businesses servicing a specific geographic area.

● Leverage the success of the first content and find more businesses to participate in another super-contest (offering further marketing afterwards for a reasonable monthly fee). Rinse, repeat.

Monthly newsletter

Publish a very simple monthly newsletter on a webpage on your website and send a link to the page every week/fortnight/month via text message.

Put some useful and interesting info (tips, tricks, money saving offers etc.) on there so people will want to receive the text message.

TIP *Put any contest details and legal info on the newsletter page. That will get people to click through to it.*

Billing problems

You wouldn't strictly use an SMS list for this purpose, but it could allow you to potentially recapture lost revenue should a customer's credit or debit card fail to be billed, especially for service providers. Again this could be a series of text messages like:

Immediate

'Hi [NAME]. For some reason, we couldn't process your last payment for [ITEM/SERVICE]. There may be an issue with your payment method. Could you double check and let us know either at support@domain.com or call Accounting on [NUMBER] Thanks!'

Second reminder

'We've tried to process your billing for [ITEM/SERVICE] and it has failed again. Could you check or change your payment method so we can try once more? Help at support@domain.com or [PHONE]'

Final reminder

'Sorry. Your payment method has failed a third time and we've had to cancel [SERVICE]/pause your order. Contact the office on [PHONE] if you need any help.'

Customer surveys

This kills two birds with one stone. It gives you an excuse to capture a customer's mobile phone number but can also give you valuable feedback to improve how your business operates.

Offer a discount or an entry into a prize draw to win something as the 'carrot' for doing the survey and it's all good.

You can either use a service to handle the entire survey through text messages, or just capture the phone number and send a message with a link to a web-based survey that is mobile-responsive (automatically formats to fit a mobile phone's smaller screen).

Immediate
'Thanks for your custom today. Would you be willing to take a short survey to improve our service? We'll give you a 20% discount coupon for helping. Text SURVEY to 12345 to begin.'

Example message 1
'How satisfied were you with the service you received today? Reply with the appropriate number.'
1 – Very satisfied
2 – Somewhat satisfied
3 – Neutral
4 – Dissatisfied
5 – Very dissatisfied

Here's a great list of 30 SMS advertising examples: http://bit.ly/2ythjkt

And here are 42 SMS marketing templates to jumpstart your own messages: http://bit.ly/2yvnDHQ

Automated SMS marketing solutions

Trying to remain in constant contact with all your leads, prospects, customers and clients regardless of where they are in your sales 'pipeline' becomes an almost impossible task, especially when it's *you* servicing your customers and clients.

You don't want to have to think about hiring a full-time 'customer liaison' to do nothing but this but you don't see any other way.

One of the great things about mobile marketing in general and SMS marketing specifically is now technology has matured to the point where it's easy and cost effective to set up an automated SMS marketing system without having to sell your firstborn.

There are solutions now for every business size and budget: from the 'one man band' to a global multi-national corporation.

SMS delivery gateways

Regardless of what system you choose, you'll also need an account with an SMS Delivery Gateway. Normally when you send a text message from your phone, you connect with your mobile network and the message is sent directly via them to the recipient's phone. When you're using a third-party software or service, you're generally not able to directly connect to a mobile network since they're not being operated from a mobile phone with a mobile number. So, we need to link our software or service account to an SMS gateway which will route our text messages via their system and onto the mobile networks and eventually to the recipient's phone.

Depending on which country you're in and which countries you need to send SMS to will depend on the gateways you can choose from and the cost of each message – with International SMS being generally more expensive than domestic. Some gateways will allow you to buy SMS in bulk ahead of time to ensure you get the lowest cost possible.

I'd advise searching for terms like:

● 'bulk sms [your country]'
● 'bulk sms pricing [your country]'
● 'sms gateway [your country]'

Automated systems

There are various types of SMS automation systems out there. Some just do one job and many can handle multiple types of automation tasks. I've listed a few below to give you an idea of costing and functionality but there are many, many more out there.

As ever, spend a little time doing your due diligence before signing up to any service or buying any software. Speak to the companies to make sure there are no compatibility issues with the service or software working in your country.

If you need any help with this, feel free to email me on: nick@traxxon.co.uk and I'll try to steer you in the right direction.

Autoresponder systems

These allow you to schedule sequences of text messages ahead of time, configure delays between each automated message, group users into lists and assign sequences to them and more.

I've used http://textdeliver.com before and can recommend them and I've heard http://txt180.com is a good service as well but again, do your research first.

SMS marketing legalities

Each country has its own rules and regulations regarding how text messages can be used in a commercial setting and so before you do any SMS marketing you should research your country's specific legal requirements. Using a little common sense should mean you keep on the right side of the law, but it's best to know exactly what you can and can't do.

If you're intending to send commercial text messages across borders into different countries, it's also worth an email or a quick phone call to your regulatory body to clarify which country's law takes precedence. Is it the country your business is registered in, the location of the SMS service/server sending the texts, the location of the recipient or something else?

As an example of legal compliance, in the USA there is the Telephone Consumer Protection Act and there is also the CTIA, a non-profit body representing the wireless communications industry. To remain TCPA and CTIA compliant includes:

- storing each subscriber's data for a minimum of four years and that includes their phone number, IP address and any opt-in capture page URL)
- including your business name upon signup
- including the phrase 'Msg & Data Rates May Apply' upon signup
- appending T&C/Privacy Policy upon signup
- appending 'Opt-out' to each message (in bold)
- providing an 'Opt-out' confirmation message
- sending only between 8am and 9pm (relating to subscribers timezone)
- maintaining a DNC (Do Not Call/Do Not Message) list.

All common sense but nonetheless quite a bit to make sure you've taken into account.

Summary

SMS marketing is pretty cool isn't it?

Of all the techniques I have mentioned so far, this is the only truly 'mobile' exclusive technique. If only for that reason this is one you must try if you are serious about reaching the mobile generation.

It really is a great way to break through the 'noise', as it were, since people are always (at least now) checking their SMS messages nearly constantly.

Investigate setting up either a dedicated or accessing a shared 'shortcode' number so you can have 'calls-to-action' like 'Text report to 12345'.

The ways to get numbers into your database is varied and limited only to your imagination. My personal favourite is the sweepstakes method, where you get them to enter based on what they can win. Make sure what they want to win is relevant to you as a business. If you give away an iPad, everyone and their uncle will be knocking at your door.

There are also many uses for SMS. For instance, you can remind someone of a meeting they made with you, or follow up with someone whose credit card was declined. This has great uses for getting webinar traffic, or getting people to your app (if you decided to build one yesterday). Anything that your customer *has* to know. It can also be used to run surveys and other direct methods.

We also looked at a bunch of technical things in this chapter, such as SMS gateways. We touched on legalities regarding SMS marketing too, lest you fall foul of the law.

Fact-check (answers at the back)

1. SMS stands for:
a) Save My Soul ❏
b) Short Messaging System ❏
c) Send Money Soon ❏
d) Sound Mantis Sting ❏

2. SMS gets opened:
a) 98 per cent of the time ❏
b) 50 per cent of the time ❏
c) 60 per cent of the time ❏
d) Never ❏

3. You need a shortcode provided in your country to get started on SMS marketing.
a) True ❏
b) False ❏

4. The best way to get numbers is to get a massive list and bulk dial them.
a) True (I like priso ❏
b) False ❏

5. The way to get phone numbers the right way is:
a) Surveys ❏
b) % off promotions ❏
c) Contests ❏
d) All of the above ❏

6. A good idea for keeping in touch with potential clients using this technology is:
a) When you have a meeting with them. ❏
b) Their credit card was declined ❏
c) When you have a new contest running. ❏
d) When you have great promotions going on at your store. ❏
e) All of the above ❏

7. Running a survey via SMS is quick and easy
a) True ❏
b) False ❏

8. Getting an account with an 'SMS delivery service' is optional.
a) True ❏
b) False ❏

9. SMS marketing is completely unregulated and no one will ever get on you if you just start spamming people.
a) True ❏
b) False ❏

10. Automated survey and responses to queries is totally available with the tools I provided.
a) True ❏
b) False ❏

CHAPTER 28

The future of mobile marketing

A combination of ever-more powerful smartphones, costing less and less every year, connected to the internet by ever-increasing data speeds is fuelling a fundamental change in how we humans gather information and data for personal and commercial use.

Countries and locations where traditionally it wasn't cost-effective to supply phones and internet services could be helped by projects like Facebook's high-altitude solar powered 'Aquila' drone or their mesh network project to deliver high speed internet access on the ground without the need to build expensive infrastructure.

But as you and I know, time, tide and technology don't stand still and in this chapter I'd like to go over some of the newer mobile marketing concepts and ideas that are being discussed and in a few cases are already here, albeit in a very basic form.

I've picked the topics I believe to be the most important for you to begin investigating and implementing within your business or company over the coming weeks and months.

If during your research you can't find examples from others in your industry look to see what businesses in other markets have done with technologies and topics that could be tweaked for your own. Start thinking and strategizing your approaches now so you're ahead of your competitors ...

Mobile SEO (search engine optimization)

What is it?

Well, since we've already dedicated a whole section to it you should already know that it's the way of optimizing pages on your website to show in the Top 10 (and ideally the Top 3) results for a specific search term done on a mobile phone using Google's search engine.

Why is it important?

As I mentioned before, mobile *is* the internet now and with that comes changes to the ways that Google displays the results and which types of results to prioritize.

Since 2016 there have been several major updates to Google to follow their major 'Mobilegeddon' update in 2015, all of which are designed to further refine Google's index for mobile devices.

Possum V1.0: An update that altered how Google displays businesses sharing a single location, as in serviced offices. There was also a ranking boost to businesses who were physically located just outside their operating town or city to enable them to begin to be seen in Google's 3-Pack results for a given area.

This is important since a 46% of all Google searches are local (i.e. 'emergency plumber Hoboken New Jersey') and of those 60% are people searching for local businesses using mobile search (source: http://bit.ly/2Oh8BAw).

In May 2016 Google gave a boost to websites that are 'mobile-friendly' and launched AMP (more details below) to deliver content quicker to users on mobile devices.

NOTE: Facebook also deployed their version of 'AMP' called Instant Articles which I'll also cover below.

And in direct response to the rise of mobile internet usage and mobile search as a whole, Google has begun to roll out its mobile-first primary index. This means regardless of what device you're using to perform a search – phone, tablet, or desktop – it will pull the results from the index gathered by its mobile-focused content spiders and ranked by its mobile-focused algorithm, rather than its 'traditional' desktop-focused database.

Because of this fundamental change to arguably the most powerful website on the internet, as I've mentioned previously it's essential your website is at best mobile-first or at least mobile-friendly to ensure it's still shown in search results.

Google realizes non-desktop internet usage is only going to increase and are focusing all their efforts into the various ways it's going to be used and you should too.

Voice search

What is it?
It pretty much is what it sounds like: it enables you to perform searches on Google, Bing etc. just using your voice and your chosen device (mobile phone, Google Home, Amazon Alexa etc.) using natural language queries.

Why is it important?
After reading everything else in this Part it will probably come as no surprise to you that voice searching in Google (whether using Google Assistant, Siri, Bixby or some other 'Intelligent Assistant') has dramatically increased.

- 58 per cent of consumers use voice search to find a local business online.
- An estimated 163 million smart speakers were sold during 2021.
- 122.7 million Americans will be using voice search in 2021.
- Two-thirds of Google Home and Amazon Alexa owners can't imagine living without a smart speaker.
- Voice-based shopping will soar to $40 billion by the end of 2022.

(Source: https://bit.ly/3MmfGte)

The search engines are starting to see a dramatic increase in longer, more complex queries with a more natural language structure and this is only going to increase as services and tools become much smarter in interacting with us.

Search queries are going to be less 'keyword' dependent and instead be more contextual. Google have said openly that:

'The destiny of [Google's search engine] is to become that Star Trek computer, and that's what we are building.'

Right now, you can do somewhat complex keyword-less searches on Google like: 'Which team won the Superbowl when was Richard Nixon President of the United States?'

Or

'Hey Google/Siri/Alexa/Cortana ... what's showing at the cinema tonight?'

'Here are some films showing near you. What are you in the mood for?'

'[FILM TITLE]'

'OK. Here are the times and locations nearby. Tap one and we can organize purchasing the tickets!'

With a little more technological progress it won't be long before you'll be able to search and make purchases just using your voice.

AMP (Google) and Instant Articles (Facebook)

What are they?

AMP (Accelerated Mobile Pages) is an open source project designed by Google and Twitter partnering with some of the largest content publishers online to formulate a web standard for mobile-optimized webpages that are created *once* and load instantly everywhere.

Facebook's Instant Articles project is a similar initiative to show content as quickly as possible for mobile devices via Facebook but still have a visually rich display with high quality images and company branding and logos.

Think of them both as a stripped down, super-fast version of a regular page without a lot of bloated 'bells and whistles' code that can slow down the time it takes to render on a mobile device.

Both AMP and IA pages can also be cached by Google and Facebook respectively to their servers located around the world to ensure that the nearest server to a user will retrieve and display the content in question as quickly as possible.

Why are they important?

In a nutshell: bounce rate and page load time.

In layman's terms, bounce rate is described as the percentage of visitors to a page on your site who leave the site without loading another webpage or interacting with the site (like clicking a link).

Bounce rate is a major factor of Google's 'dwell time' calculations, 'dwell time' being the actual amount of time a user spends on a webpage before leaving it.

Google loves speed, so if a mobile user visits a page on a website that hasn't finished loading after 30 seconds (for example) then hits the 'Back' button on their browser, Google makes a note of that to say that page isn't mobile friendly and gives the site a 'black mark' against them. Too many black marks and that URL will either be penalized or Google will happily promote other more mobile-friendly websites above them, effectively pushing non-compliant sites down the rankings.

And it's the same principle for relevance: if a user visits a result from a specific topic and it's either not relevant or doesn't provide enough information, they'll leave the page quickly and Google makes a note that URL may not be relevant. Too many black marks and ... you know the rest.

In going forward with mobile marketing, AMP and Instant Articles, it is incredibly important that you maximize your page loading and dwell times because if Google is paying attention to this you can bet your bottom dollar Facebook is – and these factors will have an impact on their 'EdgeRank' algorithm as to whether your content will be seen more in people's Newsfeeds or not.

TIP *If you use Google Analytics, it's easy to specify the actual amount of time it takes to register a user as 'bouncing' from your site to minimize any false positives. Find an explanation and tutorial here: http://bit.ly/2R6yCD4.*

Live streaming

What is it?

Live streaming is the ability to broadcast a live audio and/or video feed directly from your phone, tablet or desktop that the rest of the world can listen to or watch.

Why is it important?

Whilst live streaming has been around for quite a while, it required a little bit of techie knowledge to get up and running and it was only for streaming from a games console or desktop computer.

However, in 2015 a small company called Life On Air Inc. released an app called Meerkat that allowed anyone to livestream directly from their mobile phone just by clicking a button.

Thanks to its exposure at the South By Southwest festival in March 2015 and its ease of use, the app's popularity exploded and a slew of competitors suddenly appeared including Blab and Periscope. Within a few months:

- Periscope was bought by Twitter for $100 million
- Twitter shut off Meerkat's access to their social graph killing the app
- Blab also died due to ever mounting costs of running livestreaming servers without large amounts of venture capital
- YouTube and Facebook launched their own livestreaming functionalities.

Right now, livestreaming is in its infancy as a marketing platform but is maturing rapidly enabling companies to build ongoing relationships with prospects, customer and clients by educating and informing them in an entertaining way.

The key here is 'building ongoing relationships' with consumers. After the outcry over the spreading of so-called 'fake news' across Facebook, Mark Zuckerberg (Facebook's founder) shared that Facebook are implementing one of the largest changes to the news feed to prioritize content from friends over content from brands and businesses.

In case you didn't read his post, here's the direct link to it: http://bit.ly/2Odk3Nk (Facebook account required).

This means you can't just use Facebook as a passive broadcasting network, throwing up videos that get mass distribution. You need to provide genuine value to your audience and engage in conversation with them to ensure your video is seen and spread to as many of your target audience as possible.

The advantage of live video over pre-recorded content is it almost always generates conversation without trying – it's just the nature of the beast. People like feeling 'significant' in the eyes of others and so asking questions being mentioned in a live broadcast is an easy way for them to get that – which is great for you as you get engaging and interesting content for your broadcast.

The other benefit to livestreaming is, it's comparatively simple to do. There's no need for huge amounts of technical infrastructure. Just your phone and hitting the 'Live' button on your app.

For maximum reach you can stream on Facebook, YouTube, Instagram and Twitter all at the same time, just by setting up four smartphones with one of the apps on each and starting streaming at the same time.

If you intend to multi-stream using your home or office Wi-Fi connection, make sure your internet connection has a fast-enough upload speed to handle that many simultaneous live streams. Here's a chart that gives you a guideline to the sort of upload speeds you'll need according the quality output you want. http://bit.ly/2OgtHi9.

If you intend to livestream using a phone's dataplan, it's worth doing a test stream for a few minutes and then checking your data allowance to get an idea of how long your livestreams will be over what timespan to make sure you don't go over your data cap.

There are online services that will syndicate your single livestream feed to other platforms at the same time but I don't have any experience using them so I can't testify as to how reliable they are:

- http://restream.io (free to 30+ destinations) with paid monthly upgrades)
- http://switchboard.live (paid monthly with additional plan upgrades) are two such services.

Restream does not natively support syndicating a livestream to Facebook for free but you can do it with their reasonably-priced paid plans.

Switchboard Live integrates syndicating a livestream to Facebook as part of their standard $10/m paid service.

So that's *how* you livestream, but *what* do you livestream?

No need to get super complex – there are a ton of things you can livestream. Here are a few to jumpstart your ideas:

- A regular Q&A livestream. Either take questions live at the time or get them sent to you beforehand.
- A behind-the-scenes at a special event. People love to see what's going on in the lead-up to an event, so show them. Don't just limit it to one or two times, do a whole series of livestreams covering different aspects of the event production.
- Related to the point above, if you're doing an event with multiple speakers, why not livestream an interview with a different speaker every week in the lead-up to the event. This will help to build up anticipation for the event and the speaker will most likely promote the interview to their subscribers and customers.
- Could you create a free training course related to your product or service? If so, then instead of using an expensive webinar provider like GotoWebinar, livestream it for free over Facebook, YouTube, Twitter etc.

Normally people would have to register with their email at the webinar-provider's URL to attend a webinar (which will likely interface with your email list provider like Aweber or Mailchimp building your email list) and you can do the same with livestreaming. All you do is schedule your live event(s) on

Facebook, YouTube or whoever you're going to use ahead of time and paste the special web addresses into a textfile for use shortly.

Now you need to create a simple registration page hooked into your mailing list provider so you have somewhere to send prospective attendees and can automatically send them an email containing the URL they need to visit when you'll be broadcasting.

If you're a fancy pants tech person, then you can either create a simple page in HTML with Dreamweaver and FTP it up to your website. If you're not a geek, don't worry – there are plenty of services that can build you any type of page based on an existing template with just a couple of mouse clicks. All you have to do is edit the text on the page.

- http://clickfunnels.com
- http://leadpages.com
- http://megaphoneapp.com
- http://sendlane.com (these guys are actually an email service provider but they have their own landing page templates as well)
- If you use Wordpress, you can get a fantastic set of predesigned templates called Thrive Architect

These are all great and will integrate directly with most of the popular email service providers (apart from Sendlane – they are themselves an email service provider).

Or alternatively, use an SMS shortcode and autoresponder service like TextDeliver and have people send a text message asking to be notified when you're streaming live!

Chatbots/conversational commerce

What is it?
Conversational commerce (CC) was a term coined by Chris Messina in 2015 when discussing the use of messaging apps like Facebook Messenger, WhatsApp, WeTalk and 'Intelligent Assistants' like Siri, Cortana, GoogleNow, Viv etc. to interact with businesses and companies to perform tasks like 'get

customer support', 'make a purchase', 'get personalized recommendations', etc.

Why is it important?
There are a couple of factors:

- With people spending more time on their phones, the limitation of the phone's screen size can sometimes make it difficult to purchase goods and services, especially with a retailer or service provider whose website is not optimized for mobile.
- Add to that messenger apps are becoming the preferred method of communication with the top four messenger apps – WhatsApp, Facebook Messenger, Telegram and WeChat – having a total of around 5 billion users worldwide (source: https://bit.ly/39L89G4) and regularly handling more than 100 billion messages a day (source: https://tcrn.ch/3sxW0e9).
- It's becoming clear that consumers are using chat from the very beginning of the customer journey (finding and researching products) all the way through to purchasing goods and services – all without leaving the chat app.

We know this because in the Far East, chatbots and CC is not a new technology. China's WeChat messaging app has been able to do all this and more for quite some time. Their 889 million active users can buy movie tickets, hail a cab, order food, send money to family and friends and much more – all without leaving the app: http://bit.ly/2R5uFyB.

Now, Western social media companies have finally woken up to the potential of supercharging the functionality (and thereby their revenues) of their messenger apps.

Facebook
Since FB spun Messenger off into its own app and released API access to its development platform over 200,000 developers have created more than 300,000 chatbots (and growing) being used in 200 countries.

Facebook are now also allowing companies to run Sponsored Message ads in Messenger to users who have an open and existing 'conversation' with the company AND anyone with a FB Ad account can also run a Newsfeed ad that takes people directly to a company Messenger chat.

Google

Because Google has two different messaging apps that basically do the same thing and a Chat service (similar to Apple's iMessage and Blackberry's BBM services) they're trying to persuade ISPs to use, none of their apps are anywhere near as popular as Facebook Messenger or WhatsApp and end up being a slightly nicer way to send and receive SMS and MMS messages.

The only useful thing you can do with Google and messaging are to run click-to-message (CTM) ads on mobile search which when clicked will trigger the text application on the user's device, prefilling the phone number and message so all the users have to do is click Send.

At its simplest, this CTM ad can come through to a dedicated customer support number where one of your staff can reply to the sender manually to keep the conversation going.

If you want to automate this, there are a few online chatbot builder services that will send and receive message via SMS like:

- Agent.ai
- Motion.ai
- Init.ai
- Reply.ai

And if you wanted to use this function to just build an SMS phone number list to promote and advertise to in the future, grab yourself phone numbers from Twilio.com and hook them into the TextDeliver.com service I mentioned yesterday on the SMS direct marketing chapter.

So the user flow would go:

C-T-M Google Ad → Twilio Number → TextDeliver → SMS List

As I said before, there are thousands of other chatbots/CC apps out there not just on Facebook and working with Google, but also Skype, Twitter, Slack, KiK and even email.

If you want to explore and see what bots are out there, here are four directories that between them should keep you busy!

- https://botlist.co
- https://www.botpages.com
- https://bots.directory
- https://botfinder.io

There's a lot more cutting-edge and future tech to start researching including: wearables, augmented reality/virtual reality, deep linking, proximity and contextual targeting and push notifications. Some are here now (push notifications) others are nearly here – but start reading up on them now to get ahead of the curve.

Summary

Wow, are you as jazzed about the future of mobile technology as I am right now?

Ok, maybe I am a geek but I bet if you have got to this point in your journey you're also thinking of some cool ideas for you and your business. There are so many opportunities out there right now it is insane.

But first and foremost, you need to ensure your website is mobile-first or mobile-friendly otherwise you risk never showing up in a Google search.

Voice search is not only going to be the future of mobile search but of search in general as it's the logical conclusion of how easy it can be made for consumers to search and purchase goods and services.

This makes it more important than ever to not only get your SEO on point, but also build up your company's branding so that people aren't asking smart speakers questions like 'I want an action camera that can livestream in 4K' but instead are saying 'Alexa, buy me a GoPro Hero7 Black.'

And if you are serious about using social media to build awareness about your brand, dip your toe into Livestreaming when you get a chance (once you've gotten going on the other things you have learned first).

Fact-check (answers at the back)

1. The future is mobile:
a) True ❏
b) False (I haven't actually read this Part and skipped to the botto ❏

2. The Google 'Possum' update:
a) Helps businesses rank outside the centre of the city ❏
b) Helps clean up dead animals on the highway ❏
c) Plays dead when startled. ❏

3. What percentage of local searches in Google are done on a mobile device?
a) 40% ❏
b) 20% ❏
c) 60% ❏
d) 50% ❏

4. AMP stands for:
a) Attention Manic Peons ❏
b) Added Machine Placements ❏
c) Another Main Portal ❏
d) Accelerated Mobile Pages ❏

5. Getting your pages 'amp'ed:
a) Makes them look better ❏
b) Helps them sound better ❏
c) Helps them load faster ❏
d) Helps click faster ❏

6. Livestreaming helps you speak to large crowds of people in real time.
a) True ❏
b) False ❏

7. Video is taking off because:
a) Facebook is going all in ❏
b) Twitter bought and is promoting Periscope ❏
c) Google is promoting Youtube in their search engine all over the place. ❏
d) All of the above ❏

8. Livestreaming is mostly a simple affair.
a) True ❏
b) False ❏

9. The most chat messages sent in a single day via the What'sApp chat app was:
a) 10 billion ❏
b) 83 billion ❏
c) 75 billion ❏
d) 102 billion ❏

10. Chatbots are the future because of the answer to #9:
a) True ❏
b) False ❏

7 × 7

1 Seven dos of mobile marketing

- Make sure you are aiming at the right avatar and not just masses of Likes/fans; the quality of your prospects is almost always more important than the amount.
- Do make fun, engaging 'informative entertainment' content that the visitors you are hoping to attract want to stay and consume even with their limited attention span.
- Do keep to the highest standards possible in your products and services. Nothing can derail you faster than a few bad reviews on your Google My Business page.
- Do aim to be as detailed as possible in your customer avatar and keep changing it as you get to know your market better.
- Be social and have active social accounts on the networks your target prospects are on (search engines and real people like this). Remember YouTube/livestreaming is video and a source of good links and mobile traffic so use them as much as possible.
- Do PPC right, make sure you have an action that you are aiming for: visiting your home page doesn't count, the goal should be tied to something monetary as much as possible as well.
- Do constantly be testing, changing, and growing. Don't ever just settle for the status quo, always be setting yourself up for that next 'wave'.

2 Seven don'ts of mobile marketing

- Don't try to find 'secret' PPC or other 'hacks' – most fail because they are short term loopholes and can get your Facebook Ad account banned once they close the loophole.

- Don't write bad or boring content for your visitors if you ever want to make sales from your efforts.
- Don't do anything without some kind of plan and an end game in sight.
- Don't outsource your work without fully making sure they understand what you are trying to accomplish.
- Don't set up your PPC campaigns and forget about them – constantly be checking them, running optimization reports and making changes.
- Don't do anything just to be 'different' – aim to follow time tested processes in similar niches to your own first before just trying something because it is new.
- Don't set up social accounts and then desert them with no interaction. This turns off mobile customers more than bad service.

3 Seven best tools and resources

- Adwords Keyword Planner: https://adwords.google.com/o/KeywordTool/
- Periscope for livestreaming: http://periscope.com
- BuzzSumo (http://buzzsumo.com) and EpicBeat (https://epicenter.epictions.com/epicbeat/#!/explore) to find interesting content on your topic to share with customers or comment on. Use the filters to find the most popular content (most liked, shared, engagement etc).
- 30 great types of SMS campaigns to run: http://bit.ly/2ythjkt
- Website Analytics Software: http://google.com/analytics
- Outsourcing: http://upwork.com
- Check and post to all your most important social accounts from one place here: http://hootsuite.com

4 Seven things to do now (if you haven't yet)

- Set up your customer avatar.

- Check your website is mobile-friendly (look at it on a smartphone) and if not find someone on Upwork.com to fix it.
- Test it out and see if it is easy to find what you need. Add one-tap phone calls and email into your site.
- Set up your 'Google My Business'.
- Set up mobile social accounts where your customers are.
- Build your Facebook page and interact to start to learn what offers to make.
- Outsource anything you can (you could even have them do all of the above).

5 Seven things to do each business day

- Try to write every day, at least a fun status update or tweet or snap, even just a little bit. You will be amazed how it adds up over time.
- Write an email every day that would be good for your customer avatar (whether you send it or not).
- Check your analytics and see how people are reacting to content as you produce it. Do they come and immediately leave? Or do they stay and visit other pages?
- Set specific goals for mobile users of your site in Google Analytics (depending on the main action that you want them to take that leads to money for you) and check if the goals are being reached. If not something is wrong with your mobile setup.
- Set up a Google alert (google.com/alerts) to monitor new instances of your business name being mentioned, enabling you to instantly respond to any queries or potential problems.
- Check your Facebook/Adwords PPC campaigns and see if there are any changes needed.
- Check your social media accounts for any activity and respond to any questions or comments.

6 Seven things to do monthly (or occasionally)

- Check your website rankings in Google Webmaster tools. No need to do it daily as it's best not to give much credence to short term gains or losses but rather look at the big picture.
- Do a full audit of your Facebook/AdWords campaign and make sure any keyword, group or interest is profitable. Pause the ones that aren't.
- Update your avatar with something that you noticed in a customer interaction you had.
- Do a full audit of where visitors are landing on your site and where they are going. They might be landing in unexpected places for unexpected reasons.
- Change your goal values in Google Analytics to more accurately reflect how much money each action earns you.
- Check how many people are coming to you via your YouTube videos or social platforms and see if you can identify what made them click. Do more of that.
- Find your most popular mobile pages using analytics and make more pages like them.

7 Seven future mobile marketing trends to look out for

- Look for Facebook and Google to clamp down more and more on spam; don't ever try and get something over on them.
- Expect the unexpected, be willing to try anything out that shows even just a little bit of promise.
- Mobile Google ads will take more and more prominence; it is best to get in on these after you have mastered Facebook.
- Keep one eye on Snapchat – there seems to be definite increase in its older user base. While most of Snapchat's

users are 18–24-year-olds there is an increase in the 25–34 demographic. Expect it to grow in power as a mobile market.

- Reviews will take more power for getting mobile traffic from Google and other sources, possibly even Facebook, so do your best to get good and solid reviews.
- Google is getting better at measuring the quality of a visitor's experience on your website every year. You must ensure your site is easy to navigate, and gives visitors the information they need to make informed decisions to move them closer towards the action you want them to take.
- Expect your customers' psychology to always be changing as new tech becomes available so always be learning more about how tech shapes minds and ideas.

Answers

Part 1: Your Digital Marketing Masterclass

Chapter 1: 1b; 2b; 3c; 4c; 5d; 6a; 7e; 8a; 9a; 10b

Chapter 2: 1b; 2a; 3c; 4d; 5c; 6b; 7c; 8a; 9d; 10a

Chapter 3: 1c; 2d; 3b; 4g; 5b; 6a; 7d; 8c; 9b; 10a

Chapter 4: 1c; 2f; 3c; 4a; 5b; 6d; 7e; 8c; 9a; 10a

Chapter 5: 1a; 2d; 3b; 4d; 5b; 6b; 7d; 8b; 9f; 10e

Chapter 6: 1d; 2a; 3d; 4a; 5c; 6c; 7d; 8d; 9b; 10c

Chapter 7: 1b; 2a; 3b; 4a; 5a; 6d; 7c; 8a; 9d; 10c

Part 2: Your Search Marketing Masterclass

Chapter 8: 1c; 2d; 3c; 4a; 5c; 6a; 7d; 8d; 9a; 10d

Chapter 9: 1b; 2d; 3a; 4c; 5b; 6d; 7b; 8a; 9d; 10d

Chapter 10: 1b; 2c; 3b; 4a; 5d; 6c; 7d; 8d; 9a & b; 10b

Chapter 11: 1d; 2b; 3b; 4b; 5d; 6b & d; 7c; 8b; 9a & b; 10d

Chapter 12: 1d; 2d; 3d; 4a & c; 5a; 6d; 7c; 8b; 9b; 10c

Chapter 13: 1c; 2a & b; 3d; 4a; 5b; 6d; 7d; 8c & d; 9a; 10b & c

Chapter 14: 1d; 2a; 3b; 4c; 5d; 6d; 7a, b & d; 8c; 9a; 10c

Part 3: Your Content Marketing Masterclass

Chapter 15: 1b; 2c; 3d; 4b; 5a; 6d; 7b; 8c; 9c; 10b

Chapter 16: 1c; 2a; 3c; 4b; 5d; 6a; 7d; 8c; 9a; 10c

Chapter 17: 1c; 2b; 3b; 4c; 5a; 6b; 7a; 8d; 9c; 10b

Chapter 18: 1b; 2c; 3a; 4d; 5b; 6a; 7c; 8d; 9b; 10d

Chapter 19: 1b; 2c; 3d; 4a; 5b; 6c; 7d; 8a; 9c; 10c

Chapter 20: 1c; 2b; 3a; 4d; 5b; 6c; 7a; 8c; 9b; 10c

Chapter 21: 1c; 2b; 3d; 4a; 5a; 6c; 7c; 8d; 9b; 10b

Part 4: Your Mobile Marketing Masterclass

Chapter 22: 1b; 2c; 3d; 4c; 5e; 6d; 7b; 8a; 9d; 10c

Chapter 23: 1d; 2a; 3b; 4c; 5a; 6b; 7b; 8d; 9e; 10d

Chapter 24: 1c; 2d; 3d; 4b; 5d; 6b; 7c; 8c; 9b; 10a

Chapter 25: 1c; 2f; 3c; 4c; 5b; 6d; 7e; 8c; 9a; 10a

Chapter 26: 1c; 2c; 3b; 4g; 5a; 6a; 7b; 8f; 9a; 10a

Chapter 27: 1b; 2a; 3b; 4b; 5d; 6e; 7a; 8b; 9b; 10a

Chapter 28: 1a; 2a; 3c; 4d; 5c; 6a; 7d; 8a; 9c; 10a

Notes